Thucydides
and the Shaping of History

Classical Literature and Society

Series Editor: Michael Gunningham

Homer: The Resonance of Epic
Barbara Graziosi & Johannes Haubold

Ovid and His Love Poetry
Rebecca Armstrong

Thucydides and the Shaping of History
Emily Greenwood

CLASSICAL LITERATURE AND SOCIETY

Thucydides
and the Shaping of History

Emily Greenwood

Duckworth

First published in 2006 by
Gerald Duckworth & Co. Ltd.
90-93 Cowcross Street, London EC1M 6BF
Tel: 020 7490 7300
Fax: 020 7490 0080
inquiries@duckworth-publishers.co.uk
www.ducknet.co.uk

A catalogue record for this book is available
from the British Library

ISBN 0 7156 3283 3

Typeset by e-type, Liverpool

Contents

Editor's Foreword

The aim of this new Duckworth Classical series is to consider Greek and Roman literature primarily in relation to genre and theme. Its authors hope to break new ground in doing so but with no intention of dismissing current interpretation where this is sound; they will be more concerned to engage closely with text, subtext and context. The series therefore adopts a homologous approach in looking at classical writers, one of whose major achievements was the fashioning of distinct modes of thought and utterance in poetry and prose. This led them to create a number of literary genres evolving their own particular forms, conventions and rules – genres which live on today in contemporary culture.

Although studied within a literary tradition, these writers are also considered in their social and historical context, and the themes they explore are often both highly specific to that context and yet universal and enduring. The ideas they conceive and formulate and the issues they debate find expression in a particular language, Latin or Greek, and belong to their particular era in the classical past. But they are also fully translatable into a form that is accessible as well as intelligible in their own vernacular to those living in later centuries. Hence all quoted passages are rendered into clear, modern English.

These are books, then, which are equally for readers with or without knowledge of the Greek and Latin languages and with or without an acquaintance with the civilization of the ancient world. They have plenty to offer the classical scholar, and are ideally suited to students reading for a degree in classical subjects. Yet they will interest too those studying modern literature, history and culture who wish to discover the roots and springs of our classical inheritance.

I wish to express my especial indebtedness and thanks to Pat Easterling, Regius Professor of Greek Emeritus at Cambridge, who has from the start (1999) been a constant source of advice and encouragement without which the series would probably never have got going at all. From Cambridge too there is Robin Osborne, Professor of Ancient History, who, if ever I was at a loss to think of an author for a particular topic, almost always came up with a suitable name or two and was never stinting of his time or opinion. More recently, I have been lucky also to receive much advice and assistance, chiefly with regard to Latin scholars in the United States, from Tony Woodman, now Professor of Classics at Virginia. And I cannot fail to mention one person whose help and criticism has been throughout invaluable to me, and that is the late John W. Roberts, editor of the recently published *Oxford Dictionary of the Classical World*. I owe him no small debt of gratitude. Finally, I should like to thank Deborah Blake, Duckworth's indefatigable Editorial Director, for her continuing support and enthusiasm.

Postscript. Owing to ill health, I have decided, reluctantly, to hand over the editorship of the series to David W. Taylor, whom I have known for many years, both professionally and as a good friend, and in whom I have the utmost confidence.

2005   Michael Gunningham

Preface

Although the focus of this book is the way in which Thucydides shapes our conception of the history about which he writes, a prominent theme in the *History* is the patterns in the human condition that shape events. Thucydides holds out his work not just as an authoritative account of a particular historical conflict, but also as a short cut to understanding all historical conflicts. Writing this book I have been struck by the enduring force of Thucydides' critique. No reader of the *History* can miss the stress on intelligence and the need for thorough inquiry, least of all at a time in British politics when 'intelligence' has become such a contested term. I have felt the full force of historical irony reading Thucydides' criticism of the sloppy search for the truth (1.20.3), over the course of a year when there has been relentless media exposure of the failure of political intelligence.

I am conscious of the fact that I have spent many years trying to grasp Thucydides, and that this experience has been influenced by a series of deft teachers, who alerted me to different aspects of Thucydides and helped me to see gaps and limitations in my understanding. Caro Spencer (now Smith) introduced me to Thucydides at Sevenoaks School; I am immensely grateful to her for bringing this difficult text alive. As an undergraduate at Cambridge I benefited from supervisions on Thucydides from Paul Millett and Pat Easterling; at the graduate level Paul Cartledge enriched my understanding of Thucydides and remains, in my view, an exemplary reader and critic of Thucydides. Finally, and by no means least, students in the School of Classics at St Andrews University have inspired me with their ability to find fresh things to say about Thucydides.

Unlike Thucydides, who was notoriously grudging about mentioning the influence of other authors, I want to acknowledge my debt to previous authors who have written on Thucydides. In addition to the face-to-face education referred to above, I have learnt and go on learning about Thucydides from a steady stream of academic publications. Our understanding of Thucydides has changed substantially in the past two decades, and this is entirely due to the incisive, original work that is being published. I acknowledge these works on every page of this book, both in the main body of the text and the notes. In particular, I am extremely grateful for the existence of Simon Hornblower's ongoing *Commentary on Thucydides* as well as the numerous articles and books that he has published.[1] Without his research current scholarship on Thucydides would be much diminished. I regret that Carolyn Dewald's monograph on

Thucydides (*Thucydides' War Narrative: A Structural Study*) had yet to appear when this book went to press.[2] I await its publication eagerly. I also regret that, owing to the slowness with which I read German, I have not been able to engage with Sonnabend's monograph on Thucydides, which was published last year.[3]

The target audience for this book spans a range of disciplines: classics, ancient Greek, ancient history, comparative literature, and history. I do not assume that readers will know Greek and therefore all the Greek passages that are cited in this work are cited in translation. The translations of Thucydides are my own, and where I cite other Greek authors I indicate the translation that I have used in the notes. Wherever I make points that hinge on the meaning and significance of specific words in the Greek texts, I supplement my translation of these words with a transliteration. When transliterating Greek words I have represented long vowels with a circumflex accent over the vowel (hence ô for omega). I have used Latinized forms of names (hence 'Thucydides', not 'Thoukydides'). The decision to use Latinized forms acknowledges the distance between the Thucydides who has come down to us via his text, and the man who wrote the work at the end of the fifth century BC. Even when we read the *History* in ancient Greek, the Thucydides of modern scholarship is invariably Thucydides 'in translation'.

I have been blessed with discerning, rigorous (and patient!) editors. I would like to record my thanks to Michael Gunningham, who devised this new Duckworth Series and invited me to contribute a book on Thucydides. He has offered valued advice and editorial guidance. David Taylor also made useful comments and saved me from many errors and infelicities. Paul Cartledge read the entire manuscript and suggested many improvements; I go on learning from him. I would also like to thank Deborah Blake at Duckworth for overseeing the production of this book. Rebecca Sweetman kindly helped me edit the maps. I alone am responsible for any errors that remain.

This book is dedicated to my parents, Margaret and Robert Greenwood, with profound thanks for their love and support, and for the gift of a wonderful education. It is also a pleasure to thank David Milne for the friendship, encouragement, and vital humour that he has brought to this project, and for sharing in the *ponos*.

St Andrews University
May 2005

Abbreviations

AJAH = *American Journal of Ancient History*
AJP = *American Journal of Philology*
ANRW = *Aufstieg und Nierdergang der römischen Welt*
BICS = *Bulletin of the Institute of Classical Studies of the University of London*
CA = *Classical Antiquity*
CJ = *Classical Journal*
CP = *Classical Philology*
CQ = *Classical Quarterly*
CR = *Classical Review*
GRBS = *Greek, Roman and Byzantine Studies*
HCT = A.W. Gomme, A. Andrewes and K.J. Dover (eds), *A Historical Commentary on Thucydides*, 5 vols (Oxford: Clarendon Press), 1945-81
HSCP = *Harvard Studies in Classical Philology*
HT = *History and Theory*
JHS = *Journal of Hellenic Studies*
JRS = *Journal of Roman Studies*
LCM = *Liverpool Classical Monthly*
LSJ = H.G. Liddell and R. Scott, *Greek-English Lexicon*, 9th edn, with supplement, revised by H. Stuart Jones (Oxford: Oxford University Press), 1968
PCPS = *Proceedings of the Cambridge Philological Association*
PP = *Parola del Passato*
QS = *Quaderni di Storia*
REG = *Revue des Études Grecques*
RIS = *Review of International Studies*
TAPA = *Transactions of the American Philological Association*
YCS = *Yale Classical Studies*

1

Whose Contemporary?

'An artist is a historical individual, but you are quite right, he is a historical *individual*. History is in him. But it's an individual presentation.'[1]

This fragment of a conversation between the Trinidadian essayist, novelist and philosopher C.L.R. James (1901-1989) and the sociologist Stuart Hall articulates one of the most fundamental challenges to confront any reader who attempts to understand the meaning and significance of a work written by an author in relation to the historical society and culture in which he or she lived, assuming that he or she belonged to just one society and one culture. This book approaches Thucydides as an historical individual, but – as in the quotation above – places the stress on the word 'individual'. It is perhaps truer for Thucydides than for any Greek author who preceded him, with the possible exception of Herodotus, that he projects his *History* as the work of an individual who is not confined by a particular historical, geographical, political or cultural context.

In intellectual history – by which I mean the study of the ideas of different thinkers in a historical perspective – there is a general academic consensus that context determines meaning, although the nature and degree of this relationship are hotly debated.[2] According to a contextualist approach to Greek historiography, an understanding of the economic, social, religious, linguistic, artistic and intellectual contexts in which Thucydides wrote will help us to make sense of his text. This is a very reasonable assumption; however, in the case of Thucydides, the way in which these various contexts elucidate the *History* is often negative: they point out what Thucydides does not do.

Thucydides' *History* is a strikingly unconventional text. Again and again, the obvious cultural, social and religious institutions that we might expect to find discussed are omitted, and many scholars feel that such omissions are purposeful and polemical. Gregory Crane has explored the counter-cultural thrust of Thucydides' work in terms of the obvious socio-cultural topics that are excluded or pushed to the margins of the text; in Crane's analysis these topics include religion, the home, women, kinship ties and social bonds.[3] In order to understand what Thucydides was doing when he wrote about the war, we must relate Thucydides to his context, but we must also concede that Thucydides' counter-cultural approach to history invites us to read him out of context, as a thinker who transcended his historical situation. This strategy is compounded by the way in which Thucydides has been read and received by modern scholars. The fact that Thucydides was so successful in creating the impression of objectivity in his narrative and projecting an image of a mind detached from its historical environment has led to his assimilation into the modern discipline of history, to the extent that it is hard for us to understand how odd the narrow confines of his account would have appeared in their contemporary context.[4] Crane surmises that 'Thucydides would be astonished (even dismayed) if he could see how readily later readers accept many notions that were extremely radical in his own day', concluding that Thucydides 'wrote to shock'.[5]

Not only is it difficult to explain Thucydides in terms of the context in which he wrote, but it is also hard to relate Thucydides' work to the other texts that have survived from the same period (roughly 431-400 BC). Such comparisons are complicated by the fact that we lack conclusive evidence for the date of the circulation of Thucydides' *History*, as well as for other works that are known to have been roughly contemporary with Thucydides. Our view of the *History* would change if we had more secure dates for the dissemination of Herodotus' work. As it is, we have to juggle with different scenarios: traditionally, it has been assumed that Herodotus was the older contemporary whose work was mostly completed and in circulation when Thucydides began to write.[6] However, scholars have now revealed passages in Herodotus which may imply a knowledge of Thucydides. If we leave the traditional assumption intact, then this could suggest that Herodotus adapted his *Histories* in the light of current research (by Thucydides and others), but it could also suggest that the two writers were actually contemporaries who engaged with what they knew of each other's work. Then there is always the proviso that Thucydides' relationship with his intellectual context would look different, and that Thucydides might look more conventional, if a greater number of contemporary works survived. As it is, very few Attic prose texts survive entire from the fifth century BC.

In recent years there have been some excellent studies that have sought to clarify the intellectual context of Greek historiography. In *Herodotus in Context*, Rosalind Thomas has argued that Herodotus' *Histories* could not have come into being without the intellectual developments of the mid to late fifth century BC, particularly the developments in Ionian and East Greek science.[7] As revealed by Thomas, the intellectual affinities between Herodotus' *Histories* and the works of the Hippocratic corpus are extremely compelling. However, while an understanding of the affinities between these authors is necessary for anyone seeking to appreciate Herodotus' work, it does not provide a sufficient explanation of his intellectual outlook or the nature of the *Histories*. Furthermore, there is no total contextual culture that we can appeal to in order to throw light on

2

Herodotus' *Histories*. This is a text that spans several different genres and cultures. Assuming we could trace all Herodotus' intellectual affinities to earlier historiography, to tragedy, to lyric poetry, to Persian records, to Greek science, to the sophists, and arguably even to Thucydides, we are still left with persistent questions about the differences between these works. Influences from other authors and genres will tell us about Herodotus' conventionality, and they will also tell us something about his original use of existing literature, but they will not explain the complex entity that is Herodotus' text, for which there is no precedent.[8]

I want to suggest that Thucydides is one of the most compelling examples in intellectual history of a text constituting its own context. In fact there is something fiercely anti-contextualist about Thucydides' intellectual agenda. By this I do not mean that Thucydides does not engage with his contemporary world, or the historical context in which he wrote. He manifestly does; the subject matter of his history is the progress of a contemporary conflict and the effect of this conflict on the Greek world. But, at an intellectual level, Thucydides' response to this conflict is informed by the conviction that the thoughts of most of his contemporaries had little value. W. Robert Connor has argued that

> Thucydides knew that his treatment of almost every major figure, Pericles, Cleon, Demosthenes, Nicias, Alcibiades, would in his own day be controversial and would cut against conventional wisdom and judgements. His is sometimes a revisionist, often a polemical work, designed to provoke rather than suppress dissent.[9]

Thucydides' text promotes the view that for the thoughts of the historian to be of value, they should resist, look beyond or transcend the historical and social circumstances of the historian. After all, this is a writer who practises self-alienation in his own text. Nicole Loraux has studied the way in which Thucydides refers to himself in his own work and has concluded that Thucydides deliberately played down the fact that Thucydides the Athenian general in Book 4, who is an active participant in events, is the same man as Thucydides the detached writer of the war.[10] Admittedly this is a rhetorical strategy, and some scholars may feel that, in reality, Thucydides was more context-bound than he cared to admit.[11] However, if we ignore the rhetoric of Thucydides' text, then we ignore one very clear guide to how Thucydides intended to be read and understood. It is just as appropriate to speak of Thucydides' alienation from this context, as it is to speak of his relation to this context. To borrow a formulation used by John Patrick Diggins, I think that Thucydides is one of those 'reflective past thinkers whose own thoughts were essentially anti-contextualist'.[12] Paradoxically, reading Thucydides 'out of context' can be reconcilable with a historically minded approach to Thucydides. Recently John Moles has put forward a brilliant discussion of Thucydides' *History* as 'a text for any context', basing his argument on the way in which Thucydides introduces his work as a text that encompasses all dimensions of time through the suggestive repetition of the adverb 'always' (*aiei*) at chs 1.21-2: 'there are repeated presents [1.21.2], there are always different presents [1.22.1], and since Thucydides' work covers both, it is an always possession [1.22.4]'.[13] Contextualism becomes a self-defeating interpretative strategy if it makes it impossible to attribute to a past thinker ideas that have no counterpart in their own time. My concern, then, is not to dispense with context, but rather to strike a balance between situating Thucydides in the context of the society, culture and literary tradition within which he composed the *History* and understanding how he attempted to move beyond these contexts.

Many contextual methodologies for interpreting texts from the past draw on the language philosophy of J.L. Austin and approach these texts as an accumulation of linguistic actions which were intended to elicit a particular response from contemporary audiences (or 'to have force', in Austin's terms); consequently, interpretation begins with trying to situate texts in a 'convention-governed linguistic context'.[14] While Thucydides clearly relied on common linguistic conventions in order to write a narrative that would be intelligible to his readers, his implied readers were not 'ordinary' Athenians. Some of the most revealing studies that relate Thucydides to the linguistic context of his contemporaries have negative conclusions: these studies are important because they reveal how frequently Thucydides diverged from standard language and, more radically still, how frequently he invented his own terms. In many passages Thucydides' language is sufficiently unintelligible and idiosyncratic to suggest that he found conventional linguistic usage inadequate for the kinds of explanation that he wanted to expound.

Writing in the last decade of the first century BC, the literary critic and historian Dionysius of Halicarnassus was convinced that Thucydides had developed a recondite, archaic, artificial, outlandish, exotic style of writing in order to set his work apart from that of his predecessors and his contemporaries.[15] In light of Gregory Crane's thesis that Thucydides deliberately suppressed the topic of the family in his *History*, it is interesting to note that Dionysius reaches for the language of the family to describe the oddity of Thucydides' language in some passages. Commenting on the speech that Thucydides attributes to Hermocrates in the debate at Camarina (6.76-80; 415/4 BC), Dionysius remarks 'if people spoke like this, not even their fathers or mothers could bear the unpleasantness of listening to them: they would need an interpreter, as if they were listening to a foreign tongue' (*On Thucydides* 49). However, linguistic oddities are not confined to the speeches; Dionysius also offers us a survey of Thucydides' narrative in its entirety:

1. Whose Contemporary?

Following after Herodotus and the others whom I mentioned before him, and perceiving their several qualities, Thucydides resolved to introduce into the writing of history an individual style (*idios tis charactêr*), which had been overlooked by his predecessors. In his choice of words (*lexis*) he preferred a diction that was metaphorical (*tropikê*), full of obscure words (*glôttêmatikê*), archaic (*apêrchaiômenê*) and outlandish (*xenê*) to one that was accessible (*koinê*) and familiar (*sunêthês*) to his contemporaries.[16]

By contrast, in an earlier section (5), Dionysius describes the diction of Thucydides' predecessors and contemporaries as clear (*saphês*), accessible (*koinos*), pure (*kathara*) and concise (*suntomos*).[17] It is notable, however, that this description excludes Herodotus, who is discussed separately. Over the course of the treatise, Dionysius compiles an off-putting inventory of Thucydides' stylistic oddities; in addition to the qualities already cited, he describes Thucydides' prose as 'complex' (*poluplokos* – 24, 35), 'convoluted' (*angkulos* – 35), 'forced' (*bebiasmenos* – 35),[18] 'difficult to unravel' (*dusexeliktos* – 24), 'twisted' (*skolios* – 24, 29), 'difficult to follow' (*dusparakolouthêtos* – 29), and comments that the sense of a particular passage is 'difficult to infer' (*duseikastos* – 40).[19] In fact, on the basis of the idiosyncrasies of Thucydides' language and style, Dionysius argues that Thucydides wrote not for his contemporaries, but for posterity (50-1).

Modern verdicts have tended to echo the terminology used by Dionsyius, stressing Thucydides' idiosyncrasy, austerity and obscurity.[20] John Moles writes of Thucydides' 'usual inspissated and unlovely style';[21] Gregory Crane describes Thucydides as 'wilful, obscure, idiosyncratic, but brilliant',[22] while Carolyn Dewald describes Thucydides' narrative as 'severely impersonal' and 'severely analytic'.[23] These judgements are substantiated by detailed studies of Thucydides' language. June Allison has surveyed the linguistic process of abstraction in Thucydides, focusing on his use of abstract nouns. She notes that in the fifth century BC, there was a marked growth in the category of abstract nouns ending in *-sis*. According to Allison's research, Thucydides used more abstract nouns of this category than any other author: inventing 40 simple nouns and 120 compound nouns.[24] The example of Thucydides' language illustrates his complicated relationship with his context: Allison's study necessarily places Thucydides in the context of a linguistic and cognitive community. After all, claims about Thucydides' use of language have meaning only through comparison with that of other writers. Similarly, the originality of Thucydides' work is discerned only through comparison with other authors. In this sense, then, context and tradition are indispensable. However, we also need to pay attention to the high proportion of neologisms in Thucydides' text; many of these neologisms are not just new words, but are also *hapax legomena* (literally 'mentioned once'; i.e. the only occurrence of the word in surviving Greek literature). This linguistic idiosyncrasy should be taken together with Thucydides' counter-cultural treatment of his subject matter as a statement of intention that his work should not be confined to the context in which it was written, and that it should preserve a critical distance from this context.[25] Thucydides is not unique in this; we can point to many polemical, counter-cultural statements in Herodotus, for example. However, Thucydides' repudiation of contemporary contexts is more sweeping.

We also need to take seriously Thucydides' claim that he composed his work as a possession to be listened to for all time (*ktêma es aiei* – 1.22.4). In stressing this claim, it would of course be wrong to imply that Thucydides was the only Greek writer who envisaged an 'afterlife' for his work. In fact, the sense of this claim is close to Herodotus' statement that he has 'published' his inquiry so that the great achievement of both Greeks and Barbarians in the past should not 'fade away', or 'become extinct' (Herodotus *Histories* 1.1).[26] The use of this metaphor arguably gestures towards the idea of an inscribed text, emphasizing the visual properties of writing: through Herodotus' words, these achievements will remain visible – as will his own intellectual achievement. However, Thucydides goes even further in stating explicitly that his account will be a possession for all time.[27] It is impossible to try to gauge the limits of Thucydides' far-sightedness (how long did he imagine his work would last; did he imagine that we would still be reading it in the twenty-first century?), but Thucydides has phrased his statement in such a way that this is not necessary. For as long as the *History* is read, the adverb 'always' (*aiei*) will encompass the present tense of the reader. As Lowell Edmunds comments, 'if the adverb *aiei* is understood in its distributive sense, the work is a possession for each successive occasion'.[28] This is a no-fail prediction.

I have referred to Thucydides' language vis-à-vis the language of other writers, and I have mentioned Herodotus as one obvious intellectual influence. However, the relationship between Thucydides' *History* and other works (both contemporary and 'classic' works – in the sense that Homeric epic was already a 'classic' in the fifth-century BC) is more complicated than I have allowed. There have been several studies of the intertextual dialogue between Thucydides' *History* and other works, focusing chiefly on Homer and other epic poetry, Greek lyric, Herodotus, tragedy, the Hippocratic treatises and the sophists.[29] If Thucydides attempts to portray himself as both of and not of his context, then intertextuality becomes a complicated exercise. According to its initial usage, intertextuality involves the intrusion of another text or speaker into a text without any explicit statement of their presence. However, although there is no explicit statement of the presence of another author or 'genre' intruding into a text, there are often signs, whether at the level of verbal echoes, tone, metre, dialect or general style.[30] When modern scholars discern intertextual relationships between the *History* and other texts, this judgement is constrained by our partial view of Greek literature at the time at which Thucydides wrote. Obviously we can posit intertextual relationships only between texts that survive in some form (whether in their own right, or as summarized in other texts).

When construing intertextual relationships between texts, it is common to appeal to contemporary audiences and their expectations. Thus Tim Rood concludes a recent discussion of the general literary milieu in which Thucydides wrote with the claim that 'this broader analysis gives us a better view of the horizons of expectation of a fifth-century audience'.[31] This approach comes close to the interpretive loop that Nicole Loraux identified as being characteristic of the way in which ancient historians interpret Thucydides as a historical source:[32] we use the text to help us build up a context, and then use this context in order to explain the text. There is also an amusing irony in the fact that verbal allusions to Homer, Herodotus and other authors are mobilized to interpret Thucydides – a writer who strenuously suppressed the fame and influence of these authors in his work. This is not to say that Homer and Herodotus are not present in Thucydides' work, but that they are there *in spite of* Thucydides' historiographical ideology. Similarly, scholars rightly point out that Thucydides' claim that he has not indulged in mythical material (1.22.4) is disproved by subsequent narrative.[33] However, in order to understand how Thucydides conceived of his work it is important to give due weight to this statement of alleged methodology which is essentially a statement of ideology.[34] In passages where Thucydides either appears to draw on Homer or mentions Homer explicitly, the emphasis is not on Thucydides as a reader of Homer, or on the centrality of Homeric epic, but rather on the assumption and assimilation of the cultural authority of epic into Thucydides' own narrative.[35]

The focus on the 'intertextual' Thucydides needs to be counterbalanced by Thucydides' drive to supplant all other literature. Josiah Ober has put forward what he calls an 'exclusivist hypothesis' about Thucydides, according to which Thucydides intended his account to wipe out the accounts of his predecessors and contemporary competitors, as well as to preclude anyone from offering an account of his subject in the future.[36] Ober explains this claim to 'exclusivity' or 'exhaustiveness' on the grounds that Thucydides' 'historical' (our term, not his) account was undertaken in the service of developing a critical political theory. Approaching Thucydides in terms of political theory is arguably just as prejudicial as approaching his work as history. However, we do not have to accept the disciplinary conception of Thucydides' *History* as political theory in order to concede Ober's observation that Thucydides ideologically excludes other literature to a remarkable degree – although, as already noted, ideological exclusion is not the same as excluding other literature in practice.

7

In a discussion that gives considerable weight to literary allusions in Thucydides (in the *History*'s first preface (1.1-23), in particular), John Moles reaches a similar conclusion, arguing that the main point of the allusions is to convey Thucydides' 'divinatory' superiority to all his rivals (the adjective 'divinatory' derives from Moles' stress on the fact that Thucydides' formula at 1.22.4 'transcends its own time frame').[37]

Although we can make wide-ranging assumptions about what élite fifth-century audiences might have read, it is much harder to identify a 'contemporary' audience for Thucydides' *History*, and Thucydides gives us little help. In recent years the most systematic attempt to construct such an audience is that of Josiah Ober in his book *Political Dissent in Democratic Athens*. In the introduction to this work, Ober lays out his vision of an Athenian company of critics who constituted a single community of interpretation:

> It is perfectly likely (if not demonstrable) that some of the authors discussed here met at actual symposia; but whether or not they were fellow symposiasts in fact, the general model of the symposium, with its connections to and self-conscious separation from the *polis*, provides a useful allegory for the critical community. That community was, however, larger and more diverse, chronologically and geographically, than any gathering of symposiasts. Its size and diversity were in large part a function of literacy. Because a number of Athenian political dissenters wrote texts, and because these texts eventually circulated outside the intimate circle of friends, students, and trusted comrades, the 'Athenian critical community' was in a sense a 'virtual community'. It was not limited to those persons who might actually meet face-to-face. *Some of its members (Thucydides) were dead before others (Aristotle) were born.* Many of its members spent considerable parts of their adult lives outside Athens. And yet, through the medium of reading and writing texts in many and varied genres, *latecomers to the community were able to learn from and to argue with their deceased elders as well as their contemporaries.*[38] (my italics)

Notice that the audience that Ober imagines for this 'interpretive community' (comprising the political theories of Ps.-Xenophon, Thucydides, Aristophanes, Plato and Aristotle) transcends any single historical, social or generic context.[39] We have to entertain two different audiences simultaneously: on the one hand, Thucydides' ill-defined fifth-century audience, and on the other hand, the even less clearly defined audiences of the future. However, the existence of future audiences and audiences of the future is an important consideration. It is notable that, insofar as Thucydides does comment on the intended audience for his *History*, this audience is projected into the future. At 1.22.4 he anticipates the fact that listeners will not enjoy the lack of story-telling in his *History*, but specifies a more discerning target audience:

8

But as for all those who will wish to gain a clear insight into things which
have happened in the past and things similar to this which will happen again
at some time in the future, according to the human condition, it will be sufficient if they judge these things useful.[40]

One can argue that these instances of the future tense are non-specific,
and may simply refer to Thucydides' contemporaries who would be
reading the work in the immediate or near future.[41] However, the addition
of the phrase 'possession for all time', in the next sentence, suggests that
the use of the future tense is deliberately open-ended. This statement
refers both to the immediate reception of the work as well as to its ongoing
reception. It is easy and tempting for each generation of readers to identify with the implied audience in 1.22.4, and this is indeed part of the way
in which Thucydides shapes us as readers and ensures the preservation of
his work.

For all that we may insist on reconstructing the literary and cultural
context for Thucydides in terms of who and what he had heard / read, and
what 'texts' (oral and written) contemporary audiences would have
brought to their encounter with Thucydides, we should ask ourselves what
part these intertextual allusions play in Thucydides' *History*. If the reader
wants to contextualize Thucydides – by which I mean to 'explain
Thucydides' *History*' in terms of its context – then this is possible at every
turn. This can be illustrated by the passage 1.22.4, which is taken to be
definitive of Thucydides' conception for his work, and offers an original
framing for his narrative. However, while acknowledging its originality,
scholars have also pointed to ways in which Thucydides is drawing on his
contemporaries. For example, when Thucydides states that perhaps the
lack of a story-telling element in his *History* will displease his audience,
Gregory Crane has argued that 'Thucydides is simply varying the hackneyed courtroom persona familiar to all contemporary Athenians. Just as
speakers regularly contrast their own inexperience with rhetoric and
necessary reliance on the plain, unpolished truth, Thucydides distinguishes himself from others.'[42]

Commenting on the same passage, indeed on the same sentence, John
Moles has identified an allusion to a formula used in Athenian inscriptions
contemporary with Thucydides' *History*. When Thucydides states that his
History is intended to satisfy 'all those who will wish to gain a clear insight
(*hosoi de boulêsontai skopein*) into things which have happened in the
past', Moles likens this wording to the declaration that an inscription is
set up 'for anyone who wishes to look' (*tôi boulomenôi skopein*) and uses
this verbal echo to support his thesis that Thucydides 'images' his *History*
as an inscription.[43] So in this one sentence we are encouraged to see
Thucydides adopting the kind of rhetorical manoeuvre familiar from the
Athenian lawcourts and adapting a formula from Athenian inscriptions.

However, in both cases it is impossible to dissociate the allusions from what Thucydides adds or changes (a point acknowledged by Moles). It is one thing to eschew crowd-pleasing rhetoric in a speech delivered in front of a mass audience, and it is another to deploy this rhetoric in a written work that criticizes the failings of contemporary rhetorical culture. When Thucydides exposes his work's lack of 'entertainment value' and subsequently rejects the institution of competitive performance, he also rejects a model where the success of his work is subjected to a single hearing by a single audience.[44]

Rather than repackaging the familiar, Thucydides plays on his audience's knowledge of contemporary oratory to highlight how unfamiliar his work will be. In fact the contrastive force of the phrase 'rather than' (*mallon ê*) pervades the entire section (1.22.4). Arguably with the phrase 'all those who will wish to gain a clear insight into things which have happened in the past' Thucydides historicizes his own time and the contemporary audience at the same time.[45] This phrase probably would have had a ring of the familiar about it, evoking an established inscriptional formula, but it also informs contemporary audiences that there will be people after them, who will reflect on (*skopein*) these present events as past events. This statement observes the pastness of the present, and commits the *History* to the future.

Within modern universities, Thucydides' text has several different lives: he is studied as the precursor of the discipline of History (political history, military history) in departments of International Relations he is studied as the founding father of that subject and the first writer in the realist tradition and, somewhere between the two disciplines, he is also studied from the perspective of Political Thought.[46] In Greek and Classical Civilization programmes students study the *History* as a work of prose literature from the late fifth century BC which can be studied in dialogue with Herodotus, the sophists, Greek tragedy and the Hippocratic corpus, not to mention archaic poetry (lyric and epic), as well as philosophical and oratorical texts from the fourth century BC. Whatever disciplinary spin is put on Thucydides' text, his work is studied as a 'classic' work of literature, and also enjoys a flourishing reception outside of the academy as part of a larger canon of literature. When we read Thucydides as a classic, we imply that his work has a value that transcends its significance as part of history.[47] One of the criteria of a 'classic' work of literature is originality, or 'newness'; as Denis Feeney comments, 'great works can or even must break the bounds of interpretative possibility, redefining the critical practice needed to read them, addressing an audience which is not (yet) there'.[48]

It is my contention that, in order to understand Thucydides' work fully, we need to sustain the tension between Thucydides' inevitable relationship to his context, on the one hand, and the strenuous efforts that he undertook to disassociate his work from this same context, on the other hand. As W. Robert Connor remarked in the Introduction to his impressive study of Thucydides' *History*, 'what we need to know is not the sociology of the readership of the *Histories* through the centuries, but the ways by which the text elicits responses and shapes its audience'.[49] Harvey Yunis has recently reaffirmed this approach: 'Little information exists about who among contemporaries actually read Thucydides and Plato and to what purpose. Yet it is possible to observe what artistic provisions these writers made to accommodate, encourage, or direct interpretation on the part of their reader.'[50] Obviously an understanding of the way in which Thucydides draws on previous and contemporary literature will help us to gain a clearer appreciation of the techniques by which he shapes our interpretation of (his) history, but I stress the fact that these influences are suppressed by Thucydides' historiographical agenda.

Shaping

Writing a book about the shaping of history at the beginning of the twenty-first century, one can take the fact that Thucydides 'shapes' history as read. In recent decades, the vocabulary of shaping has become a reflex action for scholars writing about Thucydides. In the passage from Connor quoted above, he writes of the way in which the 'text [...] shapes its audience'. Elsewhere in the same work he refers to the reader of Thucydides' work as its 'co-shaper' (ibid., 18), and in the Conclusion he refers to the 'Thucydidean shaping of the work' (ibid., 233). More recently Tim Rood has used similar vocabulary in introducing his study of the role of the narrator in the *History*, focusing on 'the choices [Thucydides] constantly had to make in shaping his account'.[51]

My title, *Thucydides and the Shaping of History*, puts the accent primarily on how Thucydides shaped and created the history that he takes as his subject. Although Thucydides did not write his work under the term, let alone the discipline, of 'history', his work is one of the best examples of the ambiguity of this noun, which can signify past events (Athenian *history*), a discipline (the 'subject' of *history*), and the textual representation of these events (a *history* of the trans-Atlantic slave trade). The slippage between 'history as events', 'history as discipline' and 'history as text' became a commonplace of historical theory in the twentieth century.[52] One of the insights of postmodernist historiography has been the realization that all historical narratives, no matter how prosaic, involve ordering and invention – there are no naturally occurring historical 'plots'.[53] More fundamentally, invention occurs not just at the level of composition, where events have to be arranged into a sequence or a nexus, but also when it comes to determining what constitutes an event. When reading and studying Thucydides at the beginning of the twenty-first century, it is easy to take these insights for granted. Although there are

11

now many excellent studies of the way in which Thucydides shapes history at the level of narrative, echoes of the frisson that this proposition might once have caused still remain. In an excellent article on 'Narratology and Thucydides', Simon Hornblower discusses the controversial reception of terms such as 'the rhetoric of history' among ancient historians.[54] Likewise, Tim Rood hints at potential controversy when he reassures the reader of his study of Thucydides' narrative, which draws heavily on narratology, that the fact that narratology emerged through the study of fictional texts is no 'threat' to the modern historian.[55] If reassurance is still needed, then I reassure the reader of this work that studying how Thucydides shapes his narrative of events is a thoroughly historical enterprise: Thucydides' text as we have it is itself a historical artefact (albeit not *the* original artefact), and in seeking to understand how Thucydides constructed his text we can at least attempt to recover and understand the perspective of one Athenian, who was also a participant in the war. This is not to say that one can no longer 'do' history with Thucydides, but rather that this kind of exercise must begin with an understanding of his text. Nor should we see his text as a means (linguistic and literary interpretation) to an end (history); the text is itself part of the history.[56]

Scholars have approached Thucydides' shaping of his *History* from different angles. These approaches can be summarized as thematic studies, linguistic studies and studies which focus on the narrative structure of the work. The majority of recent studies on Thucydides combine all three approaches.[57] For example, it is impossible to undertake a convincing study of the theme of power in the *History* – to take the subject of Lisa Kallet's *Money and the Corrosion of Power in Thucydides* – without undertaking a study of the language of power and the terms of its assessment. However, an understanding of the narrative structure of the work is equally important. To quote Kallet:

> Thucydides employs a variety of methods to develop and illuminate the themes of money and war financing and to relate them to broader issues and themes in the work. Among his strategies, temporal displacement, anticipation, negative presentation, anecdote, metaphor, intertextuality, [...] not only serve to maintain the reader's attention on the financial aspect of the war but also are designed to guide the reader to draw conclusions about the proper and improper uses of money in a military context and to understand the larger meaning of events. At the same time, such methods elegantly highlight irony and ambiguity, which form an essential part of Thucydides' approach to the themes of money and finance.[58]

The way in which Thucydides shaped his *History* and the way in which he shapes his readers[59] are an important part of the agenda of several recent and contemporary studies of his work, but the student of Thucydides also needs to be alert to how scholars and readers 'shape' Thucydides' work in their turn. By talking of scholarship in terms of shaping, I am not implying that scholars deliberately manipulate or distort the text of Thucydides in order to reflect their own agenda. As with the use of the term in relation to Thucydides' *History*, shaping is integral to the process of constructing a narrative about the past, as seen from the perspective of an individual mind, with its own individual insights, not to mention the necessity of formulating ideas and arguments rhetorically in order to persuade readers. Another of the criticisms that Dionysius of Halicarnassus levels at Thucydides is the charge that his treatment of his subject matter is 'uneven' (*anômalon*):

> One can see even better the unevenness of the historian's treatment if one considers that, while omitting many important events, he nevertheless makes his introduction some five hundred lines long as he attempts to prove that prior to this war the Greeks achieved little, and nothing worthy to be compared with it.
>
> *On Thucydides* 19

Thucydides used the same adjective to describe the uneven impression (*anômalos epopsis*) of the sea-battle in the harbour of Syracuse from the perspective of the Athenian forces watching the battle from the shore (7.71.3).[60] Thucydides built this awareness of the limitations of perspective and point of view into his *History*, acknowledging, for example, that sometimes informants would give conflicting reports about the same events (1.22.3-4). He claims that he went to great lengths to overcome the shortcomings of the individual's perspective (both his own and that of others), while constructing the narrative in such a way as to project an all-seeing, all encompassing perspective on the events that he narrates, which ranged from enabling the reader to 'see' what was going on inside the head of the different generals, to giving the reader a quasi split-screen perspective whereby we can see what was going in two different theatres of war simultaneously (see below, Chapter 2, p. 20). Obviously Thucydides was not party to the criteria of scholarship that dictate modern research into his *History*, but in spite of many innovations in technology, and the massive volume of literature which the modern scholar can draw on, we remain subject to many of the constraints on knowledge that Thucydides discusses. Scholarship also wrestles with the limitations of individual perspective and the finite capacity of the individual's memory – another limitation that Thucydides highlights when discussing his methodology (1.22.1-4).

For scholars working on Thucydides, a truly all-encompassing or comprehensive interpretation is impossible. Like the Athenians in Thucydides' *History* who watch the sea-battle in Syracuse, we cannot take everything in at once. Through a careful and painstaking process of reading what others have written about Thucydides and other academic works, scholars endeavour to be representative in their treatment of

Thucydides and submit their interpretations to scrutiny in the light of conflicting views. Even so, scholarship on Thucydides steadily accumulates in several different languages, and there is increasing pressure to take the history of scholarship into account.[61] These last two considerations (language and era) highlight another sense in which perspective 'shapes' scholarship, and this, in turn, has the potential to shape our understanding of Thucydides. Scholarship is influenced by the environment in which it is done; this includes the disciplinary affiliation of the scholars, the period in which they write, the language in which they write, the broader cultural and political environment, and the wider reading and knowledge of theory that they bring to their readings of Thucydides' text.[62] Again, responsible scholarship tries to combat these influences, insofar as they are perceived to distort the historical meaning of the text. However, as I have argued above, the *History* has different tiers of historical meaning: the text has meaning in its historical context, but also strives to mean more than it did at the time of writing. So modern readers have to engage with Thucydides' claim to timelessness while trying to resist the process of transference – of making Thucydides sound 'nearer to the twentieth century AD than he is to the fifth BC'.[63]

Writing

Behind arguments about the textualization of history lies the technology of writing as a means of representing the past. From a practical point of view writing was evidently fundamental for Thucydides' project of creating an extensive prose narrative of the war and for organizing this narrative. It has been argued that the critical project of Thucydides' *History* – to enable the reader to discern, reflect on and learn from what happened in the past – is predicated on writing. Recently Paula Debnar and Harvey Yunis have put forward this thesis independently. Debnar draws a contrast between the audiences of actual rhetorical debates (in the assembly) who cannot linger on a speaker's words if they are trying to keep up with what is being said, and the reader of the speeches in Thucydides 'who can carefully weigh and repeatedly examine a passage'.[64] Yunis has argued that the speeches are crucial to the didactic purpose of Thucydides' *History*, whereby Thucydides uses the written medium of his text to encourage the reader to reflect on the gap between words and meaning, and hence to engage critically with the problem of meaning.[65] The words of speakers gain additional significance from the narrative context that frames them, and it is possible for the reader to discern the flaws in the words of the speakers according to information given elsewhere. Thucydides' reconstruction of the speeches in writing serves then as a didactic meta-commentary on the anyway didactic institution of oral speeches which, ideally, were meant to 'educate' their audiences.[66]

14

The significance of writing in Thucydides' critical lesson is not confined to the relationship between the speeches and the surrounding narrative. Many of the points that scholars make about the intricate web of verbal echoes in Thucydides, or the ironies and ambiguities of the structure of his entire narrative, assume writing. This is not because the same intricacies and complexities would not exist in oral delivery, but because they would not be so readily discernible on being heard, no matter how adept at processing oral 'texts' we assume Athenian audiences to have been.[67] I am not arguing, then, that the written word is inherently more profound or sophisticated, but rather that the fact of a text's being written promotes reflection, in the sense that readers are able to 'look again' at what they have read, and to re-examine it countless times.[68] In fact the Greek reader in the late fifth and the fourth century BC would probably have had to examine the text again and again to determine its sense, since he would have been confronted with a difficult, unpunctuated and unaccented text. As Kenneth Dover has pointed out, for all that scholars associate the Thucydidean quality of *'to saphes'* ('clarity') with the medium of writing, we should not over-emphasize the clarity of the experience of reading Thucydides in the later fifth or early fourth century BC.[69] Notwithstanding this point about the technology of reading in Thucydides' day, Thucydides holds out his work as a permanent fixture for the discerning reader who is prepared to take the time to reflect on it. The work will not go away; it is always there, both from generation to generation, but also from moment to moment. Hence the force of the *ktêma* as a symbol for the work: this perpetual possession will not depreciate and it will not decay. Thucydides ushers in a new intellectual economy.

In addition, many scholars have argued that Thucydides made 'the fact of writing, the mode itself of communication, part of his historiographical strategy'.[70] Nicole Loraux exposed the gap between Thucydides 'the contemporary', the participant in the war, and Thucydides the 'writer', arguing that Thucydides used the reflective process of writing to absent himself as an actor in his own text in order to preserve the objectivity of the writer figure.[71] Lowell Edmunds supplemented Loraux's thesis by pointing out that Thucydides might 'disappear' in his own text, but that he does so in order to achieve the 'presence' of his writing. Edmunds distinguishes between statements that Thucydides makes about his writing that use secondary tenses in Greek (aorist and imperfect), and statements that use primary tenses (present, future, perfect).[72] Edmunds demonstrates that Thucydides uses the verb *xungraphô* ('to write down' / 'to achieve the writing of') – the verb that introduces his narration of the war – only with the secondary tenses: Thucydides wrote down the war (an action in the past that is completed). Hence the phrase that Thucydides 'wrote down the war' (*xunegrapse ton polemon*) at the beginning of the *History* is itself part of the past, a fact to be recorded along with other actions that took place in the time-frame of the war. By contrast, statements that Thucydides makes on his writing about the war in the perfect tense ('it has been stated' (*eirêtai*); 'it has been shown' (*dedêlôtai*); 'it has been set down' (*xunkeitai*); 'I have kept record' (*memnêmai*)) imply that his writing carries over (the perfect tense denoting a completed action the effects of which continue in the present) into the present day of the reader.[73]

Throughout the *History* there is an ironic gap between Thucydides the writer and his contemporaries who are framed by his historical account. He sees more, knows more, and understands more than they do. This gap even extends to Thucydides himself and is illustrated by the co-existence of Thucydides the writer and Thucydides the historical actor in the same text. The Thucydides who participated in the war (4.104-7) had a much more restricted vision than Thucydides the writer. Or, looked at another way, with the benefit of hindsight Thucydides the narrator sees more in his account of the war than he did at the time as a participant.

Against this stress on writing and the significance of the written word in Thucydides' text, some scholars object that it is much more likely that oral performance was still the dominant model for publication, and that oral performance and display are still important factors in long prose texts such as Thucydides' *History*.[74] After all, in the passage at 1.22.4 where Thucydides appears to reject competitive rhetorical performances and to construct his work on the image / model of an inscription, he nevertheless writes that the work is 'set down as a possession to hear (*akouein*) for all time'. The mention of 'hearing' is arguably an acknowledgement of oral performance. However, it is widely assumed that silent reading was not widespread when Thucydides was writing; hence the fact that he designates his text for 'hearing' is not remarkable. It may simply take for granted that readers would *read* his work out aloud and is thus compatible with the idea of Thucydides addressing readers who would study his text in private contexts.[75]

Recently Rosalind Thomas has challenged the argument that 'Thucydides' style was suited to reading (in private or silently), not to performance', on the grounds that 'the most difficult texts could be communicated by reading them aloud'.[76] She cites a passage in Plato's *Parmenides* (127d-e) where Zeno reads his complicated philosophical work out aloud and Socrates asks him to read again any passage that he did not understand. However, in this example the emphasis seems to be on reading as a group activity, keeping the written text – albeit spoken aloud – at the centre of this engagement. Insofar as Socrates is able to interrogate the text and have Zeno re-read difficult passages, we are closer to the world of the reader than that of the audience. Moreover, we should be cautious about posing analogies between the publication of Plato's dialogues and the works of other prose writers, given the very complicated and idiosyncratic intertwining of the written and spoken word in Plato's dialogues. It may be that the model of a group of philosophers listening to the reading of a text that will form the basis for subsequent discussion is a model for the reception of Plato's dialogues themselves.[77] Thomas' important study proves not that Thucydides' *History* was destined for oral performance, but that we need to entertain a scenario in which reading and oral performance could intersect.

In the absence of any secure contemporary evidence for the oral publication of Thucydides' *History*, it seems safer to work with the text's stress on the mode of writing. Recent scholarship on Herodotus has stressed the importance of the 'display lecture' (*epideixis*) as the key to Herodotus' polemical first-person style.[78] But Thomas, whose work dominates this field, concedes that what survives is Herodotus' written text, as opposed to 'texts' of the oral 'display' performances of his work, and thus the closest we can get to this performance is to envisage the written text 'replicating features of the display piece'.[79] Oral performance is undeniably a very important feature of Herodotus' text in its historical context, but the written text has a life beyond this context and the writing ensures that Herodotus' performance of his knowledge will travel long after his own travels have come to an end. Although it is possible that Thucydides may have performed sections of his work for select audiences, as a prelude to written publication, this is something that we cannot know and I stress again that it is significant that, unlike Herodotus, Thucydides has not left any discernible imprint of such performances in the written text.

Conclusion

In the first section of this chapter I discussed the fact that Thucydides alienates himself from key socio-cultural institutions in his own day. I related this to Thucydides' estranging style, which enacts a process of defamiliarization:[80] it is part of the text's ideology to withhold what many contemporary audiences wanted to hear and to approach the historical present from a future, historicizing vantage point. Finally, in the last section I related the 'defamiliarized' quality of Thucydides' text to the mode of writing.

Readers of Thucydides have to perform a subtle balancing act. They have to negotiate the complex relationship between Thucydides and contemporary literature and society in the late fifth-century BC, and to understand how Thucydides reacts to and against various contexts. At the same time, they have to understand the *History* as an original text whose author successfully predicted its timeless appeal, while resisting the conclusion that Thucydides was writing for us. He may have been ahead of his time, but he is not of our time.

In the following chapters I explore these tensions through readings of Thucydides' *History*. In Chapters 2 and 3, I examine how Thucydides constructs the position and perspective from which he writes by creating the impression of a historical vista in which the historian (in his text) can see far into space and time. Specifically, in Chapter 2 I examine Thucydides' presentation of his historical insight in terms of the visual qualities of the narrative and his interest in the vantage point of the historical participants. I argue that Thucydides envisages a theatre of war, which draws on the pervasive culture of viewing in the Athens of his day. Thucydides also uses the focus on the visual to differentiate the perspective of the historian and his readers from the myopic perspective of the participants in the war.

Chapter 3 develops the subject of perspective and vantage point. It focuses on Thucydides' position in space and time and the way in which the spatial and temporal axes of the *History* distance him from the events that he narrates and furnish his historical research with the qualities of critical distance and detachment. In Chapter 4, I approach the subject of the speeches in Thucydides by suggesting that, once technological and methodological limitations have been taken into account, the gap between Thucydides' reconstruction of speeches and the words that were actually spoken corresponds to the gap between the historical audiences to whom the 'original' speeches were addressed and Thucydides' future readership. While the speeches illustrate contemporary speech culture, they also point to all the ways in which Thucydides' project is divorced from this culture.

Chapter 5 addresses a different aspect of the 'shaping of history', by exploring the way in which the *History* is plotted. I base my reading on Book 8 of the *History* – an incomplete book, which is often neglected. Reading Book 8 in conjunction with Sophocles' *Philoctetes*, I suggest that parallels in the texts reflect a sense of the history of this period as an Athenian tragedy, characterized by complex real-life plots.

Finally, in Chapter 6, I turn to the writer Lucian of Samosata (second century AD), to examine how the reception of Thucydides by one of his ancient readers also has a role to play in shaping our image of Thucydides. Thucydides plays a star role in Lucian's commentary *How to Write History*, which is all about how history is shaped by historians. I argue that Lucian is a shrewd critic of the ways in which Thucydides created a unique identity for his work in order to set it apart from other types of narrative. Finally, I argue that Lucian presents an interesting appreciation of the paradox in Thucydides' *ktêma es aiei*. In Lucian's reading, Thucydides recommends his text to the reader on the grounds of its detachment, but this very detachment also emerges as a competitive, self-interested manoeuvre. However, Lucian's provocative critique of Greek historiography is itself shaped by debates in Thucydides' *History*.

2

Point of View and Vantage Point

The theatre of war

We use the metaphor 'theatre of war' (a phrase popularized in the Second World War) to refer to a region of the world in which a war is being fought. In modern warfare it seems more appropriate to speak of the 'cinema of war', since we can watch deadly offensives on our television screens in real time.[1] In fact, the metaphor works both ways: one of the complications of modern high-tech warfare is the intrusion of multi-media coverage into so-called theatres of war. Some soldiers in modern combat zones, used to playing video games as civilians, allegedly have trouble adjusting to the reality that the targets on their screens correspond to real people and physical buildings.[2] There is also a general sensitivity to the camera, since in contemporary warfare it is common for news correspondents and camera crews to travel with troops. The power of photography and film footage to influence public perceptions of war has been shown recently in the case of the images of the abuse of prisoners at Abu Ghraib prison in Baghdad.[3]

A huge gulf separates the technologies of modern warring states and the city-states that went to war in ancient Greece in the second half of the fifth century BC. In the case of the latter, actual theatre, rather than cinema, was the medium of mass entertainment. Several scholars have referred metaphorically to the visual and theatrical overtones of Thucydides' narrative.[4] Simon Hornblower writes of 'Thucydides' gaze',[5] and also introduces a parallel with cinema to convey the vividness of Thucydides' depiction of the trireme that was despatched to rescind the decision of the Athenian assembly to execute the adult male population of Mytilene (3.49).[6] Paula Debnar cites Plutarch *Moralia* 347A for the view that the most effective historian is one whose narrative has the visual quality of painting,[7] while June Allison has used an analogy with film footage to convey the differing style of narrative in Books 1-7 of the *History*, contrasted with the style of Book 8.[8]

Paradoxically, the anachronistic terminology of film studies may advance our understanding of Thucydides; a full study of the filmic potential of Thucydides' narrative would help to draw out the extent to which the reader is required and assisted to visualize the subject matter.[9] In addition to the passage singled out by Hornblower, there are numerous passages in the *History*, which use narrative techniques that anticipate aspects of film syntax, such as the 'split screen'. For example, at 4.26.8-9, when Spartan hoplites are marooned on the island of Sphacteria (off Pylos – Map 1: 15), the reader has to imagine the helot divers attempting to smuggle food onto the island, and the Athenian lookouts trying to detect them: one has to see both under the water and above the water, as it were:

> Divers also swam in under water by way of the harbour, dragging along with a cord skins that contained poppy-seed mixed with honey and pounded linseed. Initially the divers went undetected, but later guard-posts were stationed. So each side adopted every kind of scheme, the Spartans in an effort to send in food, the Athenians to stop them from getting away with it.[10]

By evoking the media of cinema and theatre, I do not mean to imply that Thucydides encourages us to see warfare as mere drama – far from it. However, he does emphasize the strategic importance of sight, appearance and spectacle in the Atheno-Peloponnesian War, and exposes the efforts that different generals went to in order to 'stage' power with a view to intimidating their opponents.[11] As well as being a recurrent phenomenon in the narratives of battles in the *History*, the concept of the 'theatre of war' can also help us to understand how Thucydides may have been influenced by dramatic genres in his desire to give readers a good view of the Atheno-Peloponnesian War.[12] Following other scholars, I will suggest below that Thucydides' claim at 1.22.4 that he hopes that his *History* will satisfy those who want to 'gain a clear insight' (*saphôs skopein*) into events in the past and events that may occur in the future, needs to be understood in the context of the sustained emphasis on viewing and sight throughout the *History*.[13] There has been some compelling research on the 'visual' aspects of Thucydides' *History*; Tim Rood – whose work I will return to below – has written an excellent analysis of the way in which perceptions function as an important part of the 'cognitive lesson' of history in Thucydides' text.[14] Although Rood does not broach the analogies between the visibility of the action in Thucydides' narrative and the visibility that is intrinsic to dramatic genres, his comments about 'cognitive dissonance' in Thucydides – where there is a gap between the greater knowledge of Thucydides and his readers, and the restricted knowledge of the historical agents – are reminiscent of Jean-Paul Vernant's work on tragic irony, where the tragic playwright communicates meaning to the spectators which is lost on the protagonists on-stage.[15] Like the spectator (*theatês*) of Greek drama who sees more and knows more than the characters in the drama, the reader of Thucydides views a replay of the war that offers much fuller coverage than the limited perspectives of those involved in the war.[16] This is the perspective that Thucydides himself enjoyed, writing his account of a war that he had lived through from the privileged perspective of hindsight.

2. Point of View and Vantage Point

In the chapters in Book 1 (20-2) in which Thucydides sets out both the ideology and methodology of his text, he contrasts the kind of work that he is writing with other types of literature. Thucydides disassociates himself from the example of poets who offer entertaining, aggrandizing and fictional accounts of past events, as well as prose writers (*logographoi*) who compose accounts to lead their audiences on, rather than tell them the truth (1.21.1). These accounts of the past are said to achieve success on account of their fabulous element – *to muthôdes* (ibid.). It is often assumed that an allusion to the *Histories* of Herodotus lurks behind the sweeping reference to *logographoi*. While Thucydides is much closer to Herodotus than he lets on, his rhetoric of historiography is considerably less entertaining.[17] Thucydides anticipates the criticism that audiences may find his account of events devoid of pleasure relative to these other genres (*aterpesteron*), on account of his rejection of the fabulous (*to mê muthôdes*) – 1.22.4. The claim that his *History* is not a competition piece (*agônisma*) invites a direct contrast with competitive performance, the most common term for which was *agôn* (whether of dramatic plays, speeches in the assembly and the courts, or epideictic displays of knowledge).[18] These competitive genres played to the judgement of their audiences.

Thucydides' anti-theatrical rhetoric is echoed by Dionysius of Halicarnassus, writing in the first century BC; Dionysius makes a connection between the fact that Thucydides was a real-life participant in the war that he narrates and the inappropriateness of theatrical enchantments:

> These local historians were obliged to embellish their accounts with mythological digressions. Thucydides, however, chose a single episode in which he personally participated: it was therefore inappropriate for him to adulterate his narrative with theatrical enchantments (*hai theatrikai goêteiai*) or to arrange it in a way that would confuse his readers, as his predecessors' compositions would naturally do.
>
> *On Thucydides* 7[19]

I take Dionysius to mean that when one has no first-hand knowledge of the events that one is narrating, or if the events are fictional, then one might have recourse to the attention-grabbing and enthralling plots and twists of drama as staged in the theatre.[20] However, when one has clear knowledge of the events, the narrative will vouch for itself. In chapter 37 Dionysius criticizes Thucydides for beginning his narrative of the Melian dialogue by reporting what the respective parties said (5.85-6), and then absenting himself as a narrator by switching into a dramatic dialogue (5.87-111). In Dionysius' estimation, history is ideologically anti-theatre.

When modern scholars have suggested affiliations between Thucydides and Athenian drama, they have tended to focus either on tragic thought and patterns of tragic narrative in Thucydides, or else on how parallels between argumentation and language in Thucydides and Greek tragedy (primarily Euripides) can help to clarify the intellectual context of the *History*. The first study to place Thucydides firmly in the context of mythopoetics was Francis Conford's study *Thucydides Mythistoricus* (first published in 1907), and no study since has seen such extensive analogies between Thucydides' approach to his material and that of the trage- dians.[21] In the 1930s, John H. Finley's essay on 'Euripides and Thucydides' examined parallels and resemblances between the two authors in an attempt to attribute the influences on Thucydides' prose style to intellectual ideas in the Athens of his youth and the period prior to his exile.[22] Colin Macleod's essay on 'Thucydides and Tragedy' considers the presence of tragic patterns of explanation in Thucydides, but attributes these to the context in which Thucydides lived and wrote, in which tragedy was a central socio-political, cultural and religious institu- tion, rather than to direct engagement with specific tragedies. Macleod also argued that much of the 'tragedy' that readers discern in Thucydides' work derived from Homer and Herodotus.[23] In a slightly different vein, two works by Christopher Pelling have approached tragedy as a historical source, exploring its dialogues with contemporary debates and history.[24]

Until recently, relatively little attention has been paid to the intertext between Thucydides and Athenian comedy. However, both Christopher Pelling and Paul Ludwig juxtapose Thucydides and comedy as contempo- rary genres that speak to the same concerns.[25] Although direct allusions to comedy are absent in the *History*, when the crowd start to heckle the Athenian politician Cleon during an assembly debate about the advis- ability of sending an expedition to Pylos (4.28.3), and Thucydides describes sniggers of laughter falling upon the audience at Cleon's daft- ness (4.28.5), it is hard to resist the conclusion that Thucydides and his Athenian readers would not have thought of the depiction of Cleon as an object of ridicule in Aristophanic comedy.

However, in spite of a willingness to relate Thucydides to surviving Athenian plays, relatively little attention has been paid to the way in which the broader medium of theatre, what we might call 'theatrical culture', or 'the cultural politics of viewing' – as Simon Goldhill puts it – may have influenced Thucydides' narration of events.[26] I will return to the question of the dialogue between Thucydides' *History* and Athenian tragedy in Chapter 5; in the present chapter I will focus on the influence of theatrical culture and the visual in the *History*. By 'theatrical culture', I mean the emphasis placed on viewing and spectating in many areas of Athenian polit- ical life – whether in the theatre, the law court, the assembly, or in the agora and the streets.[27] Audiences went to the theatre with the express purpose of watching (and hearing) the plays; juries in the law courts and the *dêmos* in assembly meetings were frequently called upon to scrutinize speakers by picking out their non-verbal behaviour (what they wore and their body language) as well as to 'take in' significant visible landmarks and objects in the environs of the courts or the Pnyx. Moreover, in all these locations audiences were enjoined to 'see' the facts, and the process of judgement is frequently expressed in terms of the language of 'sight' and 'insight'. Athenian audiences were required to be experienced, canny spectators and, consequently, seeing was one of the most profound ways of knowing. This privileging of sight was not exclusive to Athens; at a more fundamental level there is a linguistic connection between the verbs of seeing and knowing in Greek.[28] However, in Athens – as contrasted with the stereotype of Sparta, for example – seeing and sight were strongly linked to theatrical culture. Simon Goldhill has stressed that studies on the language of vision and insight in Athenian texts need to pay closer attention to the Athenian 'culture of viewing'; commenting that 'scrutinizing viewing is part of a self-reflexive democratic discourse'.[29]

Thucydides does not just draw on the visual medium of theatrical culture; he also draws on the prerogative of theatre to instruct through *showing* (itself part of the ideology of Athenian citizenship, which is constituted as an education in and of itself through acts of listening, watching and judging). I have already mentioned Rood's idea about the significance of the perceptions in Thucydides' narrative in delivering a 'cognitive lesson' to the reader. This theory becomes more compelling when seen in terms of the precedent set in the theatre. Thucydides' narrative hints at the paradigmatic quality of Athenian drama, suggesting that the historical participants themselves viewed the events in which they were involved as a quasi-theatrical arena in which the visual was an all-important factor. These same events are also paradigmatic for the reader, if only he or she can work out how to interpret Thucydides.[30]

This motif of Athens as a paradigm to be studied and imitated runs throughout the funeral oration. At 2.37.1 Pericles claims that the Athenians are a *paradeigma* for others to imitate, rather than the Athenians imitating others (*mimoumenoi heterous*). The participle *mimoumenoi* (imitating, acting the part of) highlights the theatrical connotations of the noun *paradeigma*. Pericles says that the Athenians behave lawfully in the public sphere out of fear, because they 'give a hearing (*akroasis*) to' both those in positions of authority and the laws (ibid.). According to Pericles, then, being an Athenian is to be an *akroatês* (listener / audience member) of the best kind of performance. This is reinforced by the claim that the Athenians do not exclude foreigners from any form of instruction (*mathêma*) or show (*theama*), and this open-door policy is contrasted with the Spartan practice of expelling foreigners (2.39.1). Pericles elaborates on the reference to *mathêma* with the famous claim that the entire city is an education for all of Greece (*paideusis Hellados* – 2.41.1). As though by way of an example of what this 'education' consists of, Pericles describes his own speech as a 'lesson' (*didaskalia* – 2.42.1). The noun *didaskalia* could also refer to the rehearsal of choruses for dramatic performances, and behind Pericles' language there is definitely a hint of the playwright running a body of actors through his script (political stage-management).[31] The irony of Pericles' claim that Athens provides an instructive spectacle for the rest of the Greek world will resonate throughout the following narrative.

The most ironic twist to this claim occurs at 5.90, where the Melian representatives tell the Athenians that their fall would prompt the greatest reprisals and would serve as a *paradeigma* for others. The vocabulary that the Melians use here evokes the language of tragedy, specifically the idea of the tragic fall (*sphallô*) and vengeance (*timôria*). Not to be outdone, the Athenians turn this back on the Melians by saying that the fact that the Melians hate them is a clear *paradeigma* ('proof') of their power (*dunameôs*) to their subjects (5.95).[32] This highhanded boast about making the Melians an example of their power makes explicit a strain that was latent in the funeral oration, and in ignoring the Melians' warning that they run the risk of becoming a negative *paradeigma*, the Athenians are blind to the trajectory of the war that Thucydides has plotted for the reader. One could argue that 5.90 recalls the passage at 2.65.11-12, where Thucydides gives readers an explicit proleptic revelation of the eventual defeat of the Athenians, and uses the verb *sphallô* ('stumble', 'trip up') to refer to their downfall – the same verb that the Melian representatives use when they raise the hypothetical possibility of the Athenians' downfall.[33]

In addition to the ambivalent uses of the noun *paradeigma* in the speeches, Thucydides also reminds the reader that a *didaskalia* can also take the form of a negative example – of learning from past mistakes. At 2.87.7, Cnemus, Brasidas and the other Peloponnesian commanders try to instil confidence in their forces by telling them that their past mistakes will serve as a *didaskalia* – a lesson / rehearsal:[34] 'And as to the mistakes which we made before, these very same mistakes will be an additional advantage in that they provide a lesson (*didaskalian parechei*)'. Theatre is certainly part of the 'rhetoric of history' in Thucydides; the participants have watched drama and it informs the way in which they respond to events.[35] For Thucydides' readers in ancient Greece, theatre forms a common bond of cultural reference, and, for all of Thucydides' other readers, the theatrical atmosphere and the interplay between vision and historical insight helps to frame all of the subordinate dramas: Pericles putting Athens on display, the Melians and Athenians disputing what constitutes the real *paradeigma*, or Cnemus and Brasidas redeeming their past mistakes as a future *didaskalia*. In Thucydides' narrative, the historical agents frequently attempt to manipulate sight and to stage displays of power. However, all these shows of strength are part of the *History's* sustained illustration of the precariousness of sight, when not disciplined by insight and reflection.

2. Point of View and Vantage Point

Lowell Edmunds has observed that Thucydides' narrative typically gives us history 'from the actor's point of view, while at the same time rendering the history more intelligible than it could have been to any actor at any time'.[36] He attributes this intelligibility to the speeches which purport to show us how events looked from the perspective of the speaker. The speeches are, indeed, fundamental to Thucydides' *History*, but I would contend that even more than the speeches, it is the visual aspect of the narrative that confers greatest intelligibility. Thucydides affords us a clearer view than the restricted view of the participants and supplies a commentary on sight as one of the determining factors in the progress of the war. This visual aspect applies equally to the speeches and to the rest of the narrative.

One of the standards that Thucydides set himself in 'publishing' his *History* was that it should enable future readers to have a clear insight (*to saphes skopein*) into what happened in the past and events that would take place in the future. As others have noted, this is not equivalent to claiming that history will repeat itself, or that the reader of the *History* will be able to predict the future clairvoyantly. Rather, the clarity of the analysis offered in Thucydides' account of past events will aid insight into future events as they happen, but not before they happen.

In recent years there has been some excellent research into the way in which Thucydides' narrative is focalized, drawing on the hermeneutic framework of narratology.[37] This approach has advanced sophisticated techniques for identifying the perspective from which the narrator projects the narrative, in terms of whose eyes we are looking through, whose voice is speaking, and the distribution of knowledge ('who knows'?). Part of the development of narratology was the move away from the notion of 'point of view' – long a staple of literary criticism. This was justified by the argument that the 'point of view' from which a narrative is narrated is not a sufficient explanation of the complex techniques of narration involved. It may, therefore, seem regressive to revive the term 'point of view' in relation to Thucydides' narrative. I use the phrase in this chapter because I am interested not so much in techniques of narration and the way in which the narrative is focalized, but rather in the emphasis that Thucydides places on literal vantage points in battle narratives and the connection between physical viewpoint and point of view.[38] Furthermore, by focusing on the theatrical overtones of acts of viewing, sight and display, I hope to emphasize the connection between 'point of view' and the theatrical culture that Thucydides shared with his audience. In the remainder of this chapter I will take Brasidas' exploitation of visibility and display at 4.124-5.11 as a case-study to illustrate what I am calling the 'theatre of war' in Thucydides. I will then relate this section of the narrative to a broader preoccupation with sight, visibility and display in battle narratives by examining other theatres of war in the *History*.

Finally, I will examine the way in which Thucydides distinguishes the kind of sight that is available to agents in history from the reflective sight and insight that is possible for readers of his *History*.

Brasidas in the theatre of war (4.124-5.11)

At the beginning of Book 5 (chapters 6-13) Thucydides gives an account of the second battle of Amphipolis fought in 422 BC. The generals involved are Cleon on the Athenian side and Brasidas, leading the Peloponnesian forces. Although this battle was the occasion of the death of Brasidas, it is the Peloponnesians who win, and their victory is attributed to Brasidas' clever and prescient strategic manipulation of viewpoint / point of view and visibility. In fact, in Thucydides' account of the battle of Amphipolis, Brasidas uses sight as a weapon.

Brasidas draws up his troops at a place called Cerdylium, which is described as elevated ground (*epi meteôrou*) on the right bank of the river, not far from Amphipolis (5.6.3 – Map 1: 23).[39] Thucydides writes that everything was clearly visible from this point (*katephaineto panta autothen*), and the significance of this oversight of the terrain and everything in it is that none of the movements of Cleon, the opposing general, would go unnoticed. According to Thucydides, who infers Brasidas' train of thought, Brasidas expects Cleon to make a move on Amphipolis because the latter will overlook (*huperoraô*) the size of Brasidas' forces, which he cannot see. The verb *huperoraô* has a range of meanings, including 'to overlook, take no notice of' and 'to despise / feel contempt for'. In his translation Rex Warner selects the latter sense and translates 5.6.3 as 'This, in fact, was what Brasidas expected – that Cleon *would be contemptuous of* the numbers opposed to him and would move up against Amphipolis with the troops that he had with him.'[40] However, according to my translation, the point about this comment is not that Brasidas thought that Cleon would 'feel contempt for' the size of the forces drawn up against him (Thucydides tells us that the two opposing forces were roughly equal – *antipala* 5.8.2), but that Cleon will not see / know the size of the forces. Given the emphasis on sight in this passage, the visual connotations of the compound verb *huperoraô* are paramount: Cleon proceeds confidently with the advance because he cannot *see* Brasidas' forces, and because he cannot *see* what is going on in the city: he quite literally *overlooks* them.[41]

Cleon responds to pressure from his troops who are frustrated by the delay (5.7.2), and advances – as Brasidas expected him to – to a hill in front of Amphipolis. He tells his troops that he is moving forward to gain a vantage point, or a 'view' (*kata thean* – 5.7.3) and when he reaches the top of the hill he gazes at the view (*etheato*, from *theaomai* – 5.7.4). When Brasidas addresses his troops, he mentions the fact that the enemy are turning this way and that to take in the view in a disorganized manner (*ataktôs kata thean tetrammenoi* – 5.9.3).[42] The adverb *ataktôs* evokes *taxis* – a noun that can mean military rank and order. Here the adverb both describes their movements and refers to the disorganized manner in which they gaze. Kleon's forces do not know what they are looking for, so even their viewing lacks discipline.

In a discussion of the vocabulary of sight in Thucydides and Herodotus, Gregory Crane notes that the verb *theaomai* ('to gaze upon') is relatively frequent in Herodotus' *Histories*, occurring forty-nine times, whereas Thucydides uses this verb only three times. Crane singles out the current passage (5.7.4) as an example of Thucydides following a Herodotean pattern: 'While the object of Kleon's gaze, a military reconnaissance, is fairly pedestrian, the paradigm of the visitor moving to a new terrain, and then gazing upon the unfamiliar, is common in Herodotus'.[43] However, I would suggest that Thucydides' pointed use of this verb is due to the fact that Cleon's attempt at reconnaissance is sloppy and unfocused, hence he 'gazes'. He does not comprehend the significance of what he sees and his gaze fails to yield any productive intelligence.[44] Paul Ludwig has detected even deeper criticism of Cleon in these lines, noting that Cleon's behaviour at Amphipolis reveals the very flaws of which he accuses the Athenian assembly in Book 3 (3.38.4 and 3.38.7 – see below, p. 95):

> In an irony of Thucydides' account, this Athenian desire to watch rather than to act, to appreciate rather than to accomplish, is a passion that turns up in Cleon himself. Thucydides describes the politician's fatal reconnoitre of Amphipolis in terms suggestive of the leisured, contemplative, theatre-going life.[45]

All this while, Brasidas can see every move that Cleon makes, but Cleon can still not see Brasidas – even from the top of the hill. Thucydides writes that nobody was visible on the walls (*oudeis ephaineto* – 5.7.5). This phrase contrasts with the verb *kataphainomai* in the previous chapter (5.6.3) where Cerdylium – the point occupied by Brasidas – is described as a vantage point from which everything was clearly visible (*katephaineto*).

Brasidas manipulates vision and visibility to create an element of surprise. Thucydides writes that he made preparations to attack with craft (*technê* – 5.8.2). He deprives the enemy of foresight (*aneu proopseôs* – 5.8.3): both literally, in that they will not see his troops until he wants them to, and metaphorically, because Cleon's projections of the battle will be based on a false impression of the situation. Throughout this section of narrative the theme of vision and sight is highly pronounced.

Brasidas instructs his men that success in such situations comes from capitalizing on the errors of the enemy, and from making an attack from a point out of view (*mê apo tou prophanous*), as opposed to being drawn up

opposite the enemy (5.9.4). We have already seen how Brasidas' preparations are described as crafty; in the speech that he composed for Brasidas,
Thucydides has Brasidas equate his own tactics with cheating manoeuvres
(*klemmata*) that deceive the enemy (*apatêsas* – 5.9.5). When Brasidas
finally chooses to reveal his movements to the Athenians, there is a
sudden emphasis on visibility, but it is belated, since the Athenians have
not seen any of the preparations. In the space of a single sentence (5.10.2),
Thucydides uses four words connected with appearance that all derive
from the same stem: the adjective *phaneros* ('visible' x 2), the adjective
epiphanês ('in full view') and the verb *hupophainô*, in the passive voice ('to
be visible under'):

> Meanwhile Brasidas had come into view (*phanerou*) making his way down
> from Cerdylium, and sacrificing at the temple of Athena inside the city,
> which was in full view (*epihanêi ousêi*) from outside, and being busy with
> these things; it was announced to Cleon, who had gone on ahead in order to
> get a view of the situation (*kata thean*), that all the forces of the enemy were
> in view (*phanera*) in the city and that the hooves of many horses and the feet
> of many men were seen underneath (*hupophainontai*) the gates, giving the
> impression that they were about to march out.

It is ironic that everything comes into view while Cleon is looking in the
wrong place. The battle of Amphipolis is stage-managed by Brasidas from
start to finish; even the arrangements for Brasidas' death involve cheating
the Athenians of sight: the Athenians do not notice that he has fallen
because he is whisked off the battlefield (5.10.8).

In Thucydides' narrative of this battle, sight is equated with foresight
(Brasidas), or lack of foresight (Cleon) on the part of the generals involved.
At another level, Thucydides' account gives his readers a bird's-eye view of
the battle, and affords them an even better insight into the events that took
place than the view enjoyed by the troops themselves. As Robbins remarks
about the familiar formula, 'I know, I was there': 'Is physical presence in a
battle really a significant guarantee of pertinent knowledge about that
battle? Is it even necessarily superior to a more distanced perspective?'[46]
Thucydides' emphasis on sight in the battle over Amphipolis is no mere
narrative spectacle for the entertainment of the audience; the narrative
exploits the very real importance of sight in contemporary military
strategy. Thucydides' ancient Greek readers (assuming that they were
men) would themselves have had direct knowledge of warfare, and, in
many cases, they would have had experience of generalship and the
strategic contests in intelligence that were required in order to out-
manoeuvre enemy generals. If we review Thucydides' narrative of the
battle of Amphipolis in light of a treatise on military strategy dating from
the mid-fourth century BC by the author Aineias Tacticus (Aineias 'the

Tactician'),[47] then Brasidas' conduct emerges as textbook strategy, whereas Cleon's conduct overlooks fundamental strategic precautions. Admittedly, this involves reading backwards from the work of a later author to an earlier author. It might also be objected that Aineias Tacticus derives some of his strategic scenarios and advice from Thucydides' *History*, leading to a circular reading.[48] However, if Aineias did draw on Thucydides, then this only serves to strengthen my argument about the practical, military significance of the prominence of sight in Thucydides 5.6-13.

Aineias concentrates on surviving the challenges of a siege, but he also offers advice about reconnaissance missions and sorties against the enemy. In these passages he places great emphasis on knowledge of local topography and the significance of sight as a source of strategic advantage. At 1.2 Aineias states that expeditionary forces should take into account the terrain through which they have to march. Among the significant landmarks, Aineias specifies 'commanding heights' (*huperdexia*).[49] At 6.1, Aineias recommends that scouts should undertake reconnaissance from an elevated point in front of the city. Cleon gets this much right when he ascends the hill in front of Amphipolis to get a better view of the situation. However, Aineias stresses that scouts must have experience of warfare so that they understand what to look for and what to see:

(6.1) At each position there should be at least three scouts, chosen not at random but for their experience in war; this is to avoid any one scout's ignorantly supposing that something is important, signalling or reporting it to the city, and causing needless trouble to the people there.
(6.2) Such mistakes tend to be made by men who know nothing of warfare and how troops are used: they fail to recognize which of the enemy's operations and activities are intentional and which are accidental.
(6.3) The experienced man, by contrast, understands the enemy's preparations, his numbers, his line of march and the other movements of his army, and so will communicate the reality.[50]

By contrast, we have seen how Thucydides (sometimes using Brasidas as a focalizer) emphasizes Cleon's shoddy reconnaissance and his failure to discern the enemy's tactics. And Cleon is no mere 'scout', but an Athenian general. Aineias Tacticus further suggests that scouts should undertake their reconnaissance at night / dawn, so that their manoeuvres cannot be seen. Cleon does not adopt this precaution. Later in the treatise, Aineias advises his reader (presumably the general) to 'exploit your familiarity with the terrain' (16.19), with a view to planning movements both secretly and in the open (*lathraiôs kai phanerôs*).[51] Again, compare Brasidas' ability to exploit the landscape around Amphipolis both so as to gain superior insight into his enemy's tactics, and so as to control exactly how the enemy will view his own movements.

Brasidas' tactic of concealment is underhand – he says so himself (see above, p. 28). We might be tempted to interpret this as a case of Thucydides characterizing Brasidas in line with the 'national' stereotype that Spartans were deceivers whose military training promoted subterfuge and trickery. This stereotype is aired in the *History*, most prominently in the funeral speech attributed to Pericles. For Pericles it is a point of pride that Athens is an 'open' society that does not bar outsiders from any lecture or performance, neither does it keep anything hidden for fear that one of its enemies might benefit from seeing it, and nor does it set store by preparation and tricks (2.39.1). When read in the light of this passage from the funeral oration, Brasidas' tactics at the battle of Amphipolis look like an ironic antitype of the Athenian character idealized by Pericles. His preparations are very deliberate, he has recourse to trickery and he keeps his manoeuvres hidden from the enemy.[52]

One of the last military actions that occurs before the second battle of Amphipolis in Thucydides' account is a skirmish between Brasidas' and Perdiccas' forces, and the forces of Arrhabaeus – king of the Lynkestian Macedonians – backed up by Illyrian deserters (the Illyrians had previously been fighting for Brasidas' ally Perdiccas of Macedon) (4.124-8). When they realize that the Illyrians have deserted them, Perdiccas' forces fall into a blind panic at nightfall. Thucydides glosses this panic with the comment that this is characteristic of large armies that are subject to an unseen attack (*asaphôs ekplêgnusthai* – 4.125.1). Perdiccas' forces jump to conclusions about the size of the enemy and take flight, and at first Perdiccas does not realize what has happened (*ouk aisthanomenon* – ibid.). When he does realize that his forces have deserted, he leaves without seeing Brasidas (*prin ton Brasidan idein* – ibid.). This short encounter – or rather non-encounter – is a catalogue of obscure fears and obscured vision.

In order to extricate his own forces from this mess, Brasidas gives them a pep-talk, which contains instruction (*didachê*) about how to overcome their fear of the Barbarians by not being intimidated by what they see and hear (4.126.1). Brasidas' lesson is very much 'on message' in that it echoes Thucydides' own reservations about the tendency of visual appearances (*phanerê opsis*) to create a misleading impression of reality (1.10.2-3).[53] Clarity is both a historiographical desideratum in Thucydides' account and a positive advantage on the battlefield. Brasidas makes a general point about enemies whose fearfulness consists in having an appearance of strength (*dokêsin ischuos* – 4.126.4) when they are really weak. In such cases true instruction (*didachê alêthês*) instils confidence in the forces under attack (ibid.). He then adds that the enemy are terrifying because of their visible mass and hard to stand up to because of the volume of their cries and the way in which they brandish their weapons in a threatening demonstration (4.126.5). In fact, Brasidas distinguishes between two different categories of seeing: on the one hand, what the soldiers can 'see' (= understand) as a result of his instruction and, on the other hand, the sight before their eyes. 'You see clearly (*saphôs ... horâte*) that the danger that existed from the enemy before is in fact small, although it is harrowing to look at (*opsis*) and listen to (*akoê*)' (4.126.6). More than just the visible impact of the barbarian enemy (*opsis ... dêlôsis*), Thucydides' Brasidas mentions the noise as well, making it easier for the reader to see and hear the enemy on the page. Brasidas' awareness of his troops' sensitivity to *opsis* is shared by other generals in the *History*; for example at 2.88.3, the Athenian general Phormio gives the Athenians a pep-talk prior to a sea-battle with the Spartans, because he sees that they are disheartened by the sight (*opsis*) of the enemy fleet.

In the first engagement at Pylos (Book 4.11-13), Brasidas is described as the Spartan who was 'most visible' in the fighting (*phanerôtatos* – 4.11.4). He urges on his men and goes out onto the gangway of his ship in an attempt to be the first to land.[54] Lucian singles out the conflict between Demosthenes and Brasidas at 4.11-12 as an example of a vivid episode, where it is appropriate for the historian to 'zoom in' on a particular part of the action and abandon, temporarily, a panoramic perspective.[55] Brasidas' rousing show of strength at Pylos positively influences his men, whereas the visual appearance and sound of the Illyrians and Arrhabaeus prove a dispiriting threat at 4.126.4. As a consummate director / actor, who uses visual techniques of intimidation himself, Brasidas is suitably placed to lecture his forces on the dynamics of the gaze.[56]

Brasidas' instruction of his forces is reminiscent of Virginia Hunter's analysis of social control in Thucydides: 'in Thucydides social control is the countervailing force of a single individual who understands crowd psychology and who has the rhetorical skill to make practical use of that understanding'.[57] Hunter adds that the Thucydidean crowd is characteristically 'addicted to sight and sound rather than rational argument'.[58] Contrasted with Perdiccas' forces, who succumb to mob psychology and behave 'just as large forces are accustomed to behave when threatened by an obscure attack' (4.125.1), Brasidas schools his forces in how to overcome this tendency and behave rationally.

Brasidas' show

As we have seen, for all that he warns his forces of the dangers of succumbing to a mere 'show' of strength, there is much that is showy about Brasidas in Thucydides' depiction. Brasidas' conduct is often portrayed in theatrical terms in the *History*, with a strong emphasis on how his actions appear and the reactions that they elicit. Recently Tim Rood and Jonathan Price have discussed this aspect of Brasidas' characterization.[59] The latter argues that Thucydides' analysis of the reality of Spartan policy towards the cities in Thrace is played out in the figure of Brasidas. Price points out that Thucydides employs the language of show and reputation in relation to Brasidas (referring to Thucydides' description of Brasidas at 4.82.1), and that Thucydides expresses uncertainty about the qualities of justice and moderation that were attributed to Brasidas:

> The nuances in Thucydides' syntax and word choice stress a carefully orchestrated perception of him rather than his true nature: he 'showed himself to be' or 'gave the impression of being' just and moderate 'at that time' or 'while he was there'. There is no certainty that these are inherent characteristics.[60]

In another theatre of war, Tim Rood has analysed the depiction of Brasidas at Megara in terms of what he calls 'self-fulfilling perceptions'.[61] He suggests that Brasidas' successful confrontation of the Athenians at Megara and the Athenians' subsequent withdrawal give rise to a 'perception of failure' both on the part of Athens' allies and the Greek world at large.[62] Rood also comes very close to analysing Brasidas' approach to waging war in terms of theatre with the phrase 'didactic arena': 'The Athenians fail to realize that the plain of Megara is a "didactic arena" both for the men within the city and for the wider Greek world' (ibid.).[63] The lessons 'learned' in this arena, in which Brasidas plays to both hearing and sight, are misleading; this is demonstrated by Athens' northern allies who make overtures to Brasidas with a view to revolt (4.108.4):

> They were under the impression that they could act without fear, partly because they were deluded (*epseusmenoi*) about the power of the Athenians, the true extent of which only became manifest later, but mostly because they based their judgement on obscure acts of will, rather than a reliable projection of the future; most people are accustomed to entrust what they desire to hope devoid of circumspection, while they reject what does not appeal to them with all-empowered acts of reason.[64]

Brasidas' rhetoric makes it 'seem' as though the Athenian allies have immunity from harm by deluding them (*epseusmenoi*) about the reality of Athens' power (4.108.4). Thucydides uses the language of appearance to draw an ironic contrast between the appearance (*ephaineto*) of safety in the winter of 424/3 BC, and the subsequent manifestation (*diephanê*) of Athens' power (ibid.).[65] The significance of the allies' error is emphasized by terms that have deep historiographical significance in Thucydides' *History*.[66] The allies are said to reject a safe projection (*pronoia asphalês*) of future events in favour of blind wishing (*boulêsis asaphês*).[67] Again and again, Thucydides shows decision-making at the collective level to be dominated by wishful thinking: men want to hear, and do indeed hear, that which they want to be true.[68] The allies base their judgement on an act of will that lacks clarity (*asaphês*), whereas Thucydides privileges clarity (*to saphes*) as one of the guiding principles of the *History* (1.22.4). The fact that Thucydides mentions *pronoia* serves to remind us how much value he places on fore-sight and reasoned projections of the future (see below, pp. 53-4). There is a statement in Bernard Williams' study on *Truth and Truthfulness* about the 'virtue' of objectivity in Thucydides (as well as other thinkers) that could have been written as a commentary on this passage:

> Self-conscious pursuit of the truth requires resistance to such things as self-deception and wishful thinking, and one component of the virtue of Accuracy – which, once again, is why it is a virtue and not merely a disposition of reli-ability – lies in the skills and attitudes that resist the pleasure principle, in all its forms, from a gross need to believe the agreeable, to mere laziness in checking one's investigations.[69]

The language in which battles are narrated is continuous with the histo-riographical concerns of the author. Thucydides signals his criticism of the allies' judgement by accusing them of opting for *boulêsis asaphês* (obscure acts of will) over *pronoia asphalês* (secure projections of the future). Clarity and the lack of it are equally critical in military terms; several of the battle narratives in the *History* are framed by a contest for clarity, where power and success consist in depriving the enemy of vision and sight, while at the same time gaining insight into their planning and actions. A brief snap-shot will suffice for the time being: when a party of Plataeans escape from their besieged city under cover of darkness (3.20-4), the Plataeans contrive in advance that those left inside the walls should light torches, in order to obfuscate the fire signals of the Peloponnesians, which would be used to give warning of an attack (3.22.8).

Other theatres of war

The synoptic view of the (second) battle of Amphipolis (5.6-11) enables the reader to make an appraisal of what happened in a particular battle. The visual re-enactment of the battle in Thucydides' version of events, coupled with his critique of the fallibility of sight, is an important part of the historical explanation offered to the reader in the *History*. However, this is just one section occupying a mere six chapters in Thucydides' narrative, and the real challenge for the reader is to be able to view this battle in the context of a much larger vista – that of the *History* as a whole.[70]

What the respective armies can or cannot see is an integral part of the battle narratives in the *History*. Drawing on his own experience as a general, Thucydides depicts the generals in the *History* as being fully aware of the need to gain a visual advantage over the enemy, either by ensuring that they can see more than the enemy or by staging an intim-idatory display of power. Brasidas' strategy at Amphipolis consisted largely in exploiting the fact that the enemy could not see what he was doing, and only revealing what he wanted them to see.

At 3.16.1 the Athenians are said to have been aware that the Peloponnesians' decision to lead an allied invasion into Attica in the summer of 428 BC was due to the fact that they themselves were perceived to be weak. Consequently, they put on a demonstration (*epideixis*) of their military power to make it clear (*dêlôsai*) that this was a mistaken perception. This demonstration had the required effect because the Spartans reconsidered the reports that they had received about Athens' power and, in the face of other obstacles, cancelled the invasion (3.16.2). We can compare 6.11.4, where Nicias informs the Athenian assembly that 'the Hellenes there will be most intimidated by us if we do not go there at all, or – second best – if we make a demonstration of our power (*ei deixantes tên dunamin*) for a short period of time and then go away again'. Furthermore, Nicias endorses the idea of power as 'mere' show by claiming that 'we all know that the greatest objects of wonder are those which present the fewest opportunities to have their reputations tested' (ibid.). As important as projecting a show of strength to intimidate the enemy is creating a conviction of strength in one's own forces. At the outset of the war, Pericles addresses the Athenian assembly and gives an inventory of the city's resources to serve as a demonstration (*apodeixis*) that they would win the war (2.13.9). Even Pericles' demonstration via argument has a significant visual element in that some of the resources that he enumerates are tied up in highly visible monuments, and Thucydides describes Pericles 'revealing' these resources to the Athenians (*apophainô* – 2.13.5; 2.13.8).[71]

In his narrative of the stand-off at Pylos, Thucydides implies that sight was crucial in determining the outcome of the battle. The Athenians and Messenians make little progress in their blockade of the Spartans who are trapped on the island of Sphacteria. We are told that initially the Athenian general Demosthenes was reluctant to risk an attack because the island was wooded and they would not be able to see the enemy's movements clearly. In this situation the Spartans would have the advantage of attacking from an invisible location (*ex aphanous chôriou* – 4.29.3); consequently the preparation of the Spartan forces would not be nearly as visible (*dêla*), whereas mistakes made by the Athenian generals would be clear for all to see (*kataphanê* – ibid.). Furthermore, the Athenian forces might attack each other because they would not have a good view of what was going on (*prosopsis* – 4.29.4). When a freak forest fire burns down a huge section of forest, the visual (dis)advantage is suddenly redressed and the Athenians have the confidence to attack.[72] Demosthenes orders the Athenian contingents to seize the highest points of ground (*ta meteôrotata* – 4.32.3), hence affording them the advantage of good vantage points.[73] The Athenians' gaze is both self-reflexive and other-directed: they gain confidence from seeing the enemy's weaknesses, but even more so from the sight (*opsis*) of themselves, when they realize how numerous they are, and when they realize that the enemy no longer appears as fearsome as it used to (4.34.1).[74] In contrast to the Athenians who have a good vantage point and take strength from what they see, the Spartans literally lose sight of what is happening. The ashes from the forest-fire create a dust cloud that obscures their vision ('there was no way to see' – *aporon te ên idein*, 4.34.2), and Thucydides repeats this detail for emphasis ('they were prevented from seeing what was in front of them' – 4.34.3).

The role of sight in establishing military superiority is particularly evident in a string of decisive battles in the Sicilian campaign (7.42-72), which are described in terms of a competition, with connotations of spectatorship (*agôn, agônisma*).[75] In this section of the narrative several visual themes converge: war as theatre; the connection between vantage point on the battlefield and military advantage; and the theme of historical insight. At 7.42, Thucydides describes the arrival of the Athenian generals Demosthenes and Eurymedon with reinforcements and the effect of the sight of this fleet on the Syracusans and their allies. They are stunned (*kataplêxis* – 7.42.2) seeing that the Athenians have somehow managed to muster another expedition almost as large as the first and that Athens' power appeared great in all respects (*dunamin pantachose pollên phainomenên* – 7.42.2). The effect on the Athenian forces is also noted: the appearance of the fleet causes them to regain strength.[76] Through the device of inferred motivation, Thucydides gives us an account of what was allegedly going through Demosthenes' mind:[77]

> For his part Demosthenes saw how things stood and thought that he could not afford to waste time or to suffer what Nicias suffered (for when Nicias first arrived he inspired fear (*phoberos*), but when he did not attack the Syracusans immediately, but spent the winter in Catana, he was held in contempt (*huperôphthê*) and then Gylippus got ahead of him by arriving with forces from the Peloponnese which the Syracusans would not have had an opportunity to send for if he had attacked immediately) [...] Reflecting on these facts (*anaskopôn*), and realising (*gignôskôn*) that in the present situation on his first day [on the island] he himself was most intimidating towards the enemy, Demosthenes wanted to exploit the enemy's state of shock (*ekplêxis*) as swiftly as possible (7.42.3).[78]

Thucydides treats us to the sustained thought-process of a general calculating how he can look as intimidating as possible, and how he can exploit the fear caused by the sight of his troops. There are two different processes of sight in operation here: on the one hand the actual sight of the fleet and the gaze of the Syracusans and their allies, and on the other hand, the insight of Demosthenes who reflects on what he sees (*anaskopôn ... gignôskôn*). Ironically, for all that he is mindful of sight and how things appear, Demosthenes precipitates a battle at Epipolae which takes place in the dark, and in which lack of vision proves disastrous for the Athenians.

In his narrative of the battle at Epipolae, Thucydides draws a parallel between the conditions of the military struggle and his own historical endeavour.[79] At 7.44.1, Thucydides observes that participants in a daylight battle can never see everything and that their knowledge is often confined to what has happened directly around them. This situation is exacerbated in battles fought at night; in daylight people have a clearer (*saphestera*) idea of what has happened in a given battle, but at night Thucydides asks, 'how could anyone know clearly (*saphôs*) what had happened?' (7.44.1-2). In spite of this pessimistic statement about the possibility of reconstructing the battle at Epipolae, Thucydides offers us a reconstruction in which confusion caused by sight and sound is a fundamental part of 'what happened': 'The moon was bright, but they saw each other in the way that is to be expected in moonlight: that is they would see the sight of a body, before they could be sure if it belonged to one of their own men' (7.44.2). Owing to the level of noise, the Athenians find it very difficult to discern everything and end up shouting out their password to each other, thereby rendering it obvious (*saphes*) to the enemy (7.44.4).

Thucydides has it both ways; it is as though he allows us to be readers and spectators at the same time. He manages to impress both sights and sounds on us, gratifying the desire for entertainment which he dismissed at 1.22.4, while still maintaining an impression of historiographical rigour and circumspection: Thucydides readily concedes how difficult it is to establish the precise details of the battle at Epipolae and offers a speculative analysis of visibility conditions at 7.44.2. However, because he informs us that a sense of confusion and an inability to distinguish what was going on were themselves determining factors in the battle, Thucydides' account reads convincingly.[80]

This entire section of narrative (7.42-72) involves a subtle interplay between the poor degree of visibility and clarity enjoyed by the historical participants and, correspondingly, the reader's impression of the clarity of Thucydides' account. The emphasis on display and how things *appear* to the enemy persists; whereas, prior to the battle at Epipolae, Demosthenes was eager to make a show of the Athenians' power, after their setback the Athenian generals are keen *not to reveal* their vulnerability.[81] Hence, when Demosthenes and the other generals want to leave Sicily and return to Attica, Nicias is anxious that their weakness should not be revealed (*apodeiknunai* – 7.48.1), and that the Syracusans should not find out that they are discussing withdrawal for all to see (*emphanôs*).[82] Just as Demosthenes made sure that they began the assault on Epipolae unobserved (*lathein* – 7.43.2, *lanthanein* – 7.43.3), Nicias' concern is that any retreat should be unobserved (*lathein* – 7.48.1-2).

Thucydides depicts the Athenian generals as being preoccupied with dissembling the reality of their situation, but then reveals an additional layer of dissembling in terms of the difference between what Nicias says openly to his fellow Athenians and the thoughts and plans that he keeps to himself:

> Nicias was aware of these factors and although he really delayed them because he was in two minds and still considering matters, in his visible speech he said no to the withdrawal of the army (7.48.3).

'Visible speech' is not idiomatic English, but I have retained the literal sense of *emphanês logos* because of the strong emphasis placed on sight in this section of the narrative. The point is that members of audience cannot see straight into the mind of a speaker, although they may infer what he or she is really thinking based on various strategies of interpretation, some involving words and some involving non-verbal cues.[83] In introducing a gap between the Athenian army, who can only 'see' what Nicias says, and his (and our) privileged insight into what Nicias was really thinking, Thucydides reminds us of one of the distinguishing features of his account. When Thucydides launches his narrative of the events leading up to the war at 1.23.6, he claims that the 'truest' (*alêthestatê*)[84] reason given for the outbreak of war was one that was 'least visible in argument' / 'least visible in the words spoken' (*aphanestatên*). He then proceeds to describe the reasons which were voiced 'into the open' / 'in plain view' (*es to phaneron*). Coming immediately after Thucydides' rejection of the audience-pleasing culture of poets and speech-writers at 1.21, this statement reinforces his suspicion, which, paradoxically, draws on a well-established tradition in Greek poetic thought that speech often conceals the truth.[85] Thucydides' written account, which is ideologically opposed to the spoken word, holds out visible words to its readers so as to give them a clear view of what happened in a way that was not visible to audiences listening to speeches at the time.

The potential duplicity of the spoken word is revealed by Nicias' words in reported speech at 7.48.3-4. Thucydides has already prejudiced the reader with the statement that Nicias suppressed what he was really thinking. Nicias establishes solidarity with his audience by contrasting what they can all see and know to be true with the misleading version of events that might be reported to the Athenians at home:

> He was well aware that the Athenians would not accept these actions of theirs unless the Athenian assembly had voted for a withdrawal. For the people who would be voting about them were not in the same position as they were themselves, who could see matters and whose knowledge was not based on the hostile evaluation of others. This was not the case with voters at Athens, who would be persuaded by the slander of a clever speaker.

This is similar to the kind of solidarity that Thucydides establishes with his 'audience' of readers: 'we' know what really happened. Nicias gives the Athenian army a Thucydidean style lecture on 'cognitive dissonance', to use Rood's phrase (see above, p. 20). However, because he is keeping the facts from his audience, Nicias is misleading them when he says these words. Like Brasidas, who lectured his troops on the capacity of men to be misled by visual appearances while all the while taking advantage of this fact and stage-managing events at every opportunity, Nicias lectures his troops on the difference between a clear view of a situation and the potential for a clever speaker to give a false representation of the same situation, while himself attempting to give a clever speech that is not a true representation of the situation as he sees it. Thucydides takes a contrast – familiar in established genres such as epic, tragedy and political / judicial oratory – between the words that someone speaks and what they are really thinking, and uses it in the service of a much more ambitious claim. This is the claim that his *History* is the only account that that will provide the reader with a clear view of what really happened – all other versions will distort the truth (whether through lack of intellectual ability, fallibility of memory, or because of a desire to please audiences).[86] Although Thucydides' account is ideologically untheatrical, he draws on his experience of living in a theatrical culture in which acts of viewing and making visual inferences were pervasive. Thucydides' narrative draws on highly visual reconstructions of events to 'show' the reader what happened in the past.

In his description of the decisive naval battle in the harbour of Syracuse that brings about the collapse of the Athenian invasion of Sicily (7.59-71), Thucydides shows both sides preparing for a full-scale *agôn*.[87] The emphasis on the point of view from which each side sees the action persists, but, in addition, on the Athenian side the participants act as if they know, proleptically, that they are taking part in an action that will assume the significance of a tragedy in the future. Nicias tells the allies of the Athenians to 'show' (*deixate*) that their skill, albeit impaired, is superior to the strength of others, which derives from having luck on their side (7.63.4). Thucydides comments that Nicias succumbs to the mindset that affects people who are caught up in big struggles (*megaloi agônes* – 7.69.2), and appeals to old-fashioned values (*archaiologein*) and hackneyed sentiments in his address to the captains of the triremes.[88] Nicias appeals to anyone who has an illustrious reputation (*lamprotês*) not to betray it, and anyone who has distinguished (*epiphaneis*) ancestors not to 'remove from view' (*aphanizein*) the virtues of their fathers. Nicias' rhetoric is at odds with his rhetoric elsewhere in the *History*.

In one of the debates in the Athenian assembly prior to the launching of the Sicilian expedition, Thucydides has Nicias lambasting 'individuals who want to endanger the city in order to enhance their own brilliance' (*eklamprunesthai* – 6.12.2).[89] Although Nicias does not mention Alcibiades by name, this is clearly a reference to him. In the speech of Alcibiades that follows, Alcibiades cites and glories in the very traits that Nicias will later appeal to at 7.69.2. He refers to the way in which people regard him (*axiôma* – 6.15.3); he mentions the fact that he is widely spoken about (*epiboêtos* – 6.16.1, *epiboômenos* – 6.16.6), and speaks openly about having gained a reputation for brilliance through performing liturgies (*lamprunomai* – 6.16.3). At 6.16.5, Alcibiades also speaks generally about 'people who are prominent on account of their brilliance (*lamprotês*)'. However, Alcibiades' most flagrant act of rhetorical self-projection is when he claims at 6.16.2 that the other Greeks overestimated Athens' power on the strength of his performance at the Olympic games (6.16.2).[90] Like a latter-day Achilles, Alcibiades implies that his presence alone will be enough to intimidate the Greeks and convince them of Athens' power.

The Sicilian expedition begins with the lavish spectacle of the Athenian fleet sailing from the Piraeus (6.30-2) and ends with the spectacle of the fleet being destroyed in the harbour of Syracuse (7.71).[91] The motif of sight and show runs throughout the entire narrative of the Sicilian expedition. Thucydides claims that the Athenians became apprehensive about the expedition as the time for departure approached, but that when they saw the scale of the fleet, the sight (*opsis*) filled them with confidence (6.31.1). At the same time an audience composed of foreigners and the general populace assembled to see the view (*kata thean*). The intimation that the Athenians are susceptible to visual appearances is compounded if the reader recalls that they have been duped into sending the expedition by the visual deception staged by the Egestaeans.[92] At 6.31.4, Thucydides comments that the rest of the Greeks likened the expedition to a demonstration (*epideixin*) of Athens' power and sway, rather than a military expedition. Thucydides also comments at 6.31.6 that the expedition was acclaimed (*epiboêtos*) on account of its 'dazzling daring' (*tolmês thambos*) and the 'brilliance of the sight' (*opseôs lamprotês*).[93] This is an expedition that mirrors Alcibiades' ambitions since, according to Thucydides, he was obsessed with being acclaimed for his brilliance.

Nicias ends up appealing to his trierarchs on Alcibiades' terms – terms that he had previously rejected as being characteristic of selfish members of the élite. The terms of his appeal are also suggestive of the hero of the tragic stage, acting as an isolated agent and staggering under the burden of ancestral expectation. While the perspective of the Athenians is overshadowed with imminent tragedy, the Syracusans' Spartan commander Gylippus attempts to exhort his forces by painting a very forceful rhetorical picture of the tragedy that the Athenians intended to inflict on the Syracusans (7.68.2). Gylippus uses four superlative adjectives (in bold), which serve to raise the stakes and to intensify the tragic outcomes for the losers of the forthcoming battle:

You all know that these men are our most hated enemies (*echthroi echthistoi*), who invaded our land with a view to enslaving us; if they had succeeded in this goal they would have inflicted the most painful sufferings (*algista*) on the men, the most humiliating sufferings (*aprepestata*) on the children and women, and the most shameful name (*aischistên epiklêsin*) on the entire city.

In the battle itself, the helmsmen on both sides stage a contest of their skill and compete in front of each other (*agônismos pros allêlous* – 7.70.3).[94] In fact every individual strives to appear best in executing his own duty (*prôtos phainesthai* – 7.70.4). Thucydides narrates the battle in such a way that the crews and hoplites behave, self-consciously, as though they are putting on a play for the armies spectating on the shore; concomitantly, the armies on shore act like spectators of a play.[95] Once again, Thucydides' audience of readers can see more than the spectators in the history.[96] Thucydides writes that those on shore had an 'uneven view', because the sea-battle was uneven, with the Athenians prevailing in one area and the Syracusans in another (7.71.2-3).[97] The spectators on shore are unable to get an accurate perspective on the action because the 'show' (Thucydides uses the noun *thea* – show / sight / view) was close-up (*di'oligou gar ousês tês theas*) and because they were not all watching (*skopountôn*) the same spot at the same time (7.71.3).[98]

Conclusion

Already in the first chapter of the *History*, Thucydides refers to the activity of historical research in visual and spatial terms: 'looking as far as I can on the basis of the evidence' (1.1.3).[99] The verb that he uses here is *skopeô*, which is his preferred verb to denote reflection, or what we might call 'the exercise of the mind's gaze'.[100] In fact, part of Thucydides' authority in the initial chapters of the *History* (1.1-22) derives from the impression that Thucydides has a reliable gaze (see 1.3.1 *dêloi de moi* – it is clear/ transparent to me'),[101] which is bolstered by the fact that he is so sceptical about 'mere' visual appearances (1.10). I have already commented on the fact that Thucydides explains the intended appeal of the *History* by saying that he hopes it will prove helpful for those who want to look clearly (*saphôs skopein*) at events in the past and events that may occur in the future (1.22.4). Elsewhere, Thucydides holds his research up to inspection by inviting any reader to examine / view (*skopeitô*, *athreitô* – both third person imperatives) the events as he has narrated them (5.20.2 and 5.26.2 respectively).

Although the reader is not treated to a literal show of the kind that audiences of Greek drama enjoyed, Thucydides exploits the fact that, as a medium, the written word is visible in a way that the spoken word is not.[102] To borrow an analogy used by Charles Segal, 'the graphic space of writing', in which events are played out on the page in front of our eyes, can mimic 'the theatrical space of drama'.[103] Thucydides' prose does not lend itself to easy listening and makes unpleasant entertainment for most audiences; but instead it gratifies the reader who is able to look at the text at his / her leisure. However, as John Moles has observed, Thucydides requires more of his readers than mere 'looking': 'for the readers, as for the historian himself, the process of "looking" is complex: to "look" is not only to "see" in a physical sense, but to "contemplate", to "attempt to understand", to "reflect on".'[104] The motif of intellectual insight draws heavily on techniques of visualization as Thucydides constructs a narrative in which sight, point of view, vantage point and show are significant factors in history and also assume importance in the writing of history.

3

Temporal and Spatial Perspectives

In the previous chapter I suggested that one of the ways in which Thucydides commends his account to his readers is by offering us a synoptic view of what happened. The reader gets to see not only what different historical agents could see (or not see) in certain situations, but also how these visions affected them. In real historical time it is impossible to take in everything at once, even within a single theatre of war. Recall the scene in the harbour at Syracuse where the audiences on shore cannot take in everything at the same time (7.71.2-3; see pp. 13 and 40 above). According to Thucydides, their inability to comprehend fully what was going on in the battle was due to the fact that their perspective on events was literally near-sighted – they were too close to what they are looking at (*di' oligou gar ousês tês theas*). He also adds that they were not all looking at the same thing simultaneously (*ou pantôn hama es to auto skopountôn*). In Thucydides' narrative the temporal equivalent of a panoramic view is simultaneity – being able to comprehend a sequence of events all at once: to see the present in light of the past, the past in light of the present, the future in light of the past, and the future in light of the present.

The most obvious respect in which time and space are superimposed is when events that happen broadly at the same time, but in different places, are grouped together in the same chronological unit of narrative. For example, at the beginning of Book 5, Thucydides builds up a layered picture of the different events that were occurring in the Thracian area and elsewhere in the summer of 422 BC. He writes that 'at the same time' (*hupo ton auton chronon*) as the Athenians captured the town of Torone in Thrace, the Boeotians captured Panactum – an Athenian fortress on the frontier of Attica (5.3.5-6). And, also at the same time (*hupo ton auton chronon* – 5.4.1-2), Phaeax embarked for Sicily as an ambassador for Athens. The narrative follows events in three different theatres of war simultaneously. Obviously these events did not happen at exactly the same time, so it is potentially misleading to speak of 'simultaneity'. The preposition which Thucydides uses (*hupo*) can mean both 'at the time of' and 'about the time of'; hence we should probably understand the force of the preposition *hupo* as modifying the claim that these events happened at the same time.[1] However, through his conscious selection and ordering of events Thucydides accentuates the effect of simultaneity. The suggestion that these events were simultaneous is reinforced by the fact that they are placed together in Thucydides' text: they coincide in the same space of the narrative.[2]

One of the constraints of linear narratives, where events are recounted in their chronological sequence, is that events cannot be narrated simultaneously.[3] When commenting on his method of writing the history of the war at 5.26.1, Thucydides uses the adverb *hexês* (in succession): 'Thucydides the Athenian also wrote down the subsequent events in succession, as each event occurred, in periods of summers and winters'. However, although Thucydides implies that his process of writing was synchronous with the unfolding of events, from its outset the *History* is a narrative loop in which the end is already known at the beginning. In fact, the coherence that scholars now detect in Thucydides' *History*, and which enables them to propose interpretations that apply to the text as a whole, depends, in large part, on the assumption that Thucydides had an overview of the entire work (to use a spatial metaphor) and the fact that he was able to see the different parts of his narrative simultaneously (to use a temporal metaphor).

In recent years, several scholars have used the interpretative framework of narratology to demonstrate the extent to which Thucydides manipulates time and tense in the *History*.[4] This is particularly evident in the case of passages where Thucydides imparts information out of its chronological sequence, either by jumping forward to a later point in time (prolepsis) or jumping back to an earlier point in time (analepsis). Over and above the striking passages in which Thucydides disrupts the chronological flow of events in the narrative, the entire *History* is informed by hindsight to varying degrees. I say 'to varying degrees' because we have no sure method for distinguishing between passages that were written soon after the events that they relate, and passages that were written entirely retrospectively after the end of war. While acknowledging the important contribution of narratology to the way in which scholars now read Thucydides, in this chapter I want to explore another aspect of the significance of time and tense in the *History*. I shall argue that one of the most important dynamics in Thucydides' narrative is his struggle to transcend the limiting factor of a present-centred approach to events. Unlike the historical agents whom he frames in his narrative, Thucydides had the benefit of foresight gleaned from hindsight. He lived to see the outcome of the war and was thus able to analyse events more knowingly than the actors involved in them. This divide between the narrator and the characters in the *History* is most evident at 4.104.4-5, where Thucydides the narrator describes himself in the role of Athenian general rushing to reach Amphipolis before it surrenders to the Spartans. Unlike Thucydides the narrator, Thucydides the general is subject to the ordinary flow of time and a restricted flow of information.[5]

In the previous chapter I examined Thucydides' knowing perspective on events in terms of the motif of the physical vantage point. In this chapter I will consider the temporal dimensions of his vantage point. The rationale for Thucydides holding out his account as a possession for all time is that he aims to analyse events in a historical perspective (in the context of both the past and the future), rather than with a view to the sensibility of a particular audience at a particular point in time. The fact that Thucydides attempted to look beyond the immediate present when writing his *History* is an important aspect of the timelessness that he claims for the work. While the success of this aim is open to debate, the seriousness of the aim is indubitable.

There has been much debate in the scholarly literature about the role of foresight in Thucydides' historiography. In particular, scholars have been reluctant to credit Thucydides with the view that he, or his readers, can predict the future on the basis of past events. This reluctance stems from the fact that this view is associated with theories of cyclical history, and Thucydides nowhere expounds such a theory. However, putting theories of cyclical history to one side, it is important not to overlook Thucydides' interest in the extent to which the future can be known on the basis of past and present history.[6] Thucydides' mindfulness of the transience of his own historical present, and of the relationship of the present to both the past and the future, is an important part of his claim to authority. Note the use of the future tense at 1.22.4; Thucydides' implied readers are all those in the future (this can embrace both the near and distant future) who will want to have a clear insight into past events and similar events that are likely to take place at some point in the future.[7] In framing the appeal of the *History* in these terms, Thucydides is able to envisage a time when his own narrative will itself be part of history – part of the past. Having been so critical about accounts of the past in the preceding chapters, Thucydides presents his own historical research in self-historicizing terms, aware that the act of narration in the present is destined to become part of the past as soon as it is set down as narrative.[8] Paradoxically, it is Thucydides' very awareness of his relationship to historical time that enables him to stake his claim for the permanence of his work.

The *History* is constructed in such a way as to suggest Thucydides' fore-knowledge of later events.[9] Granted, this is artificial foresight, in that it derives from hindsight: it is knowledge of what had already happened at the time of writing, rather than knowledge of what had yet to happen. However, in the narrative the rhetorical tone of such passages is one of prediction; some of these passages are quite unobtrusive, such as the aside at 8.47.2 where Thucydides states that 'he [Alcibiades] thought that he would persuade them most of all on the following grounds: if Tissaphernes should evidently appear to be a close associate of his; and indeed *this is exactly what happened.*' Indeed, for Thucydides and his contemporaries, prediction was an important skill in politics. This is suggested by the speeches in the *History* and is confirmed by the surviving sumbouleutic speeches of later politicians such as Demosthenes.[10] These politicians justify their advice in terms of its usefulness as a guide to the future, and they offer scenarios of the future (*to mellon*) in competition with other political advisers. Consider the framing of Demosthenes' *Olynthiacs*: at *Olynthiac* I.1, Demosthenes begins by stating that his audience would pay a large sum of money 'if the course of action which will benefit the city in the future should become visible'. At the close of the third *Olynthiac*, Demosthenes concludes that he has said what he considers to be in the city's interest and entrusts the decision about what is best for the city to his audience. The implication is that his speech has now revealed to them what will benefit the city in the future, as implicitly promised at the beginning of the first *Olynthiac*.

Moreover, the forecasts of politicians were supplemented by religious predictions from prophets and oracle-analysts. We get rare glimpses of the activity of these other predictors in Thucydides' account (2.8.2-3, 5.26.4 (implied) and 7.50.4). The scope of their influence is attested at 8.1.1, where Thucydides states that, when the Athenian *dêmos* learned of the failure of the Sicilian expedition, they 'took it out on the politicians who had encouraged them to undertake the expedition [...], and vented their anger on oracle-analysts and prophets and anyone who at the time, through recourse to divination, had made them expect in the slightest respect that they would capture Sicily'. Thucydides makes his dim opinion of the authority of prophets clear at 7.50.4, when he comments, in parenthesis, that Nicias paid heed to the prophets who interpreted the lunar eclipse, 'because he was somewhat over-inclined to divination and that sort of thing'. Although he shows contempt for prophecy, Thucydides reflects a culture in which political commentary and analysis contained implicit, and sometimes explicit, narratives about the future.

Thucydides was certainly not the first ancient Greek narrator to be preoccupied with the lure of a timeless perspective. In Book 2 of the *Iliad* the Homeric narrator concedes the superior narrative powers of the Muses on the grounds that they are 'ever-present': everything is 'contemporary' to them (2.484-93). Thucydides states that it was impossible to gain clear information about the conflicts prior to the Atheno-Peloponnesian War, on account of his distance from these events in time (*dia chronou* – 1.1.3). Even in the case of events that were 'contemporary' to him, Thucydides found himself up against the unreliability of his own memory and that of others, a situation that was further complicated by the fact that those who were 'present' at particular actions told differing accounts, swayed by bias and affected by failure of memory. In order to establish an unchanging record of events Thucydides stands back from the present. His *History* is written at a remove from his contemporaries and the actions that it features.

The accent placed upon the past at the beginning of the *History* is striking; the fact that we have become accustomed to accept the work as 'ancient history' risks obscuring Thucydides' emphasis on the remoteness of the distant past as well as the inevitability, for humans, of viewing the present in terms of the past.[11] In the opening chapters of the *History* Thucydides distinguishes, very clearly, between his own era and events in the past (*ta palai*), and events in the more distant past (*ta palaitera*)[12] – to say nothing of markers such as *prôtôi* (the first to ...), *prôton* (for the first time), *nun* (now / in the present day), or *eti* (still / to this day). Thucydides has it both ways in the sense that he pours scorn on the mythistorical tone of accounts of the past as found in the poets and speech-writers, and yet concedes a skein of reality / truth to their narratives so as to furnish material on which he can base a comparison between the present war and wars in the past. This clears the way for the authoritative statement at 1.21.2, that, even allowing for a present-centred bias, it will be clear to all who look at the facts that this war was greater than all the preceding wars.

No small part of what sets Thucydides' work apart from preceding works is its respect for quantifiable time. In place of the vague temporal adverbs which predominate in the 'Archaeology', when the narrative of the war begins Thucydides marks the occasion with a display of comparative chronology, drawing on calendars from different Greek states and 'standardizing' these different ways of marking time by relating them to his preferred method of splitting up the year into summers and winters.

> The thirty years' truce that took place after the capture of Euboea stayed in place for fourteen years. In the fifteenth year, when Chrysis in Argos was in the forty-eighth year of her priestess-ship, the year when Aenesias was ephor at Sparta and, at Athens, when Pythodorus still had two months of his archonship left to serve, in the sixth month after the battle at Potidaea, and at the beginning of spring, a Theban force of slightly more than 300 men, commanded by the Boeotarchs Pythangelus, the son of Phylides, and Diemporus, the son of Onetorides, came at about the first watch of night and made an armed entry into Plataea (2.2.1).[13]

Thucydides recognizes that his contemporaries see time in terms of local perspectives and accommodates this, but he also piles up different systems of chronology in order to transcend the limits of local knowledge. Thucydides begins his account of war with an attitude of geographical and chronological independence.[14] However, at another level, the polyvalent temporal framing for the beginning of the war *proper*, after the pre-beginning in Book 1, also works to focus the reader on the exact moment in time: decades cede to single years, which cede to months, which cede to a seasonal transition, finally concentrating on a point in time 'about' (*peri*) the first watch of the night. By using chronological systems that span

46

several different regions, Thucydides creates the impression that he has space and time covered – unlike most of his contemporaries.

In the opening chapters of the *History*, Thucydides merges local ignorance with ignorance of the past, focusing on the Athenians' ignorance about the assassination of Hipparchus (1.20.2-3). His correction of popular misconceptions about the assassination has been interpreted as part of his campaign to undercut democratic knowledge, on the grounds that he divests many of his contemporaries of a confident identity by revising the history of this identity.[15] Although Thucydides puts his native *polis* at the beginning of the *History*, his relationship with Athens is distanced. In the same way that Thucydides is capable of viewing his present age in the perspective of historical time, he is also capable of viewing his own *polis* from the outside.[16] Like Herodotus before him, Thucydides uses the leverage of an historical perspective to attain a critical distance from which to re-order the familiar co-ordinates of place and the present time. The collapsing of space and time is evident in the passage on the assassination of Hipparchus,[17] in which Thucydides comments that 'people accept reports about the past from others without painstakingly extracting the details, even when these events are in their native domain (*epichôria* – 1.20.1-2). The adjective *epichôrios* – 'pertaining to one's native environment',[18] suggests the following analogy: if the Athenians have slender knowledge of what happened locally, they can hardly claim knowledge about the 'distant' past (*ta palaia*). In this analogy the past is figured as a foreign country. The idea of geographical proximity present in *epichôria*, which provides no guarantee against ignorance, reinforces the idea of the past as distinctly foreign.

To pursue this logic, since Thucydides occupies a superior vantage point of enquiry into the past, he can claim enhanced knowledge into both events in the 'present' and 'local' events. This metaphor is repeated when Thucydides justifies his decision to write about the interim period between the Persian Wars and the present conflict, on the grounds that previous writers have bypassed this field. The word Thucydides uses is *chôrion* (an area / territory), here applied to a chronological period.[19]

> I wrote about these things and made a detour in my account for the following reason, because in the works of all the authors before me this region of history was omitted and they composed works either about Greek affairs before the Persian Wars or else about the Persian Wars themselves (1.97.2).

Without naming him, this passage alludes to Herodotus, who took the Persian Wars as the focus of his historical narrative. The passage is also Herodotean in tone; the decision to call attention to the digression recalls Herodotus' meandering narrative which gains authority from the geographical span which it embraces and the assurance that the narrator has covered the historical past *and* the geographically remote in their totality, since he can offer obscure counter-traditions, in addition to a more mainstream account (I discuss the Herodotean echoes in this passage further in Chapter 4).[20] The motif of the 'reach' of the narrative is fundamental to the way in which Herodotus constructs his authority. For example, in discussing the regions which lie beyond the country of the Issedones, Herodotus observes that although Aristeas' poem, *The Tale of the Arimaspians*, does not contain any solid information about these regions, he has ventured to give an accurate report for 'as far as' he is able: 'according to the furthest extent (*epi makrotaton*) that we were able to reach reliably on the basis of hearsay' (4.16.2).[21] The Herodotean association between knowledge of distant lands and the distant past is reflected in Thucydides' turn of phrase at 1.1.3, where he refers to his researches into ancient history in the same terms: 'looking back as far as possible' (*epi makrotaton skopounti*).[22]

The introspective and localized world-view of the Athenians is put on display in the funeral oration, where Athens is staged as the epicentre of the Greek world – the school of all Hellas (2.41.1), which prides itself on drawing others to it, rather than its being drawn to them (2.37.1) and being needed by others as opposed to needing them (2.40.4). This trait is already marked out as a hallmark of the Athenian character in the Archaeology at the beginning of the *History* where Attica is a static point (*astasiastos*) in the midst of surrounding upheaval, cherished as a refuge by talented exiles who had fallen victim to *stasis* (civil unrest) in their own city-states (1.2.6). Against this complacent backdrop it is significant that Thucydides presents and justifies his subject matter as the greatest upheaval (*kinêsis gar hautê megistê*) hitherto experienced by the Greek world, if not by all mankind (1.1.2).[23] Through his insistence upon the historical dynamics of the present conflict – the long-term view – (as illustrated by the Pentekontaëtia or the account of Sicilian history at 6.1-6) and his professed avoidance of partiality, Thucydides estranges himself from the Athenians, making a virtue out of his involuntary exile (5.26.5-6) and, in turn, portrays them as isolated and out of touch with the past, with the result that they inhabit a false present and are ill-equipped to plan for the future.

Elsewhere Thucydides notes the interference and distortion that local-mindedness can impose on enquiries into the truth. Discussing the sizes of the Spartan and Argive forces at the battle of Mantinea (418-417 BC), Thucydides comments that he cannot give accurate figures. In the case of the Spartans the size of their army was not known because of the secrecy with which they conduct their affairs, and in the case of the other forces Thucydides comments that the numbers were unreliable because of the human habit of exaggerating where one's own forces are concerned (5.68.2; see also Chapter 6, p. 124 below). The adjective that Thucydides uses for 'one's own' is *oikeios* (lit. 'domestic,' but Thucydides uses this term to refer to ties at the level of city states): 'domestic' allegiances present an obstacle to the truth.[24]

As represented by Thucydides, not only are the Athenians (and people in general) undiscriminating in their approach to the past, but they are also unduly mesmerized by the present and what is to hand (1.20.3). This theme also surfaces in the debate in Sparta in the first book of the *History*, in which the Corinthians caricature the Athenians as up-to-date tireless innovators in order to put pressure on the Spartans whose way of life they characterize as old-fashioned (*archaiotropos* – 1.71.2). Furthermore, they volunteer the insight that, 'of necessity, as is evident in the arts, new developments take precedence' (1.71.3). This is followed up by the accusation that Athens' wealth of experience (*polupeiria*) has meant that she has innovated (*kekainôtai*) more than the Spartans (1.71.4). The myth of the ever-innovating, progressive Athenian spirit is discredited by correspondences with other passages in the *History*. At 6.1.1 the majority of Athenians are ignorant (they lack *peira*) of the size of Sicily and of its history and population – in spite of the fact that this is precisely the sort of new and radical venture that the Corinthians associated with the Athenians in Book 1. In fact, in Book 6 we see Alcibiades putting pressure on the Athenian assembly by using arguments very similar to those that the Corinthians brought to bear on the Spartans. The argument that Alcibiades articulates recalls the Corinthians' character-sketch of the Athenians at 1.71.3, but proves even more extreme than the stereotype. In Thucydides' account of the assembly meetings at which the Sicilian expedition was debated, Athenian politics is polarized between the old and the young. Nicias tries to prejudice the audience against Alcibiades by hinting at the latter's youthful irresponsibility and impulsiveness, while Alcibiades fights back by making Nicias look 'past it' and incapable of action. At 1.71.3, the Corinthians presented the view that a city in times of peace should best preserve its established institutions unchanged (*akinêta*),[25] but that a city that is under pressure on many different fronts needs resourcefulness. Addressing the Athenian assembly at 6.18.6, Alcibiades puts forward the more radical view that stability is detrimental for Athens:

> If the city is allowed to rest, she will wear herself out, just like any other thing, and its knowledge in all areas will become geriatric (*engêrasesthai*). Conversely, when it is involved in struggles it acquires experience.

The metaphor of the city's expertise becoming geriatric in times of stability and inactivity is a bold one. Alcibiades encourages Athens not to stop and take stock of past experience, but instead to rush to acquire new experiences.

As for the novelty of the Athenian approach to politics (*kekainôtai* – 1.71.4), as described by the Corinthians, the same verb occurs in Thucydides' description of the breakdown of Corcyrean society,[26] where reports of previous goings-on prompt people to new depths of revolutionary action which is manifested in the perversity (*atopia*)[27] of their revenge tactics (3.82.3-4). Both qualities are also present in Cleon's critique of Athenian audiences and their (in)capacity for sound judgement during the Mytilene debate (3.38.4-5).[28] Cleon's speech resonates with key Thucydidean insights, particularly as regards the psychology of verbal performance in what was famously a 'city of words'.[29] Recalling Thucydides' complaints about the sloppiness with which people accept reports of the past, Cleon rails that the Athenians make judgements about the nature of future events on the basis of fine verbal performances (3.38.4) and consider reports they have heard of past events to be more reliable than their own, direct experience. What is more, Athenian audiences are suckers for new-fangled arguments (*kainotês*), but are unwilling to go along with what is tried and tested. In sum, Cleon styles the Athenians as slaves (*douloi*)[30] of all manner of perversions who have no time for what is customary (3.38.5-6).[31] Rather than reflecting on the historical relationships between past, present and future, the Athenians are portrayed as being obsessed with the present and keeping up to date.

It is pointed out that one of the aspects which characterizes the *stasis* in Corcyra is the volatile mentality precipitated by war, which induces a present-centred mood (living for the moment) in the majority of people: it levels the emotions of most people in line with their immediate circumstances (3.82.2-3). This recalls the present-mindedness of the Athenians during the plague, when they abandon concern for existing conventions and fear of future punishment in view of the present ephemerality of life (2.53.2).

Thucydides points out how parochialism can distort information and obstruct genuine insight, and he is also sensitive to the distorting effect of too present-centred an outlook in the historiographical process. Thus his defensive qualification at 1.21.2 that people always think that the war in which they are currently fighting is the greatest, but that, in this case, it is evident from 'the events themselves' (*ap' autôn tôn ergôn*) – as if they were available to the reader through a neutral channel, independent of their representation in Thucydides' historical work. Thucydides also supplies another context in which the immediacy of present circumstances skews interpretation: just after he has discussed the climate of ephemerality brought on by the plague, he mentions a disputed oracle predicting the combined onslaught of a war with Dorians and famine / plague (*limos* / *loimos*). He notes that in view of the plague, people naturally opted for the version of the oracle predicting an Atheno-Peloponnesian War and a simultaneous plague (*loimos*): in present circumstances (*epi tou parontos*)

50

the view that the verse had said 'plague' naturally prevailed; for people invented memories in accordance with their suffering (2.54.3)

In this instance and in other passages of the *History*, Thucydides depicts memory as subject to variables in the present.[32] Accordingly, he attempts to occupy a standpoint that is historically self-aware, from which he can challenge the tendency of the present to arrange the past. As I suggested above, Thucydides uses revised notions of the past to restructure the 'history' of the present.[33] Key stages in Thucydides' account of the war are made sense of in light of the past and what passed for 'the past' at the time; indeed, as is often observed, Thucydides intimates that, at a collective level, Athens was hampered by an inadequate grasp of her own history (the *locus classicus* being the digression on the 'tyrannicides' at 6.54ff.).[34] Lack of 'historical' insight hampers Athenian internal politics and, by implication, undermines the Sicilian expedition, one of the motives for which, according to Thucydides' wry commentary, was the lust of the young to see what is distant and outside their range of experience (6.24.3). At 6.31.6, the expedition is described as a voyage away from 'home' territory (*apo tês oikeias*). Athenian audiences in the *History* are variously criticized for being overly distracted by present circumstances, but also for failing to consider the present and speculating on the future. Colin Macleod saw a connection between Cleon's criticism of the *dêmos* for not giving adequate thought to their present circumstances (*ta paronta* – 3.38.7), and the theme of 'Near and Far': 'desire for "what is not there" being a vice castigated by popular ethics'.[35] So, the Athenian *dêmos* looks to the future, but it does so with hope and desire, instead of with foresight and hindsight.[36] The Sicilian expedition is a geographical, spatial example of their temporal, historical short-sightedness. At 6.1.1 Thucydides elides geographical ignorance of Sicily with the Athenians' ignorance of the fact that they were taking on a much greater war:

> In this same winter the Athenians resolved for a second time to sail to Sicily, with greater preparation than that of Laches and Eurymedon, and to subdue it, if they could, although the majority lacked experience both of the size of the island and the number of inhabitants – Greek and Barbarian.

In this instance even the standard chronological formula 'in this same winter' is ominous, since it prompts the reader to reflect 'in the same winter as what?' – to which the answer is, in the same winter as the slaughter of the adult males of Melos and the enslavement of its women and children, the events with which Book 5 closes. In fact, as Tim Rood notes, the book divisions are misleading. In Thucydides' text, the first sentence of what we know as Book 6 follows immediately from the last sentence of Book 5 (116.4).[37] This juxtaposition implies that the Athenians are seen to conceive of the second Sicilian expedition in the aftermath of the massacre at Melos, thus the two episodes are located on the same behavioural continuum. One act of flawed judgement follows another.[38] We then progress: 'the Athenians resolved again'; the adverb 'again' is pointed, signalling that we are about to witness a replay of the fruitless expedition dispatched in 427 BC. The mention of Laches, the general whom the Athenians recalled from Sicily in 426 BC, invites us to think ahead to the fate which awaits Nicias (7.86) and indeed, to recall the fate of all the generals of the earlier expedition, who were put on trial (4.65.3-4). This mention does not bode well for the command of the present expedition.

As narrated by Thucydides, the Athenians' inexperience is a necessary condition for the voyage – had they possessed the historical knowledge that he displays at 6.2-5, they would not have embarked. We may contrast this inexperience with the considerable experience that the Athenians (and the Spartans) displayed at the outset of the first war, (1.18.3 'they had become more experienced (*empeiroteroi*) through exercises in danger'). Many critics have discussed Thucydides' description of the Athenians as '*apeiroi*' ('ignorant' / 'inexperienced'). Kenneth Dover cites the passage in Plutarch's *Life of Nicias* where veterans of the former Sicilian expedition give impromptu lessons on the topography of the island in the streets of Athens, to cater for the sudden interest in light of the approaching expedition (12.1) – a passage which indicates that not all Athenians were ignorant of Sicily.[39] Pursuing this line of argument, Kagan calculates that in 424, at the end of the first expedition, 60 triremes had returned from Sicily – a fleet numbering about 12,000 men.[40] Excluding the allies and the Athenians who may have died since then, he argues that there still must have been 5,000 Athenian sailors who knew the geography of Sicily intimately and had a rather good idea of its population. Similarly, Hornblower notes that in 457 BC the Athenians had already made an alliance with Egesta, which lies in the extreme west of the island, and presumes that there must have been a degree of general knowledge about the island.[41] He concludes that Thucydides wants to create an impression of folly at a collective level and attributes the opinionated and, arguably, distorted tone to the fact that Book 6 was written soon after the heat of the moment.

The biased claim that the Athenians were ignorant of Sicily is informed by hindsight and hence penalizes the Athenians for their lack of foresight in failing to anticipate the obstacles that the expedition encountered. However, foresight in Thucydides is premised on knowledge of the past and the patterns of the past. Thucydides exploits the ahistorical perspective of most of his contemporaries to throw his far-sightedness into greater relief. This opposition between the detached thinker, who assumes a critical distance from the present situation and is thereby wiser than his contemporaries, is also exemplified by the contrasting perspectives of Pericles and the Athenian people in the opening stages of the war when they are oppressed by the effects of his policy. Like the Thucydidean narrator, Pericles is aware of the distorting influence of immediate circumstances. At 2.22.1, he sees that the Athenian *dêmos* are angry at their present circumstances (*pros to paron*) and are not reasoning as best they might, but asserts his own view over theirs in the belief that he has the better insight.[42]

This opposition is repeated almost word for word at 2.59 where Thucydides sketches Pericles' reasoning as he prepares to confront a petulant assembly: 'and he, seeing that they were angry about their present circumstances (*pros ta paronta*) and that they were doing all the things that he was expecting them to' (2.59.3).[43] In fact, Pericles had allegedly anticipated a version of this scenario in a speech that he gave before the outbreak of the war (1.140.1). In the passage in Book 1, Pericles observes that, when people find themselves caught up in a war, they seldom retain the same state of mind that they had in voting for the war. Pericles is depicted voicing a similar insight into the changeability of people's attitudes in relation to their circumstances to that expressed by Thucydides in the passages cited above.[44]

In Pericles' final appearance in the *History* there is a cluster of verbs that underscore this foresight. At 2.59.3, Thucydides says that Pericles was expecting this reaction from the *dêmos*. At 2.60.1, Pericles reiterates that he had foreseen this turn of events (*prosdechomenôi moi*). At 2.63.1 he underlines the importance of prescience (*pronoia*) and at 2.64.6 urges the Athenians to think ahead (*es te to mellon kalon prognontes*). Furthermore, Pericles is also described as 'forecasting' (*prognous* – 2.65.5) Athens' capability, and Thucydides comments that his foresight (*pronoia*) was acknowledged posthumously (2.65.7).[45] This overwhelming stress on foresight, which employs a historical perspective to vindicate Pericles, also turns up in Thucydides' retrospective on Themistocles' life.[46] We read that, of all men, Themistocles was most adept at inferring what would happen in the future (1.138.3), followed by the claim that, even while things were still obscure, he foresaw which would be the worse and which the better course of action (ibid.).[47]

The practical implications of foresight are illustrated at 2.21.2, where Thucydides notes that the ravaging of the countryside of Attica was all the more provocative and hard to bear for the younger men, since they had never *seen* this before (2.21.2). The historical virtue of foresight which Thucydides champions is not an obscure, mantic quality, but stems from processing past experience so as to have a degree of knowledge with regard to future probabilities.[48] This is how the plague passage is introduced, so that, should such a plague recur, the reader should not be ignorant, having encountered it before (*proeidôs mê agnoein* – 2.48.3). And at 2.51.6 those who have recovered from the plague are in a position to help and pity the sick, *dia to proeidenai* – of course, in this case, they are also literally immunized against future outbreaks, and some scholars have read this metaphor into Thucydides' broader ambitions for the *History* as stated at 1.22.4.[49]

At 3.56.3-4, the Plataean spokesmen Astymachus and Lacon put it to the Spartan judges who have come to evaluate Plataea's behaviour towards Sparta that, in making their immediate interests the standard of justice, they are evidently not truthful judges of what is right.[50] They then proceed to introduce an historical perspective, reminding Sparta of past ties and allegiances:

> If you are going to determine what is just with reference to your own imme-
> diate advantage (*to autika chrêsimon*) and their [sc. the Thebans'] hostility
> towards us, you will be seen to be serving your own interests, rather than as
> judges of what is right. What is more, if the Thebans seem useful to you *now*,
> we and the Hellenes were much more useful to you *at that time when* you
> were in greater danger (3.56.3-4).

The exhortation not to overlook the past out of concern for immediate interests concurs with Thucydides' historiographical perspective.[51] As we saw above, the criterion of expediency is commonplace in Attic rhetoric, with speakers typically vying to demonstrate that their action or proposal is both expedient and justifiable, while deriding 'mere' expediency. Having rebuked the Spartan judges for betraying the spirit of their office in focusing unduly on notions of usefulness, the Plataeans themselves use considerations of usefulness as a bargaining tool – but they broaden the frame of the discussion, moving away from what is immediately useful (*to autika chrêsimon*) to what is good for the Spartans in the long term. It is interesting to review Thucydides' purported aspirations for his work at 1.22.4 in light of this diplomatic exchange, which typifies the opposition between the ideal of impartial, principled judgement and the pragmatic realization, that, in politics, judgement has to negotiate in terms of useful-ness. Thucydides claims that it will be sufficient if his work is judged *ôphelimos* (helpful / constructive) by those who want clear insights into what happened in the past and the kind of things that are likely to happen in the future. The criterion of usefulness is maintained in the next sentence where the *History* is envisaged as a possession for all time. This wording both reaffirms the idea that the book one is reading may have material value since it is a *possession* that one can store up, but unlike most possessions, it is of eternal value. Positioned as it is in the program-matic introductory chapters to the *History*, Thucydides' statement proclaims his work as a critical account that is based on a long-term perspective which privileges clear-sighted reflection on events (*to saphes skopein*). However, this insight is then provocatively packaged in terms of popular, material considerations. The implication is that the reader will gain from this intellectual possession – not just once, but always.[52]

Diodotus, the opponent of Cleon's position, offers a version of the historian's position in the Athenian assembly debate on the Mytilene question: he admonishes his audience with the familiar rhetorical charge of irresponsibility in matters of judgement, but his words are given a Thucydidean spin. Diodotus introduces the distinction between the *rhêtores* who ought to counsel the assembly, having availed themselves of extensive forecasts (*peraiterô pronoountas* – 3.43.4) and the assembled citizens who give only cursory attention to matters (*di' oligou skopountôn* – ibid.). Whereas Cleon had criticized the same audience for treating the assembly like the theatre and behaving as 'spectators' (3.38.4; 3.38.7), Diodotus adapts the visual metaphor and criticizes not the habit of 'viewing' politics per se, but the short-sightedness of their perspective. It is interesting to juxtapose this passage with the description of the audience watching the final battle in the harbour of Syracuse (see above, pp. 13 and 40). Whereas they have a restricted view because of the proximity of the ships, in this passage, Athenian assembly audiences are said to be short-sighted because they consider matters for only a brief while. This is another instance of the way in which Thucydides uses both spatial and temporal metaphors to reinforce the inferior historical perspective of his Athenian contemporaries: they are neither far-sighted, nor do the majority possess adequate foresight.

Even the corrupt politicians, whose judgements are undermined by Thucydides, are seen to possess a degree of insight that their audiences lack. In the Mytilene debate Diodotus explains this differential possession of insight / foresight on the grounds that the *rhêtores* are held to account for the advice which they give, whereas the assembly is not accountable for its audienceship (3.43.4-5).[53] If it were, he continues, and all Athenians were equally accountable for the outcome of policy, then the assembly would judge more prudently (3.43.5).

Conclusion

Much scholarship has been devoted to exposing Thucydides' biases about different Athenian politicians in the *History*. In terms of the present question, more telling than his individual moral preferences is the kindred sense of isolation and responsibility that unites the various political players and assimilates their position to that of Thucydides. The various *rhêtores* who, in their capacity as advisers, come forward and berate the vagaries of collective judgement, contribute to a composite picture of the detached historian. The crucial difference between Thucydides as historian and the politicians in the *History* (with the exception of Pericles) is that they all, to a greater or lesser degree, submit to the moderating influences of Athenian audiences.[54] For example, Cleon commends less intelligent audiences and less learned and sophisticated speeches on the grounds that such a levelling-out of intelligence promotes the efficiency of civic business, but he does so in a speech that is a model of aggressive intellectual argument (3.37.4-5).[55] Moreover, Cleon criticizes the Athenian audiences for turning political debates into theatre, but still gives his audience a good show.

Thucydides highlights the importance of distancing oneself from the immediate pressures of the present in order to gain a clear view of events. This happens to fit his own circumstances very neatly: the fact that he was sent into exile for twenty years gave him the opportunity for the critical distance that is fundamental to his ideology of history-writing. It is generally assumed that Thucydides wills the reader to credit him with first-hand (or very proximate) knowledge of the events which he describes, but the motif of detachment suggests another, contending model of authority. Thucydides makes a claim to keener knowledge and discernment than all those around him, and this claim is supported in large part by his critical detachment both from the immediate present and from his accustomed locality.[56]

4

Speaking the Truth

In Thucydides' *History* the concept of 'speaking the truth' can imply several different things. First, 'speaking the truth' can have philosophical or, more precisely, ontological overtones (whether what one is speaking about exists or not). Secondly, 'speaking the truth' can have an ideological dimension: whose truth, or whose *version* of the truth (Thucydides' version, the speaker's version, or the audience's version)? Thirdly, in Thucydides' account truth has an uneasy relationship with the spoken word; hence the very idea of 'speaking the truth' is problematic. In this last case, Thucydides contrasts 'speaking the truth' with 'writing the truth.' Fourthly, since Thucydides' *History* is a literary narrative, albeit a factual narrative that concerns itself with the presentation and analysis of real events as opposed to imaginary subject matter, we also need to consider the formal, rhetorical conventions that are employed in presenting the truth (the 'form' of the truth). This chapter examines these various dimensions of truth in the context of the speeches in Thucydides' *History*.

The form of the truth

While the harmonious arrangement (*kosmos*) of a city is good quality in its men, for a body it is beauty, for a soul wisdom, for an action excellence, and for a speech / account (*logos*) truth (*alêtheia*).

Gorgias, Encomium of Helen 1[1]

The orator Gorgias might seem a perverse starting point for a discussion of speech and truth in Thucydides. After all, Gorgias would have fallen into the class of prose writers (*logographoi*) whom Thucydides criticizes for ranking audience satisfaction over truth (1.21.1).[2] However, Gorgias' treatise is an apt starting point because it demonstrates the complications involved in squaring verbal arguments (*logoi*) – both oral and written – with truth.[3] Unfortunately we have no reliable evidence that can shed light on the relationship between Thucydides and Gorgias. We do not have a date for the composition and circulation of Gorgias' *Encomium* and, given the uncertainty surrounding the composition of Thucydides' *History*, it is very hard to construct a historical dialogue between the two texts. However, since Gorgias visited Athens and addressed the Assembly as an ambassador in 427 BC, and was subsequently prominent in Athenian intellectual life, it is possible that Thucydides had heard him speak in person and certain that he would have heard recitations or read copies of some of Gorgias' works.[4] Gorgias himself may have been aware of Thucydides' work in progress, and he would certainly have been aware of a burgeoning historiographical tradition in which writers such as Herodotus were defining the limits of a new genre with its own distinctive claims to authority and truth. In what follows I assume that Thucydides knew of Gorgias and his ideas, and that Gorgias is among the anonymous writers of speeches (*logographoi*) referred to at 1.21.1. While I suggest that Gorgias reacts to contemporary historiographical discourse, I do not assume that he was familiar with Thucydides' work.

Gorgias' *Encomium* gives us an idiosyncratic example of the way in which speech-making could be theorized in the period when Thucydides was writing his *History*. In the above passage I have translated the Greek noun *kosmos* as 'harmonious arrangement'. However, *kosmos* can range in meaning from the neutral senses 'order', or 'arrangement', through to 'adornment', 'ornament' and 'jewellery', ultimately giving us the English derivative 'cosmetic'. Hence the noun *kosmos* can signify an arrangement that has been 'touched up' or 'embellished'.[5] The first use of the noun *kosmos* in Thucydides' *History* occurs at 1.5.2, where Thucydides claims that, in his day, some of the inhabitants of mainland Greece still look on skill in piracy as a decoration of honour (*kosmos*).

Gorgias' formulation is challenging since the connotations of artifice that attach to the word *kosmos* do not sit comfortably with the quality of truth (*alêtheia*), which is here imputed to be the harmonious adornment of *logos*. As noted above, *logos* can mean a spoken / written speech, argument, or account. The language of Gorgias' provocative statement jars with Thucydides' statement at 1.21.1, where he draws a contrast between the reliability of his account of early Greek history in the Archaeology (1.1-20) and the misleading accounts of poets and prose writers. The terms of this contrast associate *kosmos* with error and pit verbal entertainment against truth. Thucydides claims that the poets have for the most part embellished (*kosmountes*) their account of events (the verb *kosmeô* is cognate with the noun *kosmos*). This association between poetry and *kosmos* recalls an earlier passage, where Thucydides casts doubt on the data about the Trojan War contained in Homeric epic and reasons, on the basis that Homer was a poet, that he probably embroidered (*kosmêsai*) his account (1.10.3). In Thucydides' estimation, accounts that have recourse to *kosmos* are unreliable accounts. But Gorgias' statement anticipates this kind of objection and offers another interpretation that is more sympathetic to Thucydides' project. To say that the *kosmos* of a *logos* is *alêtheia* is rhetorically counter-intuitive. It dangles the lure of language as artifice in front of the reader's eyes and the listener's ears, but immediately suppresses this suggestion by putting *alêtheia* in its place: the only arrangement that a *logos* should have is truth.

However, another angle on how to apply Gorgias' provocative opening gambit about *logos* to Thucydides is suggested by a remark made by the literary critic and historian Dionysius of Halicarnassus in his treatise *On Thucydides*.[6] Talking about the speeches in the *History*, Dionysius singles out the speech that the Plataeans make in their defence after the fall of Plataea to the Peloponnesians in 427 BC (3.53-9):

> But most of all the speeches contained in the seven books I have been amazed by (*tethaumaka*) the defence of the Plataeans, not so much for any other reason as because there is nothing tortured or overworked about it, but it is adorned with authentic natural colouring (*alêthei de tini kai phusikôi kekosmêsthai chrômati*).[7]

When Dionysius remarks that it is adorned with authentic natural colouring, the adjectives *alêthês* ('true') and *phusikos* ('natural') are belied by the verb *kosmeô* ('to embellish / embroider'). His point here is not that the speech feels authentic and natural because Thucydides is conveying the words that were *actually* spoken, but rather that Thucydides has used his rhetorical skill to embellish language so judiciously that the words / arguments are a persuasive representation of what the reader would expect the Plataeans to say in real life. In Dionysius' statement we see how *alêtheia* could be regarded as a colouring, or a form of embellishment that touches up a *logos* to good effect: it too is a product of invention. Dionysius' idea is comparable to modern notions of literary realism, whereby skilled writers can imitate natural patterns of speech and give the impression of real life.[8] That Thucydides' speeches could be regarded as dazzling works of art is suggested by Dionysius' choice of verb: *tethaumaka* (I have been amazed). Paradoxically, he has been struck by the naturalness of the speech as opposed to any flashy, obvious artistry. Moreover, one of the reasons that this speech appeals to Dionysius is because it contrasts with the style of so many other speeches in the *History*, which he describes as 'tortured' (*bebasanisthai*) and 'overelaborated' (*katepitetêdeusthai*). According to this reader of Thucydides, who was reading and writing about Thucydides in Greek in the Roman empire in the last decade of the first century BC, too many of Thucydides' speeches reveal the laboriousness of their construction. Conversely, good *kosmos* in speeches conceals its presence and creates an impression of how people *actually* speak.

Thucydides nowhere discusses the implications of his style of writing for the accuracy and reliability of his work, but we have seen how he criticizes the reliability of versions of the past in the works of poets, on the grounds that poets are prone to embellish (1.21.1). Furthermore, in the same section he distances his account of early Greek history from the accounts of prose writers who compose their works with a view to what is more enticing, as opposed to what is more truthful. This critique of other versions of the past constructs an equation which pits highly crafted and seductive accounts against reliable accounts that are interested in truth. Although we should take Thucydides' contrast seriously, we have seen how Gorgias' *Encomium* challenges the idea that *alêtheia* (truth) and *kosmos* (both 'arrangement' and 'embellishment') are two separate things, or that they can be separated. If we translate Gorgias' statement into post-modern criticism, then this is akin to saying that truth in verbal accounts will always be subject to formal fictions: one cannot express the truth without having recourse to the various capacities of language (syntax, grammar, rhetoric). We are then justified in asking whether narrative truth, which of necessity includes formal techniques of fiction, presents a problem for Thucydides' commitment to providing a reliable account of the past, and whether Thucydides anticipated this problem. However, before addressing this problem, I want to highlight another section of Gorgias' *Encomium*, which creates additional problems for Thucydides' historical methodology.

In section 11 of the *Encomium*, Gorgias makes a connection between the limitations on human knowledge of the past, present and future, and the power of *logos*. He argues that *logos* (speech / argument / account) is able to persuade audiences precisely because of their ignorance of the past, their partial understanding of the present and their ignorance about the future. According to Gorgias, in the absence of knowledge audiences look to speech-makers to instruct them, and the fact that the audiences lack knowledge opens up the potential for false arguments / accounts:

> How many men have persuaded and do persuade how many, on how many subjects, by fabricating false speech (*pseudê logon plasantes*)! For if everyone, on every subject, possessed memory (*mnêmên*) of the past and <understanding> of the present and foreknowledge (*pronoian*) of the future, speech would not be equally <powerful>; but as it is, neither remembering (*mnêsthênai*) a past event nor investigating (*skepsasthai*) a present one nor prophesying (*manteusasthai*) a future one is easy, so that on most subjects most men make their opinion their mind's adviser (*sumboulon*). But opinion, being slippery (*sphalera*) and unreliable (*abebaios*), brings slippery and unreliable success to those who employ it.[9]

This passage supplies a fascinating, if inadvertent, commentary on the historical role of the speeches in Thucydides' *History*. Gorgias states that most people make opinion (*doxa*) the adviser (*sumboulos*) of their soul, and, in the surrounding text, states that opinion is formed through persuasion by speeches. This statement has political overtones, since *sumboulos* – the word which Gorgias uses for 'adviser' – was the standard word for one who offered advice in a political capacity in Athens and is sometimes used as a synonym for 'politician' (*rhêtôr*).[10] Many of the speeches in Thucydides fall into this category: politicians using speech to 'advise' audiences, whether Athenian, Peloponnesian or Syracusan audiences, and the advice offered pertains to the past, present and future. Thucydides often frames the speeches in such a way as to expose the errors, if not the outright falsehoods, of the speakers; and in that sense he is in agreement with Gorgias.

There are also potential analogies between Gorgias' critique of the persuasive potential of false speech and Thucydides' criticism of his contemporaries who accept erroneous information uncritically, both about the past and the present, without exerting themselves to find out the truth (1.20.1-3). One obvious difference is that, although Thucydides criticizes this tendency, he regards it as a fault to be avoided, and a potential source of error when relying upon people's accounts, whereas Gorgias seems to hold out the power of *logos* to deceive as inevitable, given the limitations of human knowledge. However, it should trouble the reader that Thucydides himself is offering a *logos*, an account, which likewise has the capacity to mislead those who read it, notwithstanding the fact that the intention to deceive is avowedly absent in Thucydides' case. Thucydides clearly wrote to persuade his readers, and it is notable that he seldom owns up to the fact that he is offering a *logos* (an account, argument). Instead, he uses this term to refer to the spoken word, and on the few occasions where it is applied to written works, it refers to other sources. For example, at 1.10.2, Thucydides speaks of the size of the Greek expedition to Troy as 'the poets have spoken of it and as the story (*logos*) goes' (*hoi te poiêtai eirêkasi kai ho logos katechei*).

Thucydides' older contemporary Herodotus explicitly refers to his entire work as a *logos* and also refers to different sub-sections as *logoi*.[11] It seems that Thucydides took a conscious decision not to follow Herodotus' practice, in part to disassociate his own work from Herodotus' *Histories*, but also so as to discriminate between the speeches that feature in his work, which he terms *logoi*, and his own narrative. By strenuously avoiding referring to his own work as a *logos*, Thucydides arguably distances himself from the deceptiveness of *logos*, as portrayed in Gorgias' treatise, for example, and transcends the contests of persuasion in which the protagonists of his narrative are embroiled.[12] In fact, the only occasion when Thucydides refers to his narrative as a *logos* is in a passage that is glaringly Herodotean.

At 1.89, Thucydides turns aside from his narration of the political debates that preceded the outbreak of the Atheno-Peloponnesian War to the broader topic of Athens' rise to power at the head of the Delian league. This section of Book 1 (89-118) is traditionally referred to as the Pentekontaëtia ('the fifty years' period') and spans the period from *c.* 479

to 432 BC – a period of not quite fifty years between the wars with the Persians and the prelude to the Atheno-Peloponnesian War.[13] At 1.97.2, Thucydides refers to this section of narrative as an *ekbolê* (a detour) in his *logos* (account). Although there are other digressions in Thucydides' text, this is the only passage where he uses an explicit term for the digression. By way of comparison, contrast the wording at 6.54.1, where Thucydides offers his version of the assassination of Hipparchus by Harmodius and Aristogeiton. Thucydides introduces this section by saying that he is going to narrate the incident in greater detail and to reveal that neither other [writers] (this is implied) nor the Athenians themselves give a precise account about the tyranny of Hippias. Although Thucydides' authorial statement *hên egô epi pleon diêgêsamenos* ('which I, narrating at greater length') announces a digression, there is no explicit term corresponding to *ekbolê* at 1.97.2.

Thucydides makes numerous metanarrative comments, which call attention to his presence as author behind the work that the reader is reading. The most obvious and frequent instances of authorial interventions are the verbs of writing and speaking that punctuate the narrative: 'this war which Thucydides wrote down (*xunegrapsen)*',[14] or 'as has been said / written by me' (*hôs eirêtai moi*). But even here, Thucydides' authorial comments are recessive. As Lowell Edmunds has described, Thucydides' preferred verb for describing 'the act of writing' is the verb *xungraphô*, which implies that this is not his independent composition, but that he is 'writing up', or 'writing out', material that already exists in some sense (see above, p. 15). This formula allows Thucydides to play down the processes of representation and interpretation that are involved in narration. Aside from this category of statements, Thucydides avoids commenting explicitly on the logic of his narrative. He is more inclined to comment on the research and the intellectual values behind his work, as opposed to the structure of the work itself. There is no equivalent in Thucydides to the passages in Herodotus' *Histories* in which the latter gives us tantalizing glimpses into the rationale behind the structure of his *logos*.[15]

However, at 1.97.2, Thucydides departs from this practice by calling attention to the digression and referring to his narrative as a *logos*. It is probable that Thucydides calls his work a *logos* at this point because he has an eye on the competition – his predecessors and contemporaries who had offered and were offering prose accounts of recent Greek history. He justifies this section on the grounds that this period of Greek history has been overlooked by his predecessors. Hellanicus is the only historian whom Thucydides mentions by name in the entire *History*, when he concedes that the former touched upon this period in his history of Athens.[16] However, Thucydides proceeds to censure Hellanicus for providing a brief and imprecise record. Although this interpretation can only be speculative, I suggest that Thucydides, while thinking of

Herodotus and other authors and comparing his work with theirs, echoes the way in which Herodotus speaks of his own work.[17] This reading is strengthened by the fact that Thucydides says that his account of the Pentekontaëtia constitutes an exposition (*apodeixis*) of the origins of Athens' empire. The use of the noun *apodeixis* in reference to a historical account evokes Herodotus, who introduces his *Histories* as an exposition of the results of his inquiry.[18]

With reference to Herodotus' *Histories*, Deborah Boedeker has suggested that Herodotus uses the term *logos* to define the boundaries of authorship and genre and to distinguish his account from that offered by authors writing in a range of different genres.[19] She highlights a passage at 2.123.3, where Herodotus appears to be associating the circulation of *logoi* with a notion that resembles our conception of intellectual property:[20] authors can lay claim to *logoi* that are not their own and can put forward *logoi* in one genre that do not meet criteria of narratability in other genres. The fact that Thucydides steers clear of drawing attention to the competition (with the exception of the methodological chapters at 1.21-2) may account for the fact that he tends not to hold out his work as one *logos* among other contending *logoi* in an intellectual marketplace. Instead he puts out his *History* as a work whose value has already been established: a *ktêma*.

We have seen how Gorgias links the power of *logos* to deceive with the limitations of human memory (*Encomium of Helen* 11). I have suggested that Thucydides disassociates his work from the charges of fallibility that could be levelled at *logoi*,[21] and that he does this by not calling his *logos* a '*logos*', which is presumably how most of his contemporaries would have conceived of it. In effect, he takes his account out of general circulation: this work is no 'mere' *logos*. However, it remains to be seen how Thucydides tackled the problem of how to represent actions and events accurately in his narrative. In the terms of Gorgias' *Encomium*, how did Thucydides reconcile truth with the craft of narrative? With a few exceptions, Thucydides confines discussion of the methodological problems that he encountered in his own work to chapter 1.22.1-4.[22] I will now turn to discuss this chapter.

Truth and methodology

In modern scholarship this one chapter (1.22.1-4) has driven the debate about the truthfulness of Thucydides' *History*. Since the interpretation of this section has been so vexed, I offer a fairly literal translation of the passage as a prelude to my discussion.

> And as for the things that they each said by way of argument,[23] either when they were about to go to war or when they were already at war, it was diffi-

cult to carry the precise details of the things that were said word for word in one's memory. This was the case both for me, where I heard them myself, and for those who reported them to me from various sources; but they have been rendered in the way it seemed to me likely that each speaker would indeed have said what was needed concerning the present circumstances on each occasion, while sticking as closely as possible to the general ideas behind what was actually said. But as regards the events of the war, I did not think it right to base my account on what I learnt from whoever happened to be at hand, nor according to ideas of my own, but by going in pursuit of information about each event with as much precision as possible, both for events at which I was present and for those which I heard from others. They were discovered through a laborious process, because those who were present at each of the actions did not say the same things about the same events, but they spoke either according to some bias for either side, or according to memory.[24]

Thucydides' description of his method for reconstructing speakers' arguments is deliberately ambiguous. Both in his reconstruction of speeches and of actions, Thucydides holds himself to realistic standards of precision. When he states that it was difficult for him 'to carry the precise details of what was said word for word' (*diamnêmoneusai*), he acknowledges an ideal standard for recording information, only to dismiss it in the context of this *History*. Instead, he adopts the more practical criterion of sticking to *the ideas behind* what speakers actually / truly (*alêthôs*) said. The criterion of truthfulness is circumscribed very carefully in this section; Thucydides attempts to render not what was actually said, but 'the ideas behind', or 'the general sense' of what was actually said. This reticence about *alêtheia* is appropriate given that Thucydides mentions the shortcomings of human memory twice in this passage (*diamnêmnoneusai* – 1.22.1; *mnêmê* – 1.22.3). The etymology of the Greek noun *alêtheia* is 'that which is not (to be) forgotten' (from the noun *lêthê* – 'forgetfulness', 'oblivion'). Hence *alêtheia* associates truth with the ability to remember, and it proves impossible to realize in absolute terms because of the limitations of human memory.[25]

The formula that Thucydides uses gives him the scope to give an accurate representation of the gist of a speaker's arguments, while also allowing him to use the speeches as a vehicle for historical interpretation without falsifying his commitment to the 'ideas behind what was actually said'. Historical interpretation might include: the characterization of individual speakers; the interrelationship between speech and actions; the expectations of different audiences; the critique of rhetorical culture; and the introduction of intratextual and intertextual allusions. It is significant that Thucydides offsets the actual words of the speakers with an emphasis on the ideas behind the words. In fact, there are numerous instances in the *History* where Thucydides portrays speech culture (particularly in

Athens) in a way that suggests the use of speech to cover up what was really going on and to mislead audiences. Even if it had been possible to record the speakers' words with precision, one gets the sense that Thucydides would still have been more concerned with the interpretation of the ideas behind the words.

As recent discussions of this passage have stressed, it is important not to make Thucydides conform, artificially, to modern historical practice, for which the standard of accuracy for a verbal account is verbatim accuracy, on the model of a transcript.[26] Modern recording technologies are a long way from Thucydides' methods for recording data for the composition of his *History*. Although we know little about the practicalities of the written word in Athens in the second half of the fifth century BC, we do have a basic knowledge of the technology of the written word. We know that it would have been a laborious task for Thucydides to sort through notes, which probably would have been written on papyrus rolls. In fact, at 1.22.1-4 Thucydides makes no mention of the written word as an aid to memory, and instead refers to spoken testimonies. In view of the limited technology that was available to writers such as Thucydides, Jocelyn Small has suggested that our criteria for accuracy are anachronistic, and that instead we need to conceive of 'accuracy as gist'.[27] However, it is wrong to imply that the only obstacles to the historicity of Thucydides' account were technological obstacles, in the same way that it is naïve to think that modern technology makes the ideal of a true historical account a realizable goal.

Consider the range of recording technologies available to modern researchers, beginning with conventional transcripts made from recordings. Although a written transcript based on an audio recording might constitute a higher standard of representative fidelity than a speech reconstructed purely on the basis of memory, the argument that it constitutes a 'true' account of the speech is flawed. We need to envisage a scale of mimetic fidelity, which never entirely fulfils the conditions of the original speech. Owing to the constraints of time, the majority of written transcripts of the spoken word do not make any attempt to record pauses, to convey the tone of voice, intonation, or emphasis, nor do they communicate the non-verbal language of the speaker. In addition, those compiling transcripts have to infer punctuation from the delivery of the speech, and can radically alter the style, and even the meaning, of the original speech: punctuation entails interpretation. Moreover, transcribers, who typically produce transcriptions so that a *written* version of a speech can be circulated or preserved, also tend to correct the words (for example, mispronunciations or grammatical infelicities).[28] On multiple levels, then, a transcription is an edited version of a speech, even when the 'words' that a speaker spoke are conveyed.

We can perform a similar thought-experiment with an audio record of a speech. A recording of a speaker's voice overcomes some of the problems of the written transcript. In the case of an audio recording we do *hear* the speaker in his or her own words, pauses, intonation and tone of voice; and there is less scope for the recorder to intervene in the transmission of the speech. However, we do not *see* the speaker speaking these words, and in this sense an audio recording is also an incomplete representation of an original speech act. And this is an ideal scenario; in reality many audio recordings, with the exception of 'live' recordings, are also polished and edited. Even higher up this scale of representational accuracy is the video recording, which communicates to both our senses of sight and hearing, and is also able to transmit some of the context in which a speech was made. With the introduction of a visual element, the representation of speech acquires a different dimension. Cognitive psychologists have documented the overwhelming influence of sight, in relation to our other senses: the visual recording is apt to reveal parallel narratives: the verbal and the non-verbal. We now get to see how the speaker's non-verbal gestures communicate meaning. However, although we both *hear* and *see* the speaker, the way in which we hear and see him or her is framed by a camera, held by an individual with a capacity to direct our sensory responses through camera angle, lighting and editing. This is true even of the 'straightest' docu-film that approximates to criteria of historicity; even so, there is no neutral, non-intrusive angle of vision.[29] Far from bypassing the formal shaping that goes into verbal narrative, film as a medium is parasitic on narrative, and like narrative it displays language, syntax and genres.

While these problems of representation may seem subtle or even trivial in comparison to the fundamental problem of getting the text of spoken words onto a page, they emphasize that all records, in all technologies, approximate but never achieve a *true* account of a speech. And the thought experiment has been restricted to recording an account of a single speech. When we speak of an historical account, we assume that this account will take the form of narrative. In other words, it will not merely present a series of disconnected pieces of information (or accounts of information), but it will arrange this information into an intelligible sequence, in order to identify events and their causes and consequences, and convey judgements about the significance of the information, and it will use the techniques associated with fiction in order to do all of this. In this sense fiction is intrinsic to historical narrative *qua* narrative, as long as we are clear that in this context, fiction is used in its primary sense to mean 'the creation of form in language'.[30]

Thucydides' intention to provide his readers with a truthful account of the war is not undermined by elements of invention (or 'improvisation') in the speeches.[31] Rather, the speeches are subject to the same conditions as the rest of the narrative: Thucydides selects the appropriate forms of language (including grammar, syntax and rhetoric) to present an account of what happened that is accurate to the best of his ability and reasoned opinion. Thucydides makes a strong commitment to precision in this programmatic section, but his intellectual judgement is the ultimate guarantor of the accuracy of the overall work. It is, in fact, possible to argue that Thucydides invites the reader to envisage his text as a transcript, but at the level of the entire work, not that of individual sections, or speeches.[32] *Xungraphô*, the verb which Thucydides uses to refer to his narrative in the opening line of the *History*, means 'to achieve the writing of', or 'to write up', often with the suggestion of documenting, or recording (see p. 62 above).[33] Hence when Thucydides uses this verb with 'the war' (*polemos*) as its object, he implies that there is parity between the war and his narrative of the war, as though he has written up, or recorded, something that already existed.[34] At 1.21.2, Thucydides implies that 'this' war itself (*ho polemos houtos*) will reveal to those who consider the events themselves the fact that it was greater than previous wars. The demonstrative pronoun 'this' (*houtos*) encourages us to identify the war with the text in our hands.[35]

Truth and ideology

One of the phrases in Thucydides' methodological chapters that has caused most consternation is the statement that he reconstructed the speeches on the basis of how he thought each speaker would have said 'what was needed' (*ta deonta*). Thucydides implies that he relied on a factual skeleton: a report, either written by himself, or informants, of what a speaker actually said, which was then supplemented with appropriate statements relating to the contexts, audiences and circumstances in which the speeches were given. This is a broad criterion:[36] 'what was needed' in a particular speech might have included citation of factual data (for example, data relating to financial resources, topography, or manpower). It could also extend to the kind of argumentation (advisory, epideictic, forensic), the values espoused, and the tone of the speech (encouraging, reproving, threatening). Many of the speeches in the *History* are prefaced by verbs that signal the emotional and psychological tone of the ensuing speech. Some scholars argue that, in this instance, *ta deonta* is primarily a rhetorical criterion, and refers to the conventional rhetorical arguments that a speaker would make in an attempt to persuade his audience.[37]

However, the perspective from which *ta deonta* were determined is vague: does it mean 'what was needed' according to the speakers' estimation, or 'what was needed' according to Thucydides' estimation of the speakers and their personal situation? Yet another dimension of the variation between speeches, even when they address the same topic, is the process of characterization at work. Perhaps this is the force of the adjective 'each' (*hekastoi*) at 1.22.1 ('the arguments have been written according to the impression I formed of how *each* (*hekastoi*) of the speakers would most likely have said what was needed').

If one emphasizes the rhetorical connotations of the phrase *ta deonta*, then arguably the internal audiences in the *History* dictated 'what was needed'. Hence Paula Debnar writes that 'Thucydides' assessment of historical audiences was a critical factor in determining what he thought was "most appropriate" for speakers to say (1.22.1)'.[38] While not wrong, exactly, this statement addresses only one dimension of Thucydides' complex procedure in composing the speeches in the *History*. We can compare this line of interpretation to J.L. Austin's 'speech act' theory, according to which speeches are conceived of as social performances that attempt to act upon their audiences; consequently, the success or failure of a speech is determined by the reaction that it elicits in the audience. Speech act theory has been applied to the texts of Athenian speeches that survive from the fourth century BC – Demosthenes' political speeches, for example – to good effect, to explore the extent to which the speeches' audiences shaped their meaning.[39] However, in the case of Thucydides' *History*, the speeches were never delivered *in this form* to any historical audience. These are Thucydidean versions of historical speeches, and consequently we need to pay just as much attention to Thucydides' readers as to the putative historical audiences in the text. After all, the most important audience in Thucydides' view was the audience for his work, which included both his contemporaries and posterity.[40]

If we look at the speeches in the context of the surrounding narrative, as we surely must, then we should bring to bear Thucydides' own judgement about what it was necessary to say *to* contemporary audiences, and *about* contemporary audiences as a historical commentator or critic. In the context of the *History*, this involves contradicting erroneous assumptions about the past and pointing out how, according to his own analysis, populist, demagogic rhetoric (what Bernard Williams calls 'audience-relative' truth)[41] played a significant role in the Athenians' eventual defeat. After the final speech that Thucydides gives to Pericles in the *History*, Thucydides draws a stark contrast between his vision of Pericles, whose political integrity meant that he did not have to say anything with a view to pleasing the *dêmos* (*pros **hêdonên** ti* – 2.65.8), and the subsequent generation of Athenian politicians whose political ambition caused them to have recourse to pleasing the *dêmos* (*etraponto kath' **hêdonas** tôi dêmôi* – 2.65.11).[42] In other words, taking the internal audiences as a guide to what Thucydides thought it appropriate for speakers to say is only one half of his historical project, the other half is a critique of the very speech culture in which the speakers are performing. Hence the speeches address both internal and external audiences.

4. Speaking the Truth

Case-study I: Pericles' final speech (2.59.3-2.64.6)[43]

I want to take Pericles' final speech in the *History* as a case-study in order to illustrate the implicit ambiguity in 1.22.1-2 between what Thucydides thought it was necessary for historical audiences to hear and learn and thus what he wanted his readers to learn, and, conversely, what it would have been expedient for a speaker to say in response to the pressure of circumstances and the mood of his audience.[44] I should begin by acknowledging that this speech is arguably the most extreme example in the *History* of Thucydides conflating two different audiences: the audience for his own work, and the audience for Pericles' speech.[45] However, insofar as every speech in the *History* develops Thucydides' argument, this difference is one of degree as opposed to procedure. Pericles' performance in this speech is non-conventional in that he upholds Thucydides' intellectual prejudices against the *dêmos*, while managing to deliver a speech that is partly successful (it achieves its immediate strategic objective, but it does not placate the Athenians' resentment about their circumstances). The speech also contains two suggestive verbal echoes of Thucydides' statement about his speeches at 1.22.1, which makes it a particularly apt example for comparing Thucydides' professed methodology with his practice. I will suggest that this speech can serve to clarify the meaning of Thucydides' opaque wording in the earlier passage.

Pericles' final speech serves as a turning point in Thucydides' depiction of Athenian speech culture.[46] Pericles is the only named Athenian politician to whom Thucydides gives 'air time' in the first two books of the *History*, and Thucydides portrays Pericles' control of the assembly in terms of an instructive climate in which the politician can tell his audience what is best for them in a responsible manner.[47] It is part of the ideological characterization of Thucydides' Pericles that he does not pay attention to what the audience wants to hear. In the last speech, Thucydides emphasizes what we might call Pericles' 'oppositional rhetoric'.[48] Thucydides uses a series of compound verbs with prepositional prefixes that denote diversion, dissolution, dissuasion and opposition (*apo-*; *para-*; *ana-*; *anti-*), all achieved by means of speech. At 2.59.3, he prefaces Pericles' speech with the claim that 'he [Pericles] wanted to give them confidence and, by diverting (*apagagôn*) their angry emotions, to render them in a calmer and less anxious state'. The significance of this verb is emphasized by the fact that it is repeated after the speech at 2.65.1, where Thucydides summarizes the intended force of Pericles' rhetoric: 'he tried to dissolve (*paraluein*) the anger of the Athenians towards him and to lead their minds away (*apagein*) from their present troubles'. Continuing in this vein, Thucydides records the successful outcome of the speech in terms of Pericles dissuading the Athenians from going out to meet the Spartan forces in battle (*anepeithonto* – 2.65.2). Finally, in his retrospective on

Pericles' career, Thucydides uses the verb *antilegein*: 'on the basis of their high estimation of him, he [Pericles] was able to oppose them in speech (*anteipein*) and rouse them to anger' (2.65.8).

The verb *agein* (to lead) is prevalent in surviving discussions of ancient Greek rhetoric (*epagein, paragein, apagein, prosagein*). A *logos* that is *epagôgos* (from the verb *epagein*) is seductive – it leads the listener on and, accordingly, *misleads* him or her.[49] At 2.64.1, Pericles warns his audience not to let citizens who advocate letting the empire go lead them astray (*paragein*). As demonstrated by the use of the verb *apagein*, Pericles also engages in this mode of rhetoric that 'leads' the audience, the difference being that Thucydides depicts Pericles leading his Athenian audience away from errors of judgement that allegedly threaten their own interests.[50]

According to Thucydides, one of the guiding principles in his composition of the speeches was the present circumstances or issues (*ta paronta*) that a given speaker would have had to address: 'what was called for by each situation'.[51] It is notable that Thucydides portrays Pericles formulating a speech that is specifically designed to meet a particular moment where his audience's minds are overwhelmed by their present straits: 'he saw that they were vexed in view of their present circumstances (*pros ta paronta deina*)' (2.59.3; see p. 53 above). This point is reiterated immediately after the speech, where Thucydides comments that Pericles tried to lead them away from their present troubles (2.65.1). We have also seen how the elusive criterion of 'what was needed' (*ta deonta*) was another guiding principle for Thucydides' composition of the speeches. Pericles actually echoes this phrase within the text of the speech. He challenges the Athenian assembly by putting it to them that he has the best interests of the *polis* at heart and that he knows what is best and is capable of explaining it to them (2.60.5):

> And then you are venting your anger on me, yet I think that I am the kind of man who is second to none in recognizing what the situation calls for (*ta deonta*) and explaining this [to you]; I also love my city and am impervious to corruption.

The phrases '*ta paronta*' and '*ta deonta*' link Pericles' speech closely to Thucydides' conception of the demands of political speeches.[52] More than this, it is as though Thucydides has written an exemplary speech for Pericles to demonstrate his own ideal of political rhetoric in action. In the words that Thucydides has written for him, Pericles shares the narrator's insights into the flaws in the system of political rhetoric as practised in the Athens of his day. In addition to the parallels between what Thucydides says about speeches in his own voice at 1.22 and the arguments expressed by Pericles in his speech, there is also an interesting parallel between 2.64.1 and 8.1.1. In the former passage Pericles rebukes the *dêmos* for taking their frustrations about the war out on him when they themselves joined with him in taking the vote for war. In fact Pericles makes this point three times in the speech, shifting the emphasis each time. In addition to the passage referred to, at the beginning of the speech Pericles tries to play down the anger with which he is regarded by implying that the *dêmos* is angry with itself as well (2.60.4).[53] He also reminds them of their responsibility in voting for the war by pointing out that if they had a favourable opinion of his character when they were voting for the war, they should not accuse him of wrongdoing in the present context (2.60.7). Pericles' argument foreshadows, or is echoed by, Thucydides' observation at 8.1.1 that the Athenian *dêmos* reacted to the devastating news of the defeat of the Sicilian expedition in 413 BC by taking their anger out on the politicians and any other advisers, including oracle-mongers, who had encouraged them to undertake the expedition 'as if they themselves had not voted [for it]'. Pericles' view that the *dêmos* has a tendency to absolve itself of any responsibility for policy, even when they have voted for this policy, is also echoed by the troubled Athenian politician Nicias (7.48.4).[54]

Some of Thucydides' readers have been disturbed by Pericles' speech and find it implausible that he would have delivered such an antagonistic speech to the Athenian assembly. Dionysius of Halicarnassus quotes the first section of Pericles' speech (2.60.1), and objects that these are not appropriate (*prosêkonta*) words for Pericles to voice when he is meant to be defending his policy in front of the Athenian assembly:[55]

> These would have been suitable words for Thucydides to use in a historical statement about Pericles, but they are not appropriate words to put in his mouth when he is defending himself before an incensed crowd, especially at the beginning of his speech, before he has said something to appease their anger. The best manner of address for this purpose would have been not this reproachful one, but rather a more conciliatory one: political speakers should soothe, not inflame the anger of the crowds.

Dionysius analyses this speech from the perspective of one schooled in models of political rhetoric surviving from the fifth and fourth centuries BC. He introduces the consideration of what an adept orator would have said in these circumstances.[56] Whereas Thucydides' criterion of *ta deonta* (what was needed) is deliberately broad, (*ta*) *prosêkonta* – the participle that Dionysius uses – means 'what is fitting / appropriate' and invokes rhetorical conventions and protocols more explicitly: the kind of thing that a speaker should say in a given context.

It is significant that historicity is not an issue for Dionysius. Unlike Thucydides' readers in the present day, he does not waste time agonizing over whether or not these were the words that Pericles actually spoke in front of the Athenian assembly. Instead, he assumes that this speech is

Thucydides' own creation. In the case of Pericles' speech, Dionysius accuses Thucydides of writing a speech for Pericles that articulates Thucydides' own opinion of Pericles and his own analysis of the historical situation in Athens in the summer of 430 BC, as opposed to writing the kind of speech that Pericles ought to have given in the circumstances. Furthermore, Dionysius states that Thucydides has failed to distinguish between judgements that belong in the narrative section of his *History* and material that is appropriate for the speeches. For instance, according to this understanding of the historian's role, it is allowable for Thucydides to record his opinion that Pericles was the most intelligent Athenian of his day, but it is not appropriate for Thucydides to make Pericles say this himself in the speech. Now obviously we should not accept Dionysius as the sole arbiter of the legitimacy of the speeches in Thucydides. This would be merely to replace the bias that Dionysius detects in Thucydides with the former's own bias about how historians should compose speeches.

Dionysius starts from the assumption that Thucydides should have composed the speech in such a way as to portray Pericles in the best light for future audiences. However, for Dionysius this seems to entail making Pericles 'look good' in front of the assembly audience and telling them what to hear. Dionysius expects a model of conventional political rhetoric. However, this is to misunderstand Thucydides' critical mode of history-writing. There are two conflicting 'models' of political rhetoric here: Dionysius' model is audience-centred, conciliatory and pragmatic: Thucydides should have made Pericles look like a good democratic leader. Conversely, Thucydides' model of political rhetoric allows politicians to speak freely (see the adverb *eleutherôs* at 2.65.8);[57] he idealizes the historical Pericles by setting Pericles at odds with his contemporaries. It is significant that Thucydides does not gloss over public resentment towards Pericles; at the end of the speech Thucydides reveals that although Pericles managed to get the Athenian *dêmos* to change its mind about going out to meet the Spartans in battle in the countryside of Attica (2.65.2), they continued to resent him and their anger ceased only when they had punished him with a fine (2.65.3-4). In its historical context this is not an entirely successful defence speech.

Rather than compare Pericles' speech with surviving examples of defence speeches made by Athenian politicians, who avail themselves of conventional arguments intended to conciliate the intended audience, it is more appropriate to compare this speech with Plato's *Apology* – the defence speech (*apologia*) that he wrote for Socrates. It is accepted that this speech is Plato's invention, and not the speech that Socrates actually delivered in front of the Athenian jury who were judging his case, if indeed he did deliver a formal speech. Although it is styled as a speech that was delivered in the law courts, its tone is more reminiscent of a private obituary: this is Plato's representation of Socrates as an individual who knew what was best for the Athenians and who was not prepared to compromise his philosophical ideals in the face of public criticism and opposition. Moreover, it is part of the characterization of Socrates' intellectual integrity that he defies popular democratic ideology. Plato's version of the defence speech is intended not to find favour with the Athenian audience in front of whom it was ostensibly delivered. Socrates was put to death in 399 BC; Thucydides may still have been alive at this point and may even have been aware of a version of the defence speech attributed to Socrates.[58] Although we do not have secure dates for Plato's *Apology*, or any of Plato's dialogues for that matter, Thucydides would certainly not have had access to Plato's version of Socrates' defence speech. However, for the comparison to be valid it is not necessary for either writer to have knowledge of the other; it is perfectly possible that both Thucydides and Plato were attempting a similar exercise in different prose genres from the common perspective of being critical about Athenian democracy and the collective wisdom of the Athenians en masse.[59] There is ample evidence in his *History* that Thucydides took an interest in how élite individuals – particularly those who took part in intellectual pursuits – defended themselves in front of the democracy.

In fact, elsewhere in the *History* Thucydides delivers two explicit obituaries to commemorate talented intellectuals who fell foul of the *dêmos*. At 1.138.3-6, Thucydides discusses the fate of the Athenian politician Themistocles and gives him a very positive write-up, dwelling on his intelligence and foresight in particular.[60] Thucydides observes, in a matter-of-fact tone, that Themistocles had gone into exile under accusation of treason (1.138.6), and his obituary stands in defiance of the consensus view about Themistocles. Similarly, at 8.68.1-2 Thucydides very deliberately rehabilitates the reputation of the orator Antiphon, who was condemned to death for his part in the Oligarchic revolution in 411 BC. Thucydides notes that Antiphon was regarded with suspicion by the majority of people and that he shunned speaking in front of the *dêmos*, but proceeds to eulogize his intellectual qualities and rhetorical ability. Thucydides even goes so far as to say that Antiphon's defence speech was the best that had ever been given. In all three cases: Themistocles, Pericles and Antiphon, Thucydides ranks their intellectual qualities over their democratic credentials. In fact, unlike the majority of Athenians in his day, Thucydides does not regard anti-democratic behaviour *per se* as a character flaw.

As a measure of Pericles' disregard for conventional rhetorical strategy, he refers openly to the fact that he is hated by a section of the Athenian *dêmos* on account of the plague, which many Athenians associated with the overcrowding that was a direct result of his own policy of encouraging them to abandon the countryside and move within the city walls: 'I know that *I am still hated* by a certain section of the population on account of this [sc. the plague]' (2.64.1). As if openly declaring his unpopularity was not enough, Thucydides has Pericles construct an implicit analogy between the hatred that some Athenians feel towards him and the hatred that her allies allegedly feel towards Athens. In an attempt to reassure them that they should persist with their empire, Pericles tells his audience that being hated is a short-term consequence for all who have taken the decision to rule (*archein*) over others (2.64.5).[61] He then adds that hatred does not endure for long, but that those who are hated leave behind a reputation for brilliance that endures for all time. This statement has different resonances, depending on whether we focus on the Athenian *dêmos* as audience (the internal audience), or Thucydides' readers (the external audience). The comment on the hatred incurred by empire serves a definite function for the primary audience and within the historical context of Pericles' speech: the Athenians were anxious about the simultaneous burden of waging war with the Peloponnesians and maintaining their empire, particularly in view of the threat of allies revolting. However, when we read Thucydides' provocative judgement that, although a democracy, Athens was under the rule (*archê*) of Pericles, as 'first citizen' (2.65.9-10), Pericles' comments acquire another dimension. In political contexts, the noun *archê* can mean political office, rule and empire. It is possible to see an analogy between the *archê* of Pericles over Athens and Athens' imperial rule over others (*archê*). And if this subtext lurks behind the words that Thucydides attributes to Pericles, then his comment about hatred being short-lived but a brilliant reputation enduring for all time can be seen as a self-regarding and self-affirming statement on Pericles' part. However, the 'everlasting reputation' (*doxa aieimnêstos* – 2.64.6), which Pericles claims for himself and the Athenians, is in the hands of Thucydides and he has not given them the untarnished legacy that they craved. As often in the *History*, we are reminded of Thucydides' claims for the eternity of his own work (1.22.4).

Another provocative element in Pericles' speech is his metaphorical use of medical language.[62] Thucydides frames the narrative of the plague (2.47-55), in between the last two of the three speeches which he attributes to Pericles: the funeral oration (2.34-46) and Pericles' final speech (2.59-65). So the plague narrative overshadows Thucydides' narration of Pericles' speech in the text. In the latter speech, Pericles intimates that not only are the Athenians allowing the fact of the plague to affect their judgement and their sense of perspective,[63] but that the plague has literally weakened their mental faculties. In other words, he treats the audience as though they are ill. Hence at 2.61.2, Pericles informs the audience that in the infirmity of their judgement (*en tôi asthenei tês gnomês*) his advice appears not to be correct, the implication being that his advice is fine but their judgement is diseased. Shortly afterwards he tells them to 'recover from their private pains (*apalgêsantes de ta idia*) and to take a share in the safety of the community' (2.61.4). Furthermore, as Stephen Halliwell has observed, Pericles also uses the noun *metabolê*, which has been used previously by Thucydides in his account of the plague to refer to both the transformation in health (2.48.3) and the reversals of social and material fortune (2.53.1) brought about by the plague.[64] As well as referring to the plague as a *metabolê* at 2.61.2, Pericles also uses the cognate verb *metaballô* (to reverse / change) when he accuses the Athenians of reversing their position, in contrast to his own constancy of judgement. Halliwell's comment is pertinent:

> It is as though Pericles wants to translate the plague from a socio-material into a psychological 'transformation'. The plague, he asserts, has disturbed the balance of Athenian political rationality: it has weakened the power of 'judgement', *gnômê* (61.2), that is fundamental to the collective working of the democracy and in which Thucydides wishes us to be left in no doubt that Pericles himself was, and was recognized to be, pre-eminent.[65]

The metaphorical use of medical language is relatively common in political rhetoric. The most pointed example in Thucydides occurs in Book 6, where the Athenian politician Nicias, addressing the Athenian assembly, exhorts the *prutanis* (the official in charge of the council who would have been overseeing the agenda for the assembly) to become a doctor (*iatros*) for the city's [bad] judgement.[66] However, in the present context Pericles' use of medical language is much bolder: in front of an Athenian audience, the majority of whom would have been directly affected by the plague, either having lost relatives or friends or having suffered from the plague themselves, he presumes to suggest that their judgement is diseased. In parts of his final speech Thucydides' Pericles carries over rhetorical tropes from the funeral oration, such as the repeated stress on the immortal fame of Athens (2.64.3 and 2.64.5-6). It is as if he is revising a lesson that he has already taught the *dêmos*.

We have seen how Dionysius objected that no politician in his right mind would adopt such a critical and antagonistic tone when speaking defensively before the Athenian democracy. This obscures the fact there was scope for Athenian politicians to criticize their audiences and to praise themselves. The difference is that Thucydides' Pericles takes this model of critical rhetoric to an extreme. Dionysius' critique of Pericles' speech fails to consider the Thucydidean agenda, or what we might call 'Thucydides' critical project' behind the speech. Moreover, although he professes to be assessing Pericles' speech in historical terms, on the basis of what it would have been appropriate for Pericles to say, it seems that Dionysius the historian cannot help thinking like Dionysius the orator, who writes with one eye on the adaptability of Thucydides' speeches, asking whether the student of rhetoric could use them as a model. For instance, in chapter 55,

Dionysius recommends that most of the narrative portions of Thucydides' *History* (as opposed to the speeches) can be used to serve many rhetorical purposes. Hence his judgement is governed by the criterion of 'correct usage' and canons of literary style ('correct,' that is, by the standards of the rhetorical schools in Dionysius' day) and tends to be highly normative (ibid., chapter 34). Dionysius does not appreciate Thucydides' idiosyncrasies or his bold and innovative use of language. For Dionysius *alêtheia* in the context of the speeches means 'realism' – imitating the kind of thing that people say in real life. Recall his approval for the speech made by the Plataeans in Book 3.53-9 (quoted above, p. 59), where he praises the fact that the speech is adorned with 'realistic and natural colouring'. But this remains an imitation, or an artist's impression of natural speech. Speech that is entirely natural tends not to make good literature.

Writing the truth

In my analysis of Pericles' final speech, I suggested that the tension between an audience-centred version of the truth and Thucydides' version of the truth, filtered through Pericles' frank speech, is an important aspect of his critique of Athenian decision-making in the context of the war. One of the contentions of Thucydides' *History* is that the true nature of the Atheno-Peloponnesian War was not apparent to most of the participants; this applies to broad misconceptions at the level of policy such as the Athenians' miscalculation of their economic resources (as analysed by Lisa Kallet),[67] through to specific instances of misjudgement, such as the inadequate inquiry about the perpetrators of the profanation of the Mysteries and the mutilation of the Herms (6.53.1-2). Thucydides' narrative of the war supplements and corrects versions of events that circulated at the time and it is particularly cogent for being both contemporary with these versions and subsequent to them (it is written in hindsight and written to outlast these versions). By a subtle process of substitution, Thucydides' contemporary history, allegedly written in 'real time,' both 'writes up' (*xungraphô*) and overwrites what was said and done in the war.[68] Thucydides implies that the activity of writing offers scope for reflection and critical distance, making it possible to review what was done and said in clearer terms.

Case-study II: Nicias' letter (7.8-16)

By Thucydides' own admission, he was not able to reconstruct the speeches as they were actually spoken, since both he and his informants had imperfect memories of the precise words. This leads Thucydides to synthesize his own commentary with the gist of what the speakers said. At Book 7.8-16, Thucydides shows us, via Nicias' letter, what an exact report of someone's arguments might look like; it is notable that the idea of an exact report relies on the written word. The reasoning that Thucydides attributes to Nicias at 7.8.2 holds that the written word is the only medium that allows an individual to communicate his ideas to an absent audience accurately. Furthermore, the language that Thucydides uses at 7.8-16 echoes his statement about the difficulty of reconstructing speeches at 1.22.1-2, and therefore acts as an ironic commentary on the relative status of the spoken word and the written word in Thucydides' *History*.[69] In addition, Nicias' letter is framed by the further irony that this supposed 'transcript' of what Nicias wrote is apparently subject to a similar process of narratorial improvisation as the speeches (both direct and reported). It is notable that Thucydides presents the text of the letter in the form of a speech, as read out by a secretary to the Athenian assembly:[70] 'The secretary of the city took the podium and read to the Athenians the letter which revealed *the following kinds of things*' (7.10); the secretary then voices Nicias' thoughts and advice. As Westlake comments, '[Thucydides] may conceivably have seen a copy of it [sc. Nicias' letter]; but he has chosen to present to his readers his own version of it, which is designed to perform the same function as his speeches [...] it is as instructive and revealing as any speech.'[71]

Thucydides focalizes his account through Nicias, by a device which Mabel Lang has called 'participial motivation', creating the impression that he knew what was going through Nicias' mind: 'Nicias realizing ... and seeing ...' (7.8.1).[72] According to Thucydides, the reasons behind Nicias' decision to commit his report to writing stem from his fear that the messengers might not announce the reality (*ta onta*) of their position in Sicily, and that his arguments (*gnômê*) might be obscured by an oral report (*en tôi angelôi aphanistheisa*). This twofold explanation corresponds to Thucydides' differentiation between the arguments that were spoken in the war, and the actions that took place in the war (1.22.1-4). However, through the device of the letter Thucydides' Nicias aims at higher standards of representational fidelity than the standards that Thucydides claims for his own historical account. The use of the phrase *ta onta* denotes what really exists / is the case. June Allison has commented on the use of the phrase *ta onta* in this passage, and has argued that the phrase suggests 'the physical reality (the historical accuracy or objective truth) of the situation in Sicily', rather than *alêtheia* – a quality that is also mentioned in connection with the letter – which, according to Allison, belongs to acts of expression and utterance, and is associated with verbs of thinking and saying.[73]

Thucydides' Nicias does not worry about the ability of the messengers to convey his report word for word, but he is keen that his arguments (*gnômê*) should be transmitted without interference. This calls to mind Thucydides' claim to have reconstructed the 'general ideas behind' –

(*xumpasa gnômê*) what speakers actually said. However, again Nicias' standards are more exacting; Thucydides qualifies *gnômê* with the adjective *xumpasa* ('general'); this careful vagueness sidesteps the task of representing speakers' arguments systematically. However, Nicias' letter does not function as a self-sufficient text, since Nicias tells the messengers what to say, in addition to giving them a written report to convey (7.8.3); at 7.10, the messengers duly announce to the assembly 'all the things that he said to them by word of mouth' (7.10). We have no way of knowing the relationship between the oral message and the written letter, and Thucydides does not enlighten us. It is almost as though the letter acts as a backup.

When we turn to Thucydides' explanation of Nicias' rationale, again there are both verbal and thematic echoes of Thucydides' methodological statement at 1.22; the messengers might distort Nicias' report for the following reasons:

first, they might be inept speakers (*kata tên tou legein adunasian*)
secondly, their memories might not be up to the task of recalling his words
    (*mnêmês*[74] *ellipeis gignomenoi*)
thirdly, they might be influenced by the desire to please the crowd (*tôi ochlôi pros charin ti legontes*).

The phrase *mnêmês ellipeis* recalls the language of recollection and memory at 1.22.1-4 (*diamnêmoneusai ... mnêmê*).[75] While the idea that the messengers might speak with a view to gratifying (*pros charin*) their audience recalls Thucydides' criticism of the *logographoi* at 1.21.1, on the grounds that they are more interested in entertaining their audiences than trying to represent the truth. There is perhaps also an 'echo' of 2.65.10-11, where Thucydides writes, proleptically, that the generation of politicians after Pericles 'handed over political affairs to the pleasures of the *dêmos*', referring primarily to the conduct of the Sicilian expedition. The mention of gratification also reminds us of Thucydides' assumptions about he priorities of audiences at 1.22.4, where he proclaims that his *History* may appear rather lacking in enjoyment (*aterpesteron*).

Whereas Thucydides does not lay claim to *alêtheia* for his account, but instead phrases the usefulness of his work in terms of a clear insight (*to saphes*) into the past (1.22.4), Nicias' letter aims at the truth – at transmitting a report that will convey everything (recall the etymology of *alêtheia* as 'that which is not (to be) forgotten', p. 64 above). We are told that Nicias had recourse to a letter so that the Athenians could reach a decision about the Sicilian expedition on the basis of the truth (*bouleusasthai peri tês alêtheias* – 7.8.2). The criterion of *alêtheia* is repeated at the end of the letter, where Nicias states that he considered it 'safer' to reveal the truth to the Athenians (*to alêthes dêlôsai* – 7.15.1).

However, the letter also incorporates the quality of *to saphes*, since Nicias accounts for the tone of his letter with the explanation that, 'I could have included other things in his report which would have been sweeter for you to hear, however, they would not be as useful insofar as it is necessary for you to base your decisions on clear knowledge (*saphôs eidotas*) of how things stand here' (7.14.4). The claim that a straight, unadorned account is more 'useful' to the audience also recalls Thucydides' claims for his *History* (cf. 1.22.4). A further correspondence between Thucydides' stated methodology in Book 1, and Nicias' letter is present in Nicias' statement (a form of *recusatio*), that he could have included other things that would have been sweeter for the audience in the assembly to hear; this comment recalls both his fear about the messengers compromising the message in order to gratify the audience (7.8.2, above), as well as Thucydides' more general depiction of an audience-centred speech culture in Athens.

The theme of clarity is reinforced by the use of the verb 'to reveal' (*dêloô*), which is used to frame the letter and also by Nicias in the text of the letter. The text of the letter is introduced with the statement that 'it *revealed* the following kinds of things' (7.10); Nicias says that he considered it safer to *reveal* 'the truth' (7.15.1), and finally, Thucydides rounds off the letter with ring composition: 'so the letter of Nicias *revealed* these things' (7.16.1). This threefold repetition of the same verb can hardly go unnoticed. Thucydides stresses that Nicias attempted to send a report that is a paragon of clarity and truthful information. This aspect of Nicias' letter recalls Pericles' straight-speaking advice to the Athenians in the early stages of the war (Books 1 and 2). In common with Pericles' speeches, Nicias attempts to give the Athenians a systematic report of their resources, but Nicias' previous attempt to wield logistics for persuasive ends was a rhetorical failure (6.20-4; see especially 6.24.1-3). We are also invited to compare Nicias' performance with Pericles' by the former's attempt to portray himself as a discerning adviser. Nicias' speech employs an intellectual vocabulary, including the verbs 'I have learned' (*punthanomai* – 7.12.2) and 'I understand' (*epistamenos* – 7.14.4); this portrait is compounded by the suggestive use of the noun *gnômê* ('reasoned opinion'). We have seen above that one of Nicias' motives for sending the letter was to make sure that his *gnômê* will get through to the Athenians. The same noun is repeated in Nicias' summary at 7.15.1 and 7.15.2. *Gnômê* is one of the character traits of Pericles in Books 1 and 2, and constitutes an important part of Pericles' vocabulary in the speeches that Thucydides composes for him.[76] More generally, Lisa Kallet has analysed the depiction of Nicias in Books 6 and 7 in terms of the relationship between *periousia chrêmatôn* and *gnômê*, and argues that Thucydides depicts Nicias as a leader who has shrewd knowledge about war-financing, but lacks intelligent judgement and the ability to get his financial insights put into practice.[77] This is Nicias trying to do a Pericles: trying to assert

79

control and prudent policy in a situation of which he has lost control and where the Athenians have committed themselves to an imprudent, expansionist overseas expedition.

There is tragic irony in Nicias' letter. The letter enjoins the Athenian audience to make the right decisions concerning their campaign in Sicily (*bouleuesthai* – 7.11.2; see also 8.2 and 14.4). However, in having to educate the Athenians about proper decision-making, and in requesting reinforcements, Nicias fulfils a statement that he made in his speech to the Athenian assembly about the logistics of the expedition: 'it would be disgraceful if we were forced to retire or to send back later for reinforcements owing to *thoughtless decision-making* to begin with' (*askeptôs bouleusamenous* – 6.21.1). In the same speech Nicias had also foreseen the predicament that he faces at 7.8: being a long way away from home, and having to rely on messengers to make a lengthy voyage back to Athens (see 7.9): 'we are cutting ourselves off from home and going to an entirely different country from which during the four winter months it is difficult even for a messenger to get to Athens' (6.21.2-22.1). In the assembly debates at the beginning of Book 6, Nicias is alienated from the majority of the Athenians by his opposition to the expedition; paradoxically he ends up as one of the commanders of the expedition and finds himself not just psychologically alienated, but also geographically alienated. There is an information gap: the Athenians at home do not know the situation in Sicily. In contrast, the reader has a full insight, which is strengthened by Nicias' letter; in addition to developing Nicias' characterization, the letter also serves to clarify the structure of Thucydides' narrative, in that it summarizes the progress of the expedition to Sicily, at what is roughly the half-way stage. The reader is familiar with many of the details that the Athenian audience are hearing for the first time.

So far I have concentrated on the *intra*textual characterization of Nicias, whereby Thucydides introduces into the letter verbal themes, which invite comparison with Pericles and prompt us to view Nicias' letter in light of his previous speeches. However, scholars have also detected *inter*textual echoes in Nicias' letter, principally to Homer.[78] Prompted by the comment of a scholiast who connects Nicias' comment about the timber of the Athenian ships rotting in Sicily (7.12.2) with *Iliad* 2.135, Zadorojnyi has seen an allusion to Agamemnon's ill-conceived speech to the Achaean army in the *Iliad* (2.110-41).[79] One does not have to accept Zadorojnyi's subtle verbal argument in order to agree with his broader point about how Nicias' inept rhetoric and the theme of premature retreat call the Homeric Agamemnon to mind.

Nicias attempts to transcend the problems of oral communication, the shortcomings of human memory and the pressures that Athenian mass audiences could bring to bear on speakers. This attempt is framed in terms that remind the reader of Thucydides' historiographical project and his discussion of the difficulties involved in conveying a clear account of speeches and events at 1.22.1-4. I have suggested that Nicias' letter poses a fascinating commentary on the methodological chapter in Book 1: it serves simultaneously as an example of how Thucydides reconstructed 'speeches', and it also articulates the historiographical themes of truth and what constitutes clarity in an account. Nicias' pitch to the Athenian Assembly is undercut by manifold ironies, but the overall effect is not entirely negative. Failure in the face of mass Athenian audiences is not necessarily a fault in Thucydides' estimation: Nicias' statement at 7.14.2 that the Athenians' natures 'are difficult to govern' finds broad confirmation in the *History* and in Book 6 in particular, and may well have been shared by Thucydides.[80] Simon Hornblower has noted that, as a former general, Thucydides would surely have sent written reports back to Athens from the field, and would presumably have been familiar with the reports of other generals. Hornblower goes even further, positing that these military reports, none of which have survived, constituted a generic influence on Thucydides.[81] Although Nicias' letter is only partially successful and further adds to his characterization as a tragic, blundering leader, Nicias is aware that his judgement tends to get lost in delivery and takes steps to counteract this. This is the closest that we get in the *History* to a character reflecting Thucydides' own attempt to fix his own judgement of the war in writing; Nicias' letter is a foil for Thucydides' own textual 'letter'.

Conclusion

At 1.22.1 Thucydides concedes that he struggled to remember the arguments that were spoken by participants in the war, and that the accounts of actions offered by various informants were also subject to interference (1.22.2-3). But elsewhere in the narrative he does not indicate how these limitations impinged upon his account. In fact, at 1.22 he mentions these problems but then gives the reader the impression that he has solved them. The wording at 1.22.2-3 states that he went in pursuit of each of the facts about each action in the war with as much precision as possible.[82] Thucydides begins the next sentence with the admission that these facts were ascertained with a great deal of labour (*epiponôs hêurisketo*). But it is equally possible to read this statement as a positive claim, as opposed to an admission of fallibility: the research was tough, but with hard work and perseverance Thucydides triumphed.

In view of the impossibility of accurate recollection, Thucydides did not attempt to render the actual words spoken, but instead he chose to move away from the actual words and to focus on ideas – both the speakers' ideas and his own judgement of these ideas in the context of the war and the broader context of Greek history. In addition, he also used the speeches to 'speak the truth' by giving his own ideas about his contemporary world and about the human condition more generally.

Thucydides' speeches also serve the meta-rhetorical role of analysing the conditions of speech-making and the constraints placed upon truth in the service of political rhetoric. It emerges that another reason for moving away from the words that were actually spoken stems from a conviction that, in most rhetorical contexts, the spoken word will deal only in relative truths: truths that relate to the audience, or to the speaker. In Thucydides' *History*, 'speaking the truth' entails writing and involves providing a commentary on what was behind the words spoken on any given occasion, for the benefit of later audiences.

Thucydides' careful calibration of accuracy in 1.22 encourages a false sense of familiarity. Much of what he writes in this chapter appeals to the conception of research in which many of his academic readers are themselves engaged. However, Thucydides offers us none of the transparency that we might, ideally, hope for, even though it is not reasonable of us to expect these standards in a writer who is pre-'history', as we know it. Nicole Loraux's words continue to resonate: 'Thucydide n'est pas un collègue' ('Thucydides is not a colleague').[83] This recognition clears the way for us to focus on understanding Thucydides' work on his own terms and in his own words, since this too is a historical exercise.

5

New Theatres of War: Book 8 and
Sophocles' *Philoctetes*

Although scholars usually turn to Book 7 in order to illustrate the influence of tragedy in the *History*, I will argue that it is Book 8 that bears the closest resemblance to the preoccupations of a surviving tragedy. Gregory Crane has summed up Book 8 as 'a bald record of quarrels, back-stabbing and inconclusive struggles that finally breaks off in midstream'.[1] This description could equally apply to Sophocles' *Philoctetes* – a tragedy produced in the same era (409 BC).

In this chapter I will construct a dialogue between Book 8 of Thucydides' *History* and Sophocles' *Philoctetes*. In particular, I will suggest analogies between Thucydides' focus on the stage-managing of political and military plots, the difficulty of discerning motives and intentions that are concealed by misleading speeches and the ironic contortions of language in the mouths of politicians. These aspects of Book 8 'anticipate' some of the recurring motifs in Sophocles' play, which is set on the island of Lemnos in the heroic past (the tenth year of the Trojan War). Although Sophocles does not make any explicit references to the oligarchic revolution and the democratic counter-revolution of 411 BC, the play was rehearsed in the immediate aftermath of these revolutions and was staged within two years. The recent political events in Athens would have provided an obvious frame of reference for the audience of Sophocles' tragedy. I am not arguing that either author influenced the other; Thucydides was in exile when Sophocles' play was produced and we have no way of knowing to what extent Sophocles was aware of Thucydides' work, if at all. Instead, reading Book 8 and *Philoctetes* as 'parallel texts', I suggest that the dialogue between these two works reveals a shared conception of the events of 411 BC as being characterized by dissembling, acting and a crisis of trust.

Before I proceed to explore the dialogue between the two texts, it is necessary to comment on the relationship between the eighth book of the *History* and the preceding books. Traditionally Book 8 has not been received with the same excitement as the other books of Thucydides' *History*. The 'final' book disappoints the reader's expectations on several levels. First and foremost, the end of the text does not coincide with the end of the war. Thucydides' version of the war ends abruptly in the twenty-first year (411/10 BC), seven years prior to the ultimate 'end' of the war in 404 BC. Consequently, Book 8 breaks the illusion of 'history as text' – the idea that Thucydides' account is commensurate with the events that it narrates, and vice versa. At several stages in the work, Thucydides has given the reader previews of how the war will end (e.g. 2.65.12), and we are led to believe that the ending of the *History* will coincide with the ending of the war (5.26.1). Not only do we not get the 'real' end of the war, but Thucydides' account of the war also has a non-ending.[2] The book stops, unapologetically, mid-way through a sentence.

One could construct any number of sophisticated readings in an attempt to account for the lack of a conventional ending. For example, one could surmise that the hanging ending was a deliberate stylistic strategy on Thucydides' part, either to create suspense, or to convey the sense of events being 'up in the air', or 'out at sea', or in order to create an impression of a 'natural' ending that peters out like the human lifespan of the author behind it. However, such readings are entirely fanciful. Hunter Rawlings has attempted to fill in the gaps by plotting outlines for the books which Thucydides never got round to writing.[3] While this scheme is less fanciful than the ideas suggested above, it is still speculative. One of the problems with such thought experiments is that they rely on patterns of interpretation based on the existing books in order to project the content of subsequent books. However, were there other books to take into account, we would surely have to modify our interpretation of the *History* and our conception of the patterns substantially.[4]

The disappointing reality is that Thucydides abandoned his project of writing (or 'writing up') his narrative of the Atheno-Peloponnesian War, and no explanation is offered. We do not know whether the lack of an ending was accidental or deliberate: either Thucydides did not finish his work owing to circumstances beyond his control, or else he gave up.[5] The biographer Marcellinus, who wrote a life of Thucydides, records that the oddity of Book 8 prompted readers in antiquity to attribute its authorship to someone else (chapter 43). In the twentieth century scholars responded to the lack of an ending in various ways: some suggested that, post-Sicily, the denouement of the real war proved hard to reconcile with Thucydides' conception of the war, and the way in which he had plotted it in the first seven books of the *History*. For instance, Stewart Flory has proposed that it became increasingly apparent to Thucydides that the characterization of Athens as a naval power and Sparta as a land power was untenable in the latter stages of the war, and he had invested too much in developing this characterization in the *History*.[6] Conversely, Josiah Ober has drawn a distinction between Thucydides' 'critical argument' (from the perspective of political theory), which he regards as complete, and the historical narrative of the war, which is incomplete.[7]

The last book of the *History* lacks many of the stylistic features that readers have come to expect of Thucydides' narrative by the time they have read through to Book 8.[8] In contrast to the earlier books, Book 8 contains not a single direct speech; instead, Thucydides employs reported speeches.[9] Perhaps in keeping with this shift away from direct speech to speeches reported by the narrator, Book 8 also has a much higher concentration of narratorial intervention than any other book.[10] Prior to Book 8 Thucydides allows very few expressions of uncertainty into his narrative and presents the reader with a confident analysis of events; in Book 8 there are frequent expressions of doubt about the reliability of accounts, as Thucydides struggles to ascertain the true motives of the protagonists, and to pinpoint a precise sequence of events.[11] The language of Book 8 also differs from that of preceding books in that it is less abstract. June Allison has argued that Book 8 has a much lower incidence of concepts of abstraction than the preceding seven books and, unlike the other books, contains no words that are *hapax legomena*.[12]

One way of accounting for the state of the narrative in Book 8 is to argue that this is a text in its unpolished, semi-worked state.[13] Some scholars make the further assumption that this 'unpolished' book offers us a window into Thucydides' workshop, and can serve as a model for the genesis of the other books. For example, scholars have suggested that Thucydides sketched out all the speeches in the *History* in indirect speech before converting them into dramatic narratives in direct speech.[14] However, the argument that the style of Book 8 must be due to the fact that it was never polished and developed overlooks the variation in narrative style in other parts of the work. For example, there is a marked preference for reported speech over direct speech in Book 5. Far more promising, in my view, is the argument that the state of the narrative is by design, and that it reflects Thucydides' attempt to represent the dramatic alteration in the progress of the war with an altered style of narration.[15]

W.R. Connor has approached Book 8 in terms of a tension between what he calls the 'symbolic' and 'factual' levels of the work';[16] the symbolic level consists of pivotal events such as the plague and the collapse of the Sicilian expedition, which resonate with strong psychological and moral overtones both in the minds of the participants and in the mind of the reader. As Connor explains, when the expedition to Sicily fails at the end of Book 7, to all appearances the war is as good as over. However, contrary to all expectation, in fact the Athenians were not beaten and continued to prosecute war.[17] Lisa Kallet has shown how Thucydides is particularly interested in the logistics of Athens' recovery from apparent defeat, since it exposes the inability of Athens' enemies to make a proper assessment of her real power and resources, as opposed to her apparent or 'symbolic' power.

Generally scholars have tended to characterize Book 8 using terms such as 'fragmentation', 'division' and 'disintegration'.[18] The book is marked by a shifting focus, as the narrative fluctuates between different locations.

Book 8 represents a period of transition; the Sicilian expedition (Books 6-7) shifted the theatre of war away from the areas of conflict in the first half of the war, and in the aftermath of the expedition Thucydides suggests that there was genuine uncertainty about where the war would be decided. With the collapse of the expedition at the end of Book 7, assumptions and values that seemed certain at the beginning of the war have either been exploded, or at the very least destabilized. The narrative of Book 8 takes this disappointment of expectations even further. Throughout the *History* Thucydides emphasizes how the pattern of the war did not proceed according to people's expectations, over and above the fact that warfare, by its very nature, is hard to predict. Book 8 narrates the most dramatic paradox in the entire work: the oligarchic revolution in Athens in 411 BC – an event which defied expectations.[19]

However, Thucydides has overlaid his commentary on the misjudgement and poor predictions of the states involved in the war, with a meta-commentary for the reader's benefit, clearly showing the direction and likely outcome of events. Thucydides has given the reader an explicit preview of the civil war (*stasis*) that would befall Athens (2.65.12), but the narrative also gestures towards this event in other ways, as well. At 1.144.1, in his first address to the Athenian assembly in the *History*, Pericles tells the Athenians that he has grown to fear their domestic mistakes (*hamartiai*) more than the strategies of the enemy. 'Domestic mistakes' could signal a number of errors of judgement that the Athenians make during the course of the narrative. For example, Thucydides refers to the Sicilian expedition as a mistake (*hamartanein ... hamartêma* – 2.65.11), and seems to include the oligarchic revolution in this category as well. However, Pericles' basic point that the Athenians have more to fear from themselves than from the enemy is borne out with a vengeance with the oligarchic revolution. Another cue is contained in Thucydides' description of *stasis* in Corcyra (427 BC), where he pinpoints this civil war as the source of the civil unrest that would later cause upheaval in the whole Hellenic world (3.82.1). The verb 'to suffer upheaval' (the passive of *kineô*) is repeated at 8.48.1, when the oligarchic revolution begins among the Athenian forces stationed in Samos.[20] The last example that I will offer is the most poignant: the Melians end their contribution to the dialogue with the following warning (5.110.2): 'Your suffering (*ponos*) will not come from a country that has nothing to do with you, but from an alliance that has closer ties and from your own land.' Ostensibly the phrase 'a country that has nothing to do with you' refers to Melos, but because this dialogue immediately precedes Athenian preparations for the ill-fated Sicilian expedition, it is possible to interpret this as an allusion to Sicily as well.[21] Hence the Melians warn the Athenians both about the dangers of getting involved in Sicily, and about the threat of *ponos* in their own land, which foreshadows the oligarchic revolution. Some of these cues are contained in speeches addressed to Athenian audiences; although the speeches are Thucydidean inventions, these cues signal Thucydides' assessment of the failure of the internal, historical audiences to interpret both speeches and events correctly.[22] The fact that the reader can see what is coming, while the Athenians cannot, contributes to the tragic irony of Thucydides' narrative.

The expedition to Sicily is generally regarded as the great Athenian tragedy in the *History*; as we saw above, Thucydides refers proleptically to the downfall of the expedition in language that echoes the errors of tragic protagonists.[23] Moreover, with the proviso that Thucydides' account is incomplete, he highlights the Sicilian expedition as the greatest campaign (*ergon*) in the war (7.87.5). Many readers of Thucydides have commented on the tragic note on which Book 7 ends, but few have commented on the continuation of the tragedy into Book 8.

> This campaign (*ergon*) happened to be the greatest (*megistos*) of the actions that took place during this war, and – so it seems to me – the greatest (*megistos*) of the Greek campaigns that we know from tradition; for those who prevailed it was the most glorious (*lamprotatos*) campaign and for those who were destroyed it was the most wretched (*dustuchestatos*);[24] for they were conquered in every single respect and their suffering was not on any small scale, but rather a case of utter destruction (*panôlethria*),[25] as it is called, both of the infantry and the fleet and everything else – there was nothing that was not destroyed, and few from the many made the journey home (7.87.5-6).

This passage represents tragedy on an epic scale, as Thucydides evokes tragedy and epic, arguably mediated through Herodotus. For Thucydides, the Sicilian expedition ranks as the 'greatest' (*megistos*) military undertaking in human knowledge; there is a grim irony to this superlative adjective. Thucydides uses *megistos* twice at 6.31.6, when he explains that the Athenian expedition to Sicily was talked about on several counts, including the fact that it was the 'greatest overseas expedition', conceived of with the 'greatest hope for the future'.[26] Although it still makes sense to describe the expedition as the greatest venture that had ever taken place at the end of Book 7, the 'greatness' of the expedition is purely a physical attribute of scale, and any connotations of glory and superiority that might have been attached to this adjective, prospectively, in Book 6 are completely overturned. The superlative adjective *lamprotatos* – applied to the Syracusan and Peloponnesian victors – recalls the fact that in Thucydides' account of the assembly debate over the Sicilian expedition, it was the 'brilliant' Alcibiades who wielded the greatest influence in persuading the Athenians to uphold the popular vote in favour of the expedition. Alcibiades is characterized by outward brilliance (see 6.12.2 (Nicias' first speech); 6.16.3; and 6.16.5 (Alcibiades' speech)), with more than a hint of scepticism about the substance of this brilliance.

Jonathan Price has connected Thucydides' use of superlatives at the end of Book 7 to the use of superlatives in the section known as the Archaeology (1.1-20). More pointedly, he refers to Thucydides' claim, in the second sentence of the work, that the Atheno-Peloponnesian War was the greatest upheaval (*kinêsis megistê*) to have taken place not just among the Greeks but also among most of humanity (1.1.2). Reading this passage in light of the end of Book 7, Price comments that:

> As the narrative unfolds, the reader comes to understand the full meaning of the superlatives in the opening statements of the work, which are at once more limited and more profound than expected. While the Peloponnesian War was a conflict on a larger scale from an Hellenic perspective and of longer duration than any war Thucydides' generation knew, the deeper significance is not what was achieved *by* Hellas but what happened *to* it.[27]

Not only does the end of Book 7 tell an Athenian tragedy, but it also shows up the huge humanitarian cost of the war. The Athenians suffer, on a greater scale, what they have previously inflicted on other states.

The end of Book 7 depicts the massive disappointment of all the Athenians' expectations, and shows the glory that they had hoped to acquire heaped onto their enemies. Thucydides echoes the Trojan War and its aftermath when he writes that few out of many made the return voyage (*apenostêsan* – 7.87.6) – a motif that may recall the epic theme of the 'return journey' (*nostos*).[28] Based on the epic poetry that survives, we associate this theme primarily with Homer's *Odyssey*, but *nostoi* were common in epic poetry and we know that there was a poem in the post-Homeric epic cycle that was simply titled *Nostoi*. If we take the *Odyssey* as the point of comparison, then the Athenians are both like the Achaeans (one of the terms used to describe the collective Greek forces in Homer's *Iliad*) in the sense that many of them do not return from their 'epic' military expedition, and unlike the Achaeans in that they fail to take Syracuse and return defeated in every way.[29] In addition to these epic allusions, Simon Hornblower has suggested that the *nostos* theme at the end of Book 7 also draws on the depiction of the homecoming of athletes in Pindar's poetry, which also has its own complicated relationship with epic.[30]

The tragedy in Sicily at the end of Book 7 is conveyed to Athens at the beginning of Book 8, and the tragic notes from Book 7 are also carried across into Book 8. The *ergon* mentioned at 7.87.5 is repeated at 8.1.1, where those soldiers who do manage to make it back to Athens are cast in the role of tragic messengers:

> When it was *announced* in Athens, the Athenians were extremely reluctant to believe that they had been utterly destroyed to such an overwhelming degree – they did not even believe those of the soldiers who had escaped from

the campaign (*ergon*) itself and who were *announcing* the news in no uncertain terms.

Thucydides depicts the emotional impact of the news on the Athenians, describing first incredulity (*apisteô* – 8.1.1), then anger (*orgizomai* – ibid.), then grief (*lupeô* – 8.1.2), fear (*phobos* – ibid.) and the stunned reaction (*kataplêxis* – ibid.). Their response to the news is supplemented by what they see: a massive depletion of resources, which, in turn, makes the Athenians feel weighed down (*barunomai* – 8.1.2) and void of hope (*anelpistoi* – ibid.). Whereas the Athenians are oppressed by grief on every side (8.1.2), the Spartans are optimistic on every side (*euelpides* – 8.2.4).[31] According to Thucydides this looked like the end, and to the reader this reads like the end; at 8.2.1 the rest of the Greek world forms an internal audience, anticipating that the remainder of the war will be of brief duration; however, we know that the narrative of the larger war still has eight years to go (although, in the event, we are only given two further years in Thucydides' text).

Tucked away in this narrative that is overlaid with tragic irony is the source of a domestic tragedy on the stage of Athens: in response to the current crisis, the Athenians appointed ten elders as *probouloi* (special advisers), a group which Thucydides describes as '*archê tis*' (8.1.3) – a vague phrase which translates as 'some kind of (political) office'. I interpret this phrase as a Thucydidean judgement on the irregularity of this office and the fact that these *probouloi* had a loosely defined role: to make preliminary recommendations concerning present circumstances whenever the need should arise. Thucydides comments that governed by fear, the *dêmos* was ready to assume good discipline (*eutaktein* – a verb with strong military nuances).[32] As events unfold it transpires that these *probouloi* have not advised the *dêmos* with a view to its best interests. The questions of what constitutes good discipline and where the best interests of the community lie emerge as the predominant issues in Book 8, as does the difficulty of reaching a correct judgement on these issues in a climate of fear and crisis. These issues also dominate the ethico-political debates in Sophocles' *Philoctetes*. I now turn to the dialogue between Book 8 of Thucydides' *History* and Sophocles' play.

The climate of Book 8

I have argued that the convoluted narrative in Book 8 is a reflection of the intricate plots that it describes, as opposed to the incomplete state of the work. There are two main theatres of war in Book 8: on the one hand Athens, on the other the east Aegean sea, with a specific focus on the islands of Chios and Samos (see Map 1). In addition, there are several individuals all trying to manipulate and stage-manage events: the Athenian exile Alcibiades, Tissaphernes, the Persian governor of the coastal region of Ionia, the Spartan general Astyochus, Phrynichus, one of the generals in charge of the Athenian fleet stationed at Samos, Peisander, another of the Athenian generals at Samos, and Theramenes, son of Hagnon, one of the instigators of the oligarchic coup who was later to take part in the democratic counter-revolution. It is also significant that Thucydides devotes a chapter to Antiphon, who he claims was the architect of the coup, but whose role was entirely behind the scenes (8.68.1-2). The events of Book 8 are characterized by deception (and counter-deception), double-dealing and the persuasive use of speech to obscure underlying realities. Recurring motifs include suspicion (*hupopsia*), acting in secret (*krupha*) and lack of trust (*apistia*). Deception is taking place on so many different levels that Thucydides himself expresses uncertainty about what was really going on (see the following passages on the difficulty of establishing the motivation behind Tissaphernes' actions 8.46.5; 8.56.3; 8.87.4-5).[33]

Thucydides builds up the climate of deception and suspicion gradually, beginning with a plot by Chian oligarchs to revolt from Athens. At 8.7, Thucydides comments that the negotiations have been carried out in secret (*krupha*). Moreover, in a passage that foreshadows the internal deceptions that will later circulate in Athens, Thucydides describes how the oligarchs in Chios – even while plotting against the Athenians – are forced to send ships to join the Athenian fleet as a token of faith. Thucydides explains that the majority of Chians had no knowledge of the plot at this stage and that the oligarchic conspirators did not want the mass of citizens as its enemy at this stage. However, the Athenians did not regard these Chian ships as reliable (*pistai* – 8.10.3).

The questions of what and who can be trusted, and what is going on in secret behind the scenes, dominate the narrative of events in Book 8. The chief mover of this climate of deception is Alcibiades, who is plotting to secure his return to Athens. Through the depiction of Alcibiades, Thucydides gives us a case-study in the dangerous powers of persuasive speaking. The persuasive speaking, which Alcibiades excels at, is opportunistic and truth-neutral: we see him persuading different audiences to contradictory courses of action. The first instance of Alcibiades' intervention occurs in chapter 12, when he sees that the Spartans have been discouraged from supporting the Chian revolt:

> Alcibiades was aware of this, and again brought persuasion to bear (*peithei*) on Endius and the other ephors not to shrink from making the voyage, stating that they would get to Chios before the Chians found out about the disaster that had befallen the ships. Once he reached Ionia, he would easily persuade (*peisein*) the cities to revolt by speaking of the weakness of the Athenians and the eagerness of the Spartans, for he would appear more reliable (*pistoteros*) than others. To Endius himself in private he said that it would be good for Ionia to revolt, and for the King of Persia to become an ally

of the Spartans as a result of his agency [...] So he persuaded (*peisas*) Endius
and the other ephors [...] (8.12.1-3).

This is not the first time in the *History* that Alcibiades has persuaded the
Spartans; at 6.89-92 he delivers a persuasive speech to the Spartan
assembly. In this instance Alcibiades exercises two strands of persuasion:
persuading the ephors in general, and addressing an additional argument
to Endius in private. According to the gist of Alcibiades' speech as reported
by Thucydides, Alcibiades *persuaded* the ephors on the grounds that he
would easily be able to *persuade* the Ionian cities both with arguments and
because he *appeared more trustworthy* to them than others. Would you
trust a speaker who is so up-front and confident in his powers of persuasion, and who bases his arguments on being able to exploit his *appearance*
of being credible? Alcibiades' claim is all the more devious, because the
reader has also read Alcibiades' boast to the Athenian assembly about his
past success in winning the trust (*pistis*) of the Spartans (6.17.1). The
effects of this earlier persuasion have worn off by 8.45.1, where the
Spartans plan to have Alcibiades executed because he is regarded as
suspect (*hupoptos*),[34] and because he appears unreliable (*apistos
ephaineto*). Although Thucydides records the Spartans' impression that
Alcibiades is untrustworthy, Alcibiades will continue to persuade other
audiences in the subsequent narrative.

At 8.45.2, Thucydides describes Alcibiades becoming Tissaphernes'
instructor (*didaskalos*). As well as meaning a teacher in a general sense,
the noun *didaskalos* was the term used for playwrights who trained their
actors and choruses in the performance of plays.[35] In this passage there is
a hint of the theatrical connotations of the noun, as Alcibiades is essentially instructing Tissaphernes how to *act* in a duplicitous way by keeping
his actions from the Spartans through dissembling. The plot of Book 8 –
both Alcibiades' internal plotting, and, correspondingly, the plot of
Thucydides' narrative – is yet more complicated, since Alcibiades is
portrayed as persuading Tissaphernes in order to be able to persuade the
Athenians to revoke his sentence of exile (8.47.1-2); the verb *peithein* (to
persuade) is used twice in this passage. In fact, Tissaphernes' behaviour is
just as duplicitous, and he has his own motives for colluding with first the
Spartans and then the Athenians. Thucydides states that Tissaphernes
knew that the Syracusan commander Hermocrates was going to denounce
him to the Spartans as *epamphoterizôn* (playing a double game – 8.85.2-
3).[36] In addition to the theme of double agency and false loyalties, note
how convoluted the chain of information is: Tissaphernes dispatches
Gaulites to make accusations against the Milesians, who were going to
accuse Tissaphernes, and to defend Tissaphernes against the accusations of Hermocrates. How did Tissaphernes – let alone Thucydides –
know all this?

In view of the climate of deception surrounding the Spartan and Athenian negotiations with Tissaphernes and, simultaneously, the deceptiveness of Alcibiades and the private and covert ambitions of the Athenian oligarchs, the suspension of direct speech in Book 8 seems likely to have been a deliberate narrative strategy on Thucydides' part.[37] There are plenty of examples of persuasive and manipulative speeches in the earlier books of the *History*, which are framed as such by the narrator. However, the persuasive reported speeches in Book 8 are distinguished by the fact that the speakers knowingly persuade their audiences about falsehoods. These are speeches that are manifestly insincere. In fact, Book 8 contains the most explicit example of false speech in the *History* (in the form of a reported speech), where the Athenian Chaireas returns to Samos and fabricates a report about the behaviour of the Four Hundred in Athens. Thucydides introduces his report of Chaireas' speech with the comment that he 'exaggerated and made things sound terrible' (8.74.3), and concludes by saying that 'he said many other things, heaping lie upon lie (*epikatapseudomenos*)'.[38] Rather than compose false speeches for the duplicitous agents of Book 8, Thucydides uses reported speech, which enables him to offer a running commentary on the apparent motives that were concealed behind the speeches and actions.

In addition to the plots that are in evidence in the reported speeches, a series of letters sent by Phrynichus and Alcibiades (8.50-51) contributes to the layers of duplicity, particularly since the letters are represented as behind-the-scenes machinations while other strategies operate in the foreground.[39] Phrynichus first sends a letter to the Spartan naval commander Astyochus exposing Alcibiades' double-dealing against the Spartans. Phrynichus sends this letter in secret (*krupha* – 8.50.2), acknowledging that he is acting treacherously in doing so (8.50.2-3). Astyochus responds by informing on Phrynichus to Alcibiades and Tissaphernes for motives of private gain (8.50.3).[40] Alcibiades responds by sending a letter condemning Phrynichus to the Athenian command on Samos (8.50.4-5), whereupon Phrynichus sends an even more treacherous letter to Astyochus, who again betrays his trust (8.50.5). Somehow Phrynichus learns that Astyochus is betraying him and anticipates Alcibiades' letter that will expose his second act of treachery by becoming an 'exposer' himself (*exangelos*). Phrynichus exposes the news that the Spartans are planning to attack Samos in view of the fact that it is not fortified; but the irony is that Phrynichus is exposing his own plot, since he is responsible for revealing the defensive weakness to the Spartans and for encouraging them to attack. Thucydides writes that Phrynichus claimed that he had accurate knowledge about this plot (*saphôs pepusmenos* 8.51.1); what Phrynichus does *not* tell the Athenians is that he has certain knowledge of the plot because *he* devised it. Phrynichus manipulates a situation in which he has twice turned traitor, with the paradoxical result that the Athenian generals do not regard Alcibiades as a credible source (*ou pistos*) when he informs against Phrynichus, even though he is telling the truth. The phrase *ou pistos* echoes the Spartans' mistrust of Alcibiades at 8.45.1, in a context where he was indeed not to be trusted. However, in this instance he happens to be telling the truth but, owing to Phrynichus' pre-emptive deception, Alcibiades' exposure of Phrynichus only serves to make the latter's account look more convincing (8.51.3).

Further ironies are present in this passage: the phrase *saphôs pepus-menos* (8.51.1) echoes 8.27.1, where Phrynichus advised the Athenian navy to withdraw from Miletus on the strength of accurate knowledge (*saphôs eputheto*) about the proximity of a superior Spartan fleet. Thucydides comments explicitly on the intelligence of Phrynichus' advice and also records that Phrynichus gained a reputation for being 'not unclever' (*ouk axunetos*) – that is, 'exceptionally clever' – in every command that he assumed (8.27.5). When Phrynichus is in command of the defences at Samos, he uses his intelligence to cover up his own treachery (8.51.1). Phrynichus' 'intelligence' proves even more sinister in his capacity as one of the oligarchic conspirators; it is notable that he is included in the roll call of clever (*xunetoi*) men who masterminded the coup (8.68.3-4).

In this passage Thucydides states explicitly that the overthrow of Athenian democracy in 411 BC was made possible by the intelligence of the conspirators (8.68.4). The gap in intelligence between the conspirators and the *dêmos* is exemplified at 8.53-4, when Peisander proposes to the Athenian assembly that they should adopt oligarchic rule in order to gain the support of the King of Persia in the war against the Spartans. Peisander overcomes the uproar in the assembly and takes on the opposing speakers one by one, challenging them to propose an alternative strategy for saving the city. Thucydides concludes this episode with an image of a docile *dêmos*, 'instructed (*didaskomenos*) by Peisander in clear terms that there was no other way to secure safety and reassured that they could always vote democracy back later if the Persians did not help' (8.54.1).[41] The reader who has been party to the web of plots and counter-plots has seen how empty is the promise of a Persian alliance, and so can see through Peisander's arguments. Thucydides' narrative of the intricacy of the plots that were practised is such that it is easy for the reader to understand the climate of suspicion, which is a feature of Thucydides' account of this stage of the war. By means of ironic intratextual echoes, Thucydides involves the reader in the process of judging the trustworthiness of Phrynichus and Alcibiades. The arts of intelligence are present in abundance in Book 8, but always in the service of deception.

It is debatable whether Thucydides intended to 'implicate' the *dêmos* in the oligarchic revolution, as Martha Taylor has argued, on the grounds that they do not pose any serious opposition to the coup, or whether the weight of blame falls rather on the abuse of cunning intelligence and political rhetoric to manipulate less intelligent audiences. Taylor rightly stresses that the portrait of the *dêmos* in the oligarchic revolution is unflattering and negatively critical, but I think the real subject of Thucydides' critique is the collapse of the ideals and values of democracy, or 'democratic ideology' and the social crisis that this precipitated. Sara Monoson has summarized Athenian democracy's view of the achievements of democracy in the following terms: 'the accomplishment of social unity, an intellectually capable citizenry, the responsible exercise of power, relations of reciprocity among citizens and between city and individual, and the defeat of tyranny'.[42]

This checklist of democratic achievements highlights the many different counts on which democracy failed in 411 BC. Mass decision-making failed to expose the flawed rhetoric of political advisers; not only was there no social unity but, worse still, the citizen body was divided both ideologically and geographically (split between Athens and the island of Samos), power was abused for private ends and, instead of reciprocity and communality, economic self-interest took hold. The idea of a divided citizen body acting against its own interests is highlighted by the ironic use of financial language to describe the way in which the behaviour of the army at Samos affected the citizens in Athens.

When the proposal for an oligarchic régime is put to the army at Samos, with a view to gaining the support of the king of Persia and recalling Alcibiades from exile, the Athenian *ochlos* (a contemptuous phrase for the masses)[43] is said to have been vexed momentarily, but placated by 'an abundance (*to euporon*) of hope for payment (*misthos*) from the king' (8.48.3).[44] The choice of the substantive adjective *to euporon* (connected with the noun *poros* – 'means', 'resources', 'revenue', 'financial provisions')[45] implies that the crews of the Athenian navy were obsessed with money, treating intangible hope as though it was an economic commodity. The fleet was the mainstay of the democratic *polis*; in Aristophanes' comedy *Acharnians* (425 BC) the *thranitês laos* (the men who sit at the uppermost of the three banks of rowing benches) is given the epithet 'saviour of the city'.[46] It is a sign of the inversion of the ideal of Athens that the crews are prepared to 'sell out' on democracy.[47]

The oligarchic revolution starts with the fleet and then later reaches Athens (8.48.1). The cruel disappointment of the anticipation of economic gain (*misthos*) is shown up in the continuation of economic language to describe the repercussions of the revolution in Athens. Thucydides notes that even the individual citizen who kept quiet considered it a 'profit' (*kerdos*) if he did not suffer violent treatment (8.66.2). One of the features of the revolution in Thucydides' account is how familiar language is used as a cover for subversive political actions. In the early stages of the revolution the *dêmos* and *boulê* continue to meet, under the same names and in the same locations, but the way in which the political business is conducted is a travesty of Athenian democracy.[48] In contrast to the ideal of extemporaneous debate in the assembly, all the speeches have been rehearsed and follow the party line (I quote this important passage at length):

> Nevertheless the Assembly and the Council chosen by lot still assembled, although they did not take any decision which was not approved by the party of the conspirators, and the speakers were also part of the conspiracy and the words that they were going to say were provided for them in advance. People were afraid when they saw their numbers, and no one from the rest of the citizen body still spoke in opposition (*antilegein*) to them, fearing when they saw that the body of conspirators was large. If anyone did happen to speak in opposition, he immediately died by some convenient means, and there was no investigation to find the people responsible, nor was legal recourse taken, even against those who were suspected (*hupopteuô*). Instead, the people were silent and in such a state of shock that the individual considered it a profit (*kerdos*) if he did not suffer violent treatment, even if he had kept quiet. And, because they thought that the conspiracy was much bigger than it really was, their judgement was weakened, and they were unable to find out about the conspiracy because of the size of the city and because of their lack of knowledge about each other. For this very reason it was not possible for an individual who was aggrieved to lament this to someone else so as to plot to avenge himself, for he would have found that the man to whom he spoke was unknown to him, or else known but not reliable (*apistos*). The population of citizens approached each other with suspicion (*hupoptôs*), as if each man had a role in what was happening. For indeed there were people in the plot whom no one would ever have imagined would resort to oligarchy. It was these men who created the greatest sense of mistrust (*to apiston*) among the mass and who, most of all, promoted the safety of the minority by establishing lack of trust (*apistia*) towards itself as a secure thing among the citizen body (8.66.1-5).

One of the tenets of Athenian democracy was that listening in common was a key mode of fostering the communality of interest, but it was vital that there was a debate.[49] In Book 3 Cleon criticizes his audience in the Athenian assembly for dramatizing political debate, by setting up contests in which they are a passive audience (3.38.4 and 3.38.7), but Thucydides records that on that occasion speakers put several conflicting points of view before the assembly (3.36.6). In Book 8 the oligarchic revolution marks the breakdown of democratic politics, which derived its stability precisely from its engagement in institutionalized conflict.[50] The dissolution of democratic ideology is reflected in the fact that nobody opposes (lit. 'speaks against') the resolution proposed by the oligarchs in the assembly (8.66.2 and 8.69.1). Subsequently, the malaise of the political climate is characterized by the prevailing silence.

The Athenians' inability to know whom to trust in the event of the

conspiracy reflects the lack of trust that has characterized political negotiations in the preceding narrative. The psychological and physical
intimidation of the *dêmos* described at 8.66 renders the citizen body
divided and prepares the way for the transition to a full oligarchic take-
over. When this transition occurs, the oligarchs further fragment the
existing political community by playing around with the topography of
government: the abuse of the democracy is accompanied by the misuse of
buildings and space. The conspirators hold the assembly on the transfer of
power at the site of the sanctuary of Poseidon Hippios in Colonus
(8.67.2).[51] It is significant that the assembly is convened at a distance of
ten stades (approximately two kilometres) from the *polis*, outside normal
civic space and outside the protection of the city wall. Other irregular uses
of space include the moderate hoplites' use of the theatre of Dionysus at
Mounychia for an assembly (8.93.1) and the attempt by the oligarchic
conspirators to build a fortification wall at Eëtionia in order to block the
Athenian fleet from the city (8.92.4). The pro-democratic hoplites subsequently tear down this wall (8.92.10-11). In turn, the return to democratic
normality is signalled by the fact that assemblies are once again held on
the Pnyx (8.97.1-2).

Conversely, although the idea of going over to an oligarchic régime had
originally come to Athens from the fleet in Samos, when the fleet hears
that the oligarchic régime is actually in place (albeit through a misleading
account from Chaireas), they hold a functional assembly (8.76.2), as
opposed to the dysfunctional assemblies in Athens. Thus, in effect, the
democratic *polis* is now located with the fleet in Samos, which is subsequently referred to as the '*dêmos* of the Athenians in Samos' (8.86.8).
According to the speakers in this assembly, with the Four Hundred in
power the *polis* has revolted from the fleet which is now construed as the
dêmos of the Athenians (8.76.3), because the citizens in Athens have
forfeited their right to this title as a result of their undemocratic behaviour (8.76.6). The account of the Atheno-Peloponnesian War began with
the disruption of the spatial organisation of Attica. Thucydides describes
the movement of the population of Attica in terms of 'uprooting' (*anas-
tasis* – 2.14.2) and 'relocation' (*metanastasis* – 2.16.1). Both of these nouns
are compounds of the noun *stasis* ('civil unrest'). Hence the language in
which Thucydides describes these upheavals, which are a direct result of
Pericles' policies, exposes the fragmentary nature of the *polis* in the minds
of many of its citizens (2.16.2).[52] This disruption is escalated in the
internal war described in the eighth book, where the organisation of the
entire *polis* is overturned. While the *polis* proper is in disarray, the fleet
takes over, grafting the ideological framework of the democratic *polis* onto
the ships that are stationed in Samos. When Nicias tells the Athenian
troops in Sicily that they constitute a movable *polis* (7.77.4),[53] his words
make fine rhetoric but the truth of the image is belied by his own conduct,

which is governed by his perceptions of how the Athenian assembly, instructed by political leaders, would want him to act.[54] In contrast, the fleet in Samos concludes that the *polis* in Athens is not fit to give it political advice, and consequently the *polis*-potentiality of the fleet is realized in actuality.

The fleet as a *polis* in its own right

Although the crews of the triremes were a vital part of Athens' manpower, in our sources they are effaced behind the mask of a voiceless collective, which was fashioned by an ideology that ranked hoplites and the cavalry over rowers.[55] Technically the *thêtes* (the lowest status of citizens, and the majority of the citizen body) who manned the ships were treated differentially in terms of the government of the *polis*; they were admitted to the assembly and the law courts but could not legally hold higher offices (cf. Ps.-Aristotle *Ath. Pol.* 7.3). The challenge from the trireme fleet to the oligarchic government of Athens in 411 BC can be seen as an affirmation of its strong group solidarity.[56] Moreover, as the source of several key victories in recent Athenian history, the fleet was often portrayed as the backbone of Athens' power and thus a symbolic city in its own right. This conception of the fleet is evident from Herodotus' account of the Battle of Salamis, which put the fleet on the map of the Athenian *polis*.[57] Herodotus records a debate, during one of the Greek councils of war before the battle of Salamis, in which Adeimantus the Corinthian tried to deny Themistocles the right to speak before the council on the grounds that he was without a *polis* (*apolis* – 8.61.1). Themistocles' rejoinder is that the Athenians have a greater *polis* and more land than the other Greeks, in so far as they have 200 manned ships (8.61.2) – the equivalent of roughly 40,000 men. The motif of the fleet as a mobile repository of the *polis* which endures regardless of what happens to the physical space of the city resurfaces in Thucydides' account of the oligarchic revolution where the speakers who address the Athenian assembly on Samos claim that the fleet is preserving the traditions of the *polis* from which the current government has diverged, and that as long as they possess the fleet they will always have access to cities and land (8.76.6-7). The functions of the city are represented as being transferable to the body of the fleet.

In Book 8 the fleet is not just politically, but also financially, independent from the *polis*, as the soldiers are financing themselves (8.76.6);[58] Thucydides records that the politicians on Samos reassured the fleet that they represented a majority and thus corresponded to the 'vote of the many' espoused by democracy (8.76.3-4). What is more, in view of the oligarchic take-over, the city can no longer provide 'useful resolutions' (8.76.6).

At crucial points in Athens' history it was certainly the case that the fleet became a symbolic *polis* that challenged the authority of the physical *polis*.[59] In Pericles' résumé of Athens' resources for the war, in Book 1 of the *History*, he singles out the superiority of Athens' helmsmen and ships' crews as one the city's most important resources (1.143.1).[60] Subsequently, in his last speech to the Athenians in the *History*, Pericles goes even further in telling the assembly that there is no power on earth that can stop the navy from sailing where it wants (2.62.2). This boast (and it is acknowledged as a boast – 2.62.1) amounts to a claim that Athens' navy is invincible:[61] a claim that will be disproved as the narrative unfolds. Lisa Kallet has argued convincingly that Thucydides criticizes the Athenians for misunderstanding the financial basis of their naval power, and for relying on the power of the fleet without giving due attention to its funding.[62] However, this argument is reconcilable with the ideological role of the Athenian fleet in the *History*: albeit on the basis of mistaken calculations, Thucydides' Athenians consistently equate their power with the navy.

A parallel text: Sophocles' *Philoctetes*

I have argued that Thucydides produced an intricate account of the negotiations leading up to the oligarchic revolution and of the revolution itself, which allows the reader to gain a sense of the politics of dissembling that dominated the theatre of war in 411 BC, and which led to a dissolution of trust not only in inter-state relations, but critically within Athens itself as well. Thucydides' narrative does not just expose the web of deceit; it also represents the apparent credibility of the false speeches that were spoken and depicts the financial interests, the fear and the lack of information that warped political decision-making. While Alcibiades is the primary exemplar of deceitful opportunism, the other key political players in Book 8 are similarly prone to change allegiance in the pursuit of selfish interests. Moreover, the characterization of many of the protagonists is ambiguous, blending true and intelligent insights with cunning and a capacity for lying. I have suggested that all intelligence in Book 8 is flawed through its close association with duplicity.

Book 8 of Thucydides' *History* is based on the events of 411 BC, whereas the subject of Sophocles' tragedy *Philoctetes* (produced in the Spring of 409 BC at the City Dionysia) is an embassy to the Greek warrior Philoctetes on the island of Lemnos, set in the heroic past. However, from another angle one might regard Book 8 of Thucydides' *History* as further away from these events than *Philoctetes*, in that Thucydides was in exile from Athens until 404 BC (5.26.5) and had no first-hand knowledge of Athenian politics at this stage in the war, whereas Sophocles had been elected to the office of *proboulos* in the summer of 413 BC, and subsequently played a role in endorsing the régime of the Four Hundred.[63] Moreover, the play was written for performance in front of an audience that consisted primarily of citizens who had experienced the oligarchic revolution in the very recent past.

Philoctetes invites many different frames of reference; many of these frames are supplied by intertextual allusions to Homeric epic, and to Sophocles' own plays. Scholars also detect allusions to the language and argumentation associated with the sophists in contemporary intellectual culture. The oligarchic revolution and the continuing war with Sparta supply yet another frame of reference for the play. For the Athenian audience watching *Philoctetes* in 409 BC, conscious of the internal war in their recent past and the foreign war that they were desperate to win, the divisions among the Achaeans, which impede the capture of Troy, must have seemed extremely close to home. The embassy to Philoctetes provides a mythological commentary on the socio-political world in which the play was staged, and comments simultaneously on a literary and cultural tradition stretching back to Homeric epic; consequently, the play challenges members of the audience to contemplate reflections of contemporary politics in the mythical past, and to consider analogies with myth in the present day.[64]

In the past, historicizing and politicizing interpretations of *Philoctetes* focused on trying to find on-stage counterparts for contemporary politicians, particularly Alcibiades.[65] Recent interpretations of *Philoctetes* have discerned contemporary ethico-political concerns in the play. Angus Bowie has written: 'The very difficulty of knowing at any stage during the play what is true and what false, what bluff and what sincere, provides an atmosphere of uncertainty which well mirrors the perplexity of Athenians looking at the current political situation.'[66] Similarly, Jon Hesk sees the play conveying 'a crisis of moral, military and political values which mark it as speaking to an Athenian audience who had experienced oligarchic revolution in 411 and who were still recovering from reverses in the war with Sparta'.[67] My approach here will be to explore points of contact between Thucydides' account of the oligarchic coup and the mythological scenario in Sophocles' play, in terms of both the geography and topography of the world on-stage and the state of the community that occupies it.[68]

The opening lines of *Philoctetes* present the audience with a bleak, uninhabited landscape (1-2). The first word of the play is *aktê* (the shore), positioning the action of the play on the margins of inhabitable land.[69] The *aktê* can both point inwards towards dry land or outwards towards the sea, depending on the perspective of the observer. For the Achaeans at Troy, as well as for Philoctetes on Lemnos, it is the dividing line between a foreign and hostile land and their *nostos*. It is important that the action of the play is staged at the point where land meets sea, since the conflict between setting sail and holding one's ground will provide a crucial backdrop to the deliberations in which the characters engage. Oliver Taplin has argued that, for the purposes of staging, one of the two entrance ways onto the stage would have been dispensed with, leaving a single, prominent exit / entrance leading to and from the ships at anchor off the coast of Lemnos ('towards the ship' is a recurrent stage direction).[70] As the play unfolds, disembarking from the island can be construed either as desertion or as the fulfilment of one's patriotic duty, depending on the direction taken. Orientation thus has clear ideological implications.[71]

Another key aspect of the scene-setting is the twofold nature of Philoctetes' cave. The cave has two mouths (*distomos petra* – 16) and provides dual (*diplos*) inlets for the sun (17-18); the idea is repeated at line 952, where Philoctetes addresses his cave as 'You rock with two entrances (*dipulos*)'.[72] Since *dipulos* is a rare epithet, the image of a rock with two entrances / gates may have evoked the Dipylon gate (one of the main entrances to the city of Athens) in the minds of the Athenian theatre audience, bringing the mythical world into contact with their own environment in an unexpected detail. At the outset of the play the two-mouthed cave offers an image of the situation of Neoptolemus who is confronted, by a two-faced Odysseus, with a polarized schema of action (either lure Philoctetes to Troy or incur the hostility of the Achaean army) where either course will entail some wrong.[73] As the play progresses, this scenic image is seen to have an even broader resonance, as the Atreidae are referred to as 'twofold' (*diplos*) generals (793 and 1024), where *diplos* can mean both 'double' – in that there are two sons of Atreus, Agamemnon and Menelaus – and 'duplicitous', because they betray the trust of the other warriors.[74]

This disjunction in the on-stage topography (mental as well as physical) is then compounded by the off-stage geography, which borders on the immediate action.[75] In the first instance there is a contingent of the Achaean fleet, moored off Lemnos – a body hostile to Philoctetes and supposedly to Neoptolemus as well (for the purposes of the deceit), yet to which both men can, in one sense, be said to owe allegiance. Then there is the island of Lemnos, beyond the strip of coast on which our attention is focused. Lemnos was construed as being hostile to Athens in mythological tradition,[76] yet, at the time when the play was produced, the island was a cleruchy (colony), which was strategically and economically vital to the Athenian *polis*.[77]

Sophocles' decision to confront his audience with a barren, uninhabited Lemnos represents a marked departure from the 'Philoctetes' plays of Aeschylus and Euripides, in which the choruses were Lemnian inhabitants. It also diverges from the Homeric picture of Lemnos, and from the audience's own knowledge of the island.[78] The denaturing of a familiar environment and the fact that it is literally void make us scan the on-stage dialogue and the allusions to off-stage locations all the more keenly for clues about how to conceive of the setting. It is significant that the play does not offset Lemnos with a viable geographical opposite, since every destination, whether Troy (where the Achaean army is stationed), Scyros (Neoptolemus' home) or Malis (Philoctetes' home in mainland Greece), is problematic.[79] Nor is the world of the Athenian audience, watching the play in the theatre of Dionysus, a safe alternative, because the problems of Athens are visible in this improbable Lemnian landscape.

The basic geographical conflict is between sailing home, on the one hand, and sailing to join the Achaean fleet, on the other (58-9). On Odysseus' instructions, Neoptolemus duly lies to Philoctetes that he is sailing home (240). The designation of certain regions of Greece as 'home', coupled with the rejection of the collective Greek fleet, raises questions about the identity of this fleet and its affiliations (see lines 1213-16 where Philoctetes apostrophizes his ancestral *polis* and rejects the Danaans – that is the Greeks – as enemies in the same breath). The fleet has banished and abandoned Philoctetes and in turn he retaliates by deserting the fleet and exhorting Neoptolemus to do so as well. This leads to a situation of mutual hostility and exclusion, hampered by the fact of mutual dependence, since the 'merchant' informs Neoptolemus and Philoctetes of a prophecy made by the Trojan seer Helenus, according to which the Achaeans cannot take Troy without Philoctetes (603-21). The Achaeans need both Philoctetes and his bow, while Neoptolemus is presented as Philoctetes' only means of leaving Lemnos and reaching home.[80]

As in Sophocles' *Ajax*, the chorus of *Philoctetes* consists of male sailors. John Gould has remarked that these two plays constitute an exception to the typical 'otherness' of tragic choruses (which are frequently composed of old men, women, foreigners or slaves), insofar as they are 'adult males *of the city*'.[81] But the homogenizing category 'adult males' plays down the distinctive identity of different groups within the city. It makes a difference that the choruses of *Ajax* and *Philoctetes* are sailors, since the rowers of the Athenian fleet were frequently construed as a separate interest group within the democratic city (particularly in anti-democratic sources).[82] Studies which have looked at the presence of the fleet in tragedy have tended to concentrate on the political symbolism of the fleet as the victorious organ of the Athenian *polis* at Salamis and thus as a way of reflecting on the politicians involved.[83] Little attention has been paid to the sociology of the fleet *qua* community (a notable exception is Felix Budelmann's discussion of the sailor chorus in *Ajax*).[84]

In *Philoctetes*, the on-stage presence of the chorus of sailors, hovering on the edge of the action, gestures towards the dynamics of the political community and of the potential of the fleet to make a difference to an action in the political sphere. The presence of a chorus of sailors is doubly pointed, because the sailors, while vital to the *polis* and while undeniably within the *polis* from the point of view of citizenship, were consigned to its edge from the point of view of representation. Given that in 411 BC the crews of the trireme fleet had in fact assumed a key political role, there are

101

contemporary resonances in the situation of the chorus of sailors on Lemnos who are party to discussions about duty and desertion.

The audience of *Philoctetes* is faced with the on-stage deliberations of 'sailors'; Sophocles repeatedly uses nautical vocabulary so that, however else we might view them, Odysseus and Neoptolemus are also sailors;[85] and we are given frequent reminders of the off-stage presence of ships. Thus the moral debates in the play take place on an island, among characters who are identified as sailors, in the absence of the commanders who have dispatched them. Moreover, the conflicting courses of action and the ethical choice that Neoptolemus has to make translate into a question of orientation: to which destination should Neoptolemus sail? At the beginning of the play he professes to be sailing in one direction (home), while in fact intending to sail in another (to Troy); but during the play he realigns himself and changes his intended destination. The play actually closes with the chorus of sailors, now bound for Troy, praying to the sea nymphs for a safe *nostos*:

> Let us go now all together,
> when we have prayed to the Nymphs of the sea
> to come as saviours of a return home (1469-71).[86]

However, there is a tension in these lines since the *nostos* that they desire is not the immediate journey to Troy, but their eventual return home.[87] Thus at the end of the play, even after the intervention of Heracles has solved the social crisis, the chorus still express the pull of conflicting directions.

While it would be misguided to try to map the divided loyalties of the different parties involved in the oligarchic revolution onto the different interest groups in *Philoctetes*, there are suggestive correspondences between Book 8 of Thucydides' *History* and Sophocles' play. The image of a fleet in the Northern Aegean, which is internally divided, and which stands in opposition to the homelands to which Philoctetes and Neoptolemus threaten to return, is reminiscent of the situation of the Athenian fleet vis-à-vis Athens at the time of the oligarchic revolution. The Athenian fleet was operating as an independent unit in the Aegean (albeit in Samos, as opposed to Lemnos), after refusing to co-operate with the oligarchic government in Athens. The eighth book of the *History* traces the complex manoeuvrings of the Athenians at a time when the *polis* is situated outside itself, in the form of the exiled fleet. Nor was this a passing phase since the fleet continued to operate with a degree of independence from the *polis* until 407 BC, when Alcibiades returned to Athens. This period in Athenian history has been referred to as a 'crisis of the centre'.[88] As Andrewes comments, 'The history of the years 410-407 is much more easily intelligible if we assume some sort of separation, even political tension, between the fleet in the Hellespont and the democracy at

Athens'.[89] Given that *Philoctetes* was produced in 409 BC, and was probably rehearsed the year after the oligarchic revolution and the democratic counter-revolution, the fact that the chorus is a group of sailors and that the Achaean fleet is such a dominant off-stage presence may have brought contemporary politics into the minds of the Athenian audience.

In relating the play to the institutional and ideological structure of the democratic *polis*, scholars have tended to focus on allusions to the hoplite ethos and the institution of the *ephêbeia*.[90] Tragedy frequently focuses on the ideology of the hoplite phalanx as the key to notions of duty, cohesion and, contrastingly, the potential for deceit; but I would argue that a substantial portion of citizens were not hoplites and that, within *Philoctetes*, the allusions to the fleet counterbalance the allusions to the hoplite ethos. It is worth considering how the sailors in the play may have evoked the *thêtes* who manned the Athenian fleet, and who are generally effaced in surviving literary sources. Within *Philoctetes* there is a tension between the Achaean army, as a community of soldiers, and the on-stage community of sailors who form a smaller group, isolated from the main expedition.[91]

The tension between hoplite prestige and the reality of Athenian manpower (as embodied in the fleet) is evident in the circumstances of the oligarchic revolution. In the first place it was easier to pass the resolution to abolish the democratic constitution in 411 BC because the constitution of the assembly was distorted by the fact that a large proportion of *thêtes* (the poorer citizens) were away on active service in Samos.[92] In Thucydides' account the army on Samos swings back towards democracy when confronted with the threat of an oligarchic coup among the Samians. It is notable that the Samian democrats focus their appeal for assistance on the crew of the trireme Paralus, 'every one who sailed on this ship was a free-born Athenian and attacked the idea of oligarchy at any time, even when it was not a present threat' (8.73.5). That this one ship could be seen as the embodiment of the ideals of the democracy is evidenced by the fact that Pericles called one of his sons Paralus.[93]

In *Philoctetes* a crisis within the Achaean army, has precipitated a crisis of values that has to be negotiated on-stage by Odysseus, Neoptolemus and Philoctetes, in the absence of the larger Achaean community. The speech of the 'merchant', played by Odysseus, who arrives with news about new resolutions (*nea bouleumata*) in the Argive camp (554-5), is intended to convey to Philoctetes, who is the internal, 'target' audience of the speech, that his own army, whom he views as 'enemies', have launched a fresh plot against him. This is intended to strengthen his solidarity with Neoptolemus who, as part of the deception, refers to the commanders of the army as his enemies. The phrase *nea bouleumata* is a contemporary idiom that evokes the political resolutions that were debated in the Athenian assembly; as such, it refers to the extra-dramatic world of the audience. In Thucydides' account, one of the arguments that was put to the Athenian fleet in favour of disowning the government of Athens was that it no longer gives them any good political resolutions (*bouleuma chrêston* – 8.76.6). Again, the idea of soldiers on an island being betrayed by their absent leaders may have brought resonances of Athens' recent history to the minds of the audience.

Although there is no stable image of a community in *Philoctetes*, the *polis* is not absent from the world of the play (see n. 91). At line 1213 Philoctetes invokes his native *polis* 'My city, my native city' (*ô polis, ô polis patria*). The fact that the *polis* is not named allows for the evocation of the *polis* in which the play was staged. The combination of the noun *polis* and the adjective *patrios* ('ancestral', lit. 'of the father') may also have spoken to the contemporary politics of the theatre audience, because towards the end of the fifth century the different political factions in Athens were involved in a debate about which configuration (or constitution) of the *polis* was more ancestral, with both sides appealing to the ancestral laws of the *polis* (*patrioi nomoi*). In Thucydides the democrats in the fleet at Samos style themselves as the defenders of the ancestral laws that the oligarchs have dissolved (8.76.6).[94] More specifically, the Athenian *polis* is brought to mind at lines 133-4 where Odysseus appeals to Athena, the patron Goddess of Athens: 'May Hermes the Escort, the Trickster, guide the two of us, / and Victory Athena the City-Goddess, who always saves me.'[95] Odysseus invokes Athena, his protectress in the *Odyssey*, but he does so anachronistically, using cult titles for Athena from contemporary Athens (*Athena Nikê* and *Athena Polias*).[96] The temple of Athena Nike on the Athenian Acropolis was completed circa 420 BC, so it would have been part of the landscape of the audience watching the play in the theatre of Dionysus beneath the Acropolis. Odysseus' confident invocation of Athena would not have been lost on an Athenian audience who themselves were surely praying that Athena would indeed fulfil her function as bestower of victory at this stage in the war.

At lines 385-7 Neoptolemus speaks generally about the dependency of the city and the army on their leaders:

> I'm sailing home, robbed of what was mine
> by the vilest offspring of vile ancestors, Odysseus.
> And I don't blame him as much as those in office (*hoi en telei*):
> a city (*polis*) as a whole belongs to its leaders.
> as does an entire army (*stratos*); and those mortals who are
> disorderly become evil through the words of their teachers (*didaskaloi*).[97]

Some editors of the play have deleted these lines as a later interpolation on the grounds that they appear to be anachronistic and out of context, and because they interpret this as a specious argument to absolve

Neoptolemus of responsibility. However, if they are genuine, then these lines speak very directly to the political context in which *Philoctetes* was staged. The expression 'those in office' post-dates the heroic world in which the play is set and gestures towards the magistracies and offices of the *polis* (many of which were military).[98] We have seen how Thucydides emphasizes the role of political 'instructors' in misleading the *dêmos*, and how the Athenian forces stationed in Samos reject the government of Athens on the grounds that it is no longer giving good counsel. Thucydides also portrays the Athenian *dêmos* as being quick to fasten responsibility for failure onto political advisers and leaders (8.1.1). The idea that the *dêmos* always blames its leaders was a *topos* of political rhetoric in the last decades of the fifth century BC;[99] consequently, we should not interpret these lines as an excuse for Neoptolemus' actions, since his statement could also have been interpreted by a contemporary audience as the flawed argument of an irresponsible individual who blames politicians for failure, while suppressing his own involvement. In fact, individual members of the audience would presumably have interpreted these lines in different ways, depending on their political sympathies.

Philoctetes wrestles with the problem of authority and whether those in power should be obeyed unconditionally.[100] Neoptolemus' father, Achilles, who opposed the unquestioned right of the Atreidae to supreme command of the Achaean forces, serves as a mythological precedent for insubordination.[101] In contrast, Odysseus is portrayed as the henchman of the Atreidae ('I was following the orders of my rulers' – 6). Odysseus also plays up the cohesion of the army and uses it to support his threats (1243, 1250, 1257-8).[102] We can perhaps discern a cue to Sophocles' Athenian audience in line 1006, when Philoctetes addresses Odysseus as 'you who think no healthy or free-spirited (*eleutheros*) thought', portraying Odysseus as a man who eschews one of the fundamental democratic qualities (*eleutheria* – 'freedom').

If we consider the portrayal of the fleet in the play in conjunction with the representation of the Athenian fleet in Book 8 of Thucydides' *History*, it becomes apparent that the contemporary problem of the fleet informs, in part, the representation of the Achaean fleet in the *Philoctetes*. The problem of the fleet was also the problem of its generals who were able to use the fleet as a self-determining power base. Hence the interest in the uses of military power set against the background of a fleet which is in a geographically indeterminate location and undecided about its orientation resounds, historically, beyond the legendary world of the play.

It is significant that the action of *Philoctetes* occurs at a late stage in the Trojan War when the old order of warriors has been killed. When informed by Neoptolemus of all of those from the initial expedition who have been killed (410-52), Philoctetes reflects on the fact that war deprives the community of the best men, leaving behind men of the worse variety, such as Thersites and Odysseus. By virtue of his name ('new-war'), his youth and his late entry into the war, Neoptolemus epitomizes the new order of warriors. Yet the fact that he is addressed repeatedly as 'Achilles' son' also connects him to the old order.[103] Moreover, the fact that his father was the most problematic warrior in the *Iliad* makes Neoptolemus a complicated model for military conduct. As such, he personifies the crisis of the Athenian *polis* at an important juncture in its history when the city itself needed to evolve with the changed circumstances of the Atheno-Peloponnesian War.[104]

While the delicate balance between deceit and persuasion, and the different manifestations of 'persuasion' (extending to violent coercion), are of perennial interest in Greek literature, the debate between Odysseus and Neoptolemus about the relative merits / efficiency of persuasion by trickery, on the one hand, and force, on the other, coincides with accounts of the use of deception and violence in the oligarchic coup of 411 BC. In Thucydides' account the oligarchs begin by persuading the Athenian *dêmos* that an oligarchic government is in its best interests (cf. Peisander's speech of persuasion at 8.53-4), but once in power they then start to resort to violence (8.66.2). In the *Politics* Aristotle looks back to the Four Hundred as an example of a régime that tried to take control of the consti-tution first by deceit and then by force.[105] Odysseus is eventually forced to adopt the same strategy with Philoctetes.

As we have seen, in Thucydides' account the oligarchic revolution is characterized by the politics of deception.[106] One of the symptoms of the political situation in 411 BC is that audiences are susceptible to manipula-tion by performers. Alcibiades is portrayed as continually exchanging roles, trying to seem one thing to Tissaphernes and another to the Athenians (8.47.1, 56.3). It is also tempting to see the image of the actor behind Chaireas at 8.74.3, whose exaggerated 'performance' is exposed by Thucydides. Even more suggestive is the case of Theramenes, who played a prominent part in setting up the Four Hundred, only to overthrow them four months later, and who earns the epithet *kothornos* (a boot worn by tragic actors, and thus synecdoche for an actor in tragedy) in Xenophon.[107] I have already commented on the motif of Alcibiades as the *didaskalos* of Tissaphernes, which has overtones of coaching an actor (see p. 91 above); subsequently, as the oligarchic revolution unfolds, politicians vie to instruct the *dêmos* in their rival ideologies (the verb *didaskein* (to teach / instruct), is used at 8.54.1; 8.72.1; 8.75.1; and 8.86.1).

Peter Wilson has discussed the metaphor of the 'political stage' in polit-ical rhetoric in the fourth century BC, where speakers depict contemporary events as real-life tragedies, with their opponents as the source of the tragedy.[108] It is striking that, in Wilson's study, Alcibiades epitomizes the tragic inversion of healthy political life (ibid., 320). Arguably, the 'political stage' metaphor has its origins in the politics of deception surrounding the oligarchic revolution. The social and political viability of lying speech and dissemblance is also richly explored in *Philoctetes* in terms that hint at the blurring of politics and theatre.[109] The play opens with Odysseus teaching Neoptolemus how to 'act' in the forthcoming deception scenes, and some scholars have interpreted the role of Odysseus as a quasi-playwright who attempts to control the on-stage action.[110] The theme of acting and dissembling complicates the characterization of Neoptolemus, making it hard to establish whether he is lying or telling the truth when he recounts the allocation of Achilles' arms. Felix Budelmann has argued that Sophocles achieves this complex characterization by making Neoptolemus use known myths with subtle distortions.[111] The Athenian audience of *Philoctetes* were confronted not just with uncomfortably familiar duplicitous political arguments, delivered against a backdrop of coercion, but also with half-echoes of myth challenging them to consider just what they knew and how reliably. This play on the knowledge and expectations of the theatre audience parallels the intellectual challenges that confront the reader of Book 8 of Thucydides' *History*, who has to follow plot and counterplot in a highly charged theatre of war.

Conclusion

This chapter has juxtaposed two radically different ways of plotting the same events: Thucydides' *History* offers his readers a prose account that purports to be as precise a representation as possible in its account of the events of the period 413-411 BC. Within this narrative I concentrated on Thucydides' presentation of the oligarchic revolution and the democratic counter-revolution. I argued that these episodes in Athenian history also lie behind Sophocles' *Philoctetes*: a dramatic text, composed for performance at a dramatic festival, which brings extra-dramatic events into dialogue with a mythological past.

The parallel plots that I have traced in Book 8 of the *History* and Sophocles' *Philoctetes* suggest a complex interrelationship between 'history' and 'text'. The plots in Book 8 correspond to real historical plots: people were killed behind the façade of the Five Thousand put forward by the 'real' government of 400 oligarchs. The overlapping themes in Thucydides and Sophocles indicate that, for Athenians, the history of this period was a rich, if tragic, text, imbued with its own plots and potential for theatre. This comes close to Hans-Peter Stahl's claim that tragedy in Thucydides emerges from the facts themselves, as opposed to deriving from a pre-formulated plot that the historian imposed on his subject matter. Stahl appeals to the idea of a 'symbolism of the facts', although he omits to discuss how facts might acquire this symbolism.[112] The relationship between tragic plots and history becomes simpler if we recall that tragedy was an institution in and of the *polis*: the metaphor of the political stage in Athenian politics, which seems to have been associated with the revolutions of 411 BC and their aftermath, has a natural affinity with the *actual* political stage in the heart of the *polis* on which the Athenians could watch a distant version of their own problems.

6

Reading Thucydides with Lucian

In Chapter 1, I examined Thucydides' claim that he established his work as a 'possession for always' – a phrase that encourages us to see the work as a super-monument. This bold claim, backed up the work's ideological (if not actual) detachment from contemporary audiences, invites successive generations of readers to envisage themselves as the true recipients of Thucydides' work. This belief is borne out by the ongoing reception of the *History*: we continue to read and interpret Thucydides and the fact of our reading confirms that the text has not been exhausted. Every reader who finds herself or himself contemplating a page of Thucydides' *History*, whether in Greek or in translation, contributes to the realization of Thucydides' ambition that his work would be a 'possession for all time'. However, we should not focus on our role as twenty-first-century readers of Thucydides to the exclusion of the interpretations of other readers in different historical contexts. Recall the distinctive ways in which Aineias Tacticus and Dionysius of Halicarnassus interpret Thucydides: diverse audiences and readers, in different historical and cultural contexts, have played a role in shaping our conception of Thucydides' *History* today.[1]

It is hard to plot the reception of a classical text such as Thucydides' *History*. Reception is a complicated process that is easy to simplify. Even within a given era, there is no single, unanimous reception of a classic work of literature. Instead, there are differing audiences for the work, who respond in their several ways to its perceived relevance. Although there are generalizable trends in interpretations, if we survey scholarship on Thucydides we see that trends in interpretation shift several times within a single generation and that individual scholars modify their views of Thucydides many times in a lifetime.

At 1.22.4 Thucydides uses two metaphors to consolidate the reader's impression of his work. First, in material terms, the noun *ktêma* invites us to conceive of the *History* as a concrete object that can be passed down and circulated like an heirloom. Then, at a temporal level, there is the phrase '*es aiei*' which opens up the work to a limitless future, which Thucydides makes no attempt to circumscribe. Within the *History*, Thucydides signals his distrust of contemporary audiences and their fickleness. Accordingly his *History* is modelled as a fixed written communication, which is guaranteed by the authority of the narrator, authority that derives from his ability to persuade the reader that his work is an accurate representation of the Atheno-Peloponnesian War.

Authority is a difficult notion where Thucydides is concerned. He marks his *History* as the work of 'Thucydides the Athenian' (1.1.1), but he does so in language that plays down the function of authorship as we know it. As we have seen, Thucydides uses the self-effacing verb *xungraphô*, which implies 'writing out', or 'writing down' something that already exists (see above, pp. 62 and 67). This choice of verb promotes the idea of the author as scribe, writing down a subject, which in some sense already exists, since the text is introduced as a literal re-presentation of the Atheno-Peloponnesian War. This impression is compounded by the anonymity that Thucydides cultivates, seldom allowing the first person pronoun, first person verbs and direct authorial statements to intervene in the narrative. Consequently, Thucydides suppresses the act of narration and his role in shaping the text that we are reading. And yet the fact remains that, in common with his predecessors Herodotus and Hecataeus, he put his name at the head of his work.

Again, as we saw in Chapter 1, another factor that complicates our understanding of Thucydides' claim to authorship is the fact that there are two Thucydideses in the *History*. Thucydides dissembles his own identity within the text: as 'author' he is 'Thucydides the Athenian', whereas when he appears as a historical agent he is 'Thucydides the son of Olorus'.[2] It is as if Thucydides did not want his authorship to be compromised by his dual role as author and agent: Thucydides the author is (almost) all-knowing, whereas Thucydides the agent, *qua* Athenian general, made errors of judgement. We face the challenge of reconciling Thucydides the retiring author with the ambition that Thucydides clearly harboured for his work in designating it as a possession for all time. The former persona implies objectivity and impartiality, relaying 'what happened' and representing the war, while the latter claim implies Thucydides' confidence in his own work and his desire to inscribe it in a literary tradition.[3] The adjective 'literary' is arguably inappropriate in this context, since it presupposes the anachronistic notion of 'Literature' as a privileged and contested body of writings – a notion that Thucydides could not have harboured. However, the ambition that one's work (whether poetry or prose) should have an afterlife and that it should continue to be read after one was dead, is already present in Homer and was well established in Thucydides' day. When I use the term 'literary tradition', I use it to refer to the awareness among writers such as Thucydides of a tradition of producing memorable words that would be preserved after one's death, and a further awareness that the written word promotes memorability.

If the idea of discerning literary ambition in the phrase *ktêma es aiei* seems fanciful, then consider how Thucydides associates previous conflicts with the accounts of these conflicts given by particular authors, whether named (Homer) or unnamed (Herodotus). Lurking behind Thucydides' survey of the significance of the conflict that he had chosen to write about, in comparison with the scale of the Trojan War (1.3-21), is an implicit claim that 'this work is better than Homer's *Iliad*'.[4]

Modern scholarship on Thucydides has always struggled with the conflicting pull of a pseudo-scientific model of historical objectivity, and the counterargument that Thucydides' *History* is polemical, biased, and aims to supplant other conceivable interpretations of events with his vision of the war.[5] The argument that Thucydides' narrative serves the simultaneous function of promoting Thucydides' own fame further undermines the ideal of an objective Thucydides. However, this is only a conflict of interests if we apply anachronistic modern expectations of historical research to Thucydides' *History*. In the context of the late fifth century BC, Thucydides presented his stringent and innovative claims to accuracy and impartiality, alongside his individual conception of the war, and held out these features as a qualification for everlasting fame.

In the remainder of this chapter I examine the interpretation of Thucydides offered by the writer Lucian of Samosata (second century AD), who regards Thucydides' *History* as a paradigm for how to achieve a successful literary afterlife.[6] In fact, Lucian's treatise *How to Write History* (c. AD 166), which styles itself as a practical, didactic treatise for the would-be historian, ultimately concludes that the key to writing successful history is to write with posterity in mind. Behind this conclusion lies an extremely clever and subtle serio-comic challenge to would-be readers and writers of history. I will argue that in *How to Write History* and in his fictional travel narrative *True Stories*, Lucian puts forward a theory about history-writing that casts light on how he read Thucydides and is relevant to the way in which we interpret Thucydides today.

Lucian is a notoriously elusive writer whose works defy straightforward generic classification. For convenience he is often referred to as a satirist, and this description is helpful insofar as it alerts us to the presence of 'serious play' throughout Lucian's oeuvre. Among the several excellent works on Lucian that have appeared in recent years, there has been a division in the scholarship between those who work on questions of cultural identity in Lucian's works, and those who work on Lucian's critique of ancient Greek historiography.[7] Scholars working on cultural identity in Lucian have tended to focus on the complex ways in which Lucian negotiates and destabilizes Greek identity and culture in the period known as the Second Sophistic (a term that refers to a period of literary and cultural activity from roughly AD 60 to 230). In these works Lucian emerges as a theatrical 'author function' whose real identity consists in the performance of multiple identities. Accordingly, if Lucian's real identity is a performance, then it is impossible to pin him down to anything he says. However, at the same time these works do pin Lucian to a particular view, albeit an elusive, protean point of view: namely, they pin Lucian to the view that Greekness is a matter of contestation and performance. Given the emphasis on performance, Lucian is not obliged to 'believe' or subscribe to any of the intellectual positions expounded by the different narrators in his works. By its very nature, this research has had little to say about Lucian's take on historiography, or Lucian as a theorist of historiography, other than to encompass all of Lucian's genres into an ironizing charade at the expense of the naïve reader.

By contrast, scholars who focus on Lucian as a literary critic and theorist of historiography operate with an image of a much straighter Lucian – a writer who offers an ironic, parodic commentary on historiography and its relationship to other genres. This is the Lucian whose ideas on history I wish to explore, while drawing on the important insights about the play of multiple identities that have emerged from studies on cultural identity in Lucian. In particular, I will examine Lucian's reading of Thucydides, in the works *How to Write History* and *True Stories*.[8] The relationship between these two works has been the subject of debate, but there is a general consensus that *How to Write History* is the earlier. Consequently, some scholars argue that *How to Write History* sets up a serious treatise on history-writing, only for Lucian to parody this treatise in *True Stories* where he breaks the rules set down in the earlier work.[9] However, this is too simplistic a version of the relationship between the two texts. After all, paradoxically, Lucian does not attempt to pass off *True Stories* as true, instead he exposes the work's bogus historicity: this is a fictional, quasi-historical, quasi-philosophical travel account. Moreover, as I shall argue below, for all that Lucian holds out the *True Stories* to the reader as a lying account, his phrasing is such that even this admission is unstable. Lucian invites us to read this contradictory text *both* as a true account of a false story and as a false account of a true story.

The notion that the more serious or 'straight' treatise can act as a control on the overtly parodic *True Stories* misrepresents the nature of parody in Lucian's oeuvre, in which all the different voices in his works speak back to each other and rewrite each other. Georgiadou and Larmour suggest the term 'polyphonic intertextuality' as a model for understanding the dialogues within Lucian's oeuvre.[10] Writing from a different angle, on one of Lucian's 'autobiographical' works, *The Apology*, Simon Goldhill calls attention to the operation of split voices in Lucian's work (*diaphônia* – 'dissonance', 'different-voicedness') and connects this phenomenon to Lucian's hypocritical exposure of hypocrisy in others.[11] Whether we adopt the model of *poluphonia* (many-voicedness) or *diaphonia* (different-voicedness), Lucian uses his intertextual oeuvre to say many things simultaneously; consequently, it is unhelpful to think in terms of a linear chronological relationship in which *True Stories* comes 'after' *How to Write History*. Nor should we envisage a hierarchical model in which different texts can cancel each other out.[12] Instead, we need to read the two works side by side. Similarly, parody is not simply a literary mode whereby a subsequent work revises, or 'writes / speaks back', to a previous work, since the act of association involved in parody also invites us to read the later work in terms of the work being parodied. In other words, parody sets up a relationship between two texts that transforms them both.[13]

Thucydides is an important presence in both works. In *How to Write History* he is cited explicitly as the best kind of history writer, while in *True Stories* there are numerous Thucydidean motifs.[14] It is broadly true that in *How to Write History* Thucydides is placed in the foreground of the treatise, while Herodotus comes in for marginal criticism, whereas the situation is reversed in *True Stories*. In the latter work Herodotus is the more obvious model for Lucian's project of telling an account of a journey made in the interests of *sophia* / *theôria*, while Thucydides is an ironic interlocutor.[15] I disagree with those scholars who argue that Lucian's knowledge of Thucydides was superficial and restricted to the rhetorical handbooks and the excerpts popular in school curricula.[16] Although it is impossible to establish just how well Lucian knew his Thucydides, I will argue that his critique of Thucydides derives from an engagement with Thucydides' work in its entirety. If Lucian shows a predilection for quoting and paraphrasing the most famous passages in Thucydides, this should not surprise us; a survey of modern scholarship on Thucydides would also reveal uneven coverage of Thucydides' work, with a bias towards many of the passages that captured Lucian's attention. The argument that Lucian's engagement with Thucydides is opportunistic and biased towards Lucian's own intellectual interests is also not a satisfactory argument for the view that Lucian had not bothered to read Thucydides at any length. Dionysius of Halicarnassus' analysis of Thucydides is also biased and reads Thucydides on Dionysius' own terms; however, Dionysius cites from the entire span of Thucydides *History*. We should not query whether ancient critics 'read' Thucydides closely on the grounds that they do not read him as we do.

How to Write History

On the surface, Thucydides is the hero of the treatise *How to Write History*. Lucian frequently cites Thucydides as an example to illustrate the criteria for good history-writing, and in chapter 42 he is envisaged as a lawgiver for the discipline. In chapter 15 Lucian criticizes an anonymous historian who is simply called a 'keen emulator of Thucydides'; this historian allegedly copied the way in which Thucydides began his history, copied the speech made by the Corinthian envoy who addressed the Spartan assembly in Book 1 of Thucydides' *History*, and copied Thucydides' plague narrative. Lucian claims that it is a current trend in historiography to think that writing like Thucydides consists in appropriating his words and making a few small adjustments to them.

However, Lucian's own practice is not much better in this respect. *How to Write History* begins with an anecdote about the Abderites succumbing to a literary plague (they 'catch' tragedy) as an analogy for the pathological history-writing which Lucian claims has gripped the Roman empire in response to the Parthian War, engendering a tide of Thucydideses, Herodotuses and Xenophons (2). This plague is a loosely constructed spoof of the famous plague narrative in Thucydides (2.47.3-54). So Lucian gets in on the act of ripping off Thucydides, while simultaneously claiming to protect Thucydides' legacy. However, it is notable that Lucian absolves himself of responsibility for the truthfulness of the anecdote about the plague with the tag 'they say' (*phasi*), which is the second word of the treatise. *Phasi*, like *legousi* or *legetai* (respectively 'they say' and 'it is said'), can serve as a distancing device that enables the historical narrator to incorporate different voices and traditions, without being held responsible for their authenticity.[17] So Lucian borrows a rhetorical device associated with historians in order to break the standards of history-writing that he is going to be expounding, with impunity. This is an early indication of the fact that Lucian will fluctuate ambiguously between parodying Thucydides and openly extolling him.[18] Presumably in this exercise there is an element of the 'pleasure of recognition' referred to at chapter 1.2 of *True Stories*, where Lucian informs his readers that he is not going to name names, since they can identify the allusions to different writers themselves. Through this sly, intertextual game Lucian tests his audience's knowledge of Thucydides.

The one overarching theme that emerges from *How to Write History* is that history should be written with a view to future audiences and readers and should transcend the concerns and interests of the social and political contexts in which it is written. All the other precepts advanced in the treatise can be seen as subservient to this ultimate aim (40). According to Lucian's survey of Greek and Roman historiography, one of the essential characteristics of good history-writing is the fact that it does not care about its reception in the present, but instead focuses on how future audiences will judge it. At the beginning of the work, Lucian likens history-writing to an edifice (*oikodomia*), and claims that by writing a treatise on the subject he will be able to make his mark on the construction (4). This is picked up in the next chapter (5), when Lucian mentions Thucydides' ambition that his history would be a possession for all time. According to Lucian, Thucydides conceived of the impartial, critical, stateless model of history-writing in response to the reception of Herodotus' work:

> Thucydides laid down this law very well: he distinguished virtue and vice in
> historical writing, when he saw Herodotus greatly admired to the point

where his books were named after the Muses. For Thucydides says that he is writing a possession for evermore rather than a prize-essay for the occasion, that he does not welcome fiction but is leaving to posterity the true account of what happened (42).[19]

This passage alludes to another of Lucian's works – a prologue that is known by two titles: *Herodotus, or Aëtion*.[20] In the first chapter of that work, Lucian describes Herodotus' rise to fame as a result of his performance of his *Histories* at the Olympic games, resulting in the books of the *Histories* being named after the muses. It is notable that Lucian depicts Herodotus playing to the crowds, demonstrating massive popular appeal, winning prizes at the Olympics and upstaging athletes, while Thucydides is aloof and shuns competition for prizes among his contemporaries. In view of Thucydides' alleged withdrawal from the competition, it is ironic that Lucian depicts contemporary historians all striving to compete with Thucydides, who has become the historian to beat (26).[21] These are two divergent routes to fame: the one (exemplified by Lucian's Herodotus) wins fame in the present tense and is subsequently read and remembered; the other (Lucian's Thucydides) focuses on, and wins, fame among future readers. Despite travelling different routes to fame, both writers are numbered among the 'best historians' in the present treatise (*How to Write History* 54).

There is a conflict between the framing of Lucian's treatise, which concentrates on literary fame, and the precepts expounded within the treatise, which address the appropriate methodology for writing history. In the case of methodology, truth is paramount, but Lucian finds an ingenious way of connecting the two concerns: the way to ensure truthfulness is to ignore the present and focus on the past, which dovetails neatly with the theme of ensuring the survival of your work. As Matthew Fox comments, 'truth is to be found in history by thinking of the future rather than the present'.[22] Wheeldon connects Lucian's strategy to a broader appreciation of the 'truth effects' of authorial distance in ancient history-writing, whether this distance is emotional, psychological, ethical ('disinterestedness'), temporal (writing some decades / centuries after the subject matter narrated) or geographical / cultural. [23] We can contrast the rhetorical approach to truth in historiography, whereby the historian manipulates the 'truth effects' of authorial distance and supposed objectivity with the philosophical conception of objectivity. Although Lucian rejects the distorting influences of present audiences, in *How to Write History* he does not advocate truth as an end in and of itself; rather, his model of historical truth is audience-centred, or 'audience relative' to use Bernard Williams' term (even if the audience is an 'absent' audience of future readers.[24] Lucian's argument undermines itself: he criticizes contemporary historians for seeking to ingratiate themselves with wealthy patrons and men of influence, and the corresponding trend for writing panegyric history. However, he ends up championing history that will ingratiate itself with future audiences. The irony is that Thucydides serves as the paradigm for both aspects of Lucian's project: Thucydides' *History* is the ultimate example of the text as an eternal monument and it also furnishes the criteria for good historiographical practice among the aspiring historians who are named as the target audience for the work. We could call this reading Thucydides against the grain: taking *bona fide* Thucydidean precepts and manipulating them in ways that undercut the ideology of accuracy, historicity and impartiality, which is such a prominent feature of the *History*.

Recalling the image of history-writing as an edifice in chapter 4, the treatise ends with the example of Sostratus of Cnidus, the architect of the lighthouse at Alexandria, who inscribed his name on the masonry of the lighthouse before covering it over with plaster and an inscription to the king of the day (62).[25] The moral of this story is that the plaster crumbled away over time to reveal Sostratus' name underneath. If we apply this analogy to history-writing, then history-writing emerges as a show-case for the name (and fame) of the historian. More pointedly, Lucian's foray into critical historiography in the current treatise enables him, Sostratus-like, to graft his name onto the edifice of history-writing.[26] John Moles has extrapolated an architectural metaphor from Thucydides' presentation of his work as a *ktêma es aiei* (1.22.4).[27] Reading backwards from Lucian to Thucydides, we might also detect an analogy with the Sostratus motif in 1.10 of Thucydides' *History*, where he anticipates, hypothetically, the impression of the ruins of Sparta, as it was in his day, on future generations (1.10.2-3):

> If the city of the Spartans were to be deserted, but the temples and the foundations of buildings were left behind, I imagine that with the passage of time future ages would greet the reputation of the Spartans' power with incredulity. And yet they control two-fifths of the Peloponnese and lead the entire region and many allies beyond its borders. Nevertheless, since the city is not centralized nor does it have the use of expensive temples and constructions but instead is settled in the old style of the Greeks, it would seem to fall short of its reputation.

Conversely, Thucydides speculates that the ruins of Athens will mislead future ages into believing that the city was twice as powerful as it really was. As Guy Rotella has observed in the context of a study of the theme of monumentality in twentieth-century poetry, 'falsification by enlargement is a besetting sin of monuments'.[28] However, Thucydides' work is liable to the same charge. When it came to fashioning his subject matter he amplified and enlarged the war, running together the different conflicts into a monumental war, which, thanks to Thucydides, we now know as the Atheno-Peloponnesian War.[29] The criterion of scale is paramount in Thucydides' presentation of his subject: 'this war ... will emerge as manifestly greater than previous wars' (1.21.2). Since the comment about the potential for architectural monuments to mislead posterity about past greatness occurs in a passage where Thucydides is comparing his estimation of the Atheno-Peloponnesian War with Homer's account of the Trojan War, it is tempting to see Thucydides anticipating a future contest between conflicting versions of the past. In 1.10 there is a scale of representational accuracy: physical remains constitute the least reliable guide to the past, poetic accounts are an improvement but also reveal exaggeration and embellishment, and then there is Thucydides' work which attempts to present a precise account of past and present history. Taken together with 1.22, this passage implies that Thucydides' *History* will be the only true remnant of his era.

While Lucian's architectural metaphors for history-writing are germane to Thucydides' presentation of his work, he also employs more subversive metaphors. For example, he states that he has written the current treatise so as not to be the only man without a voice in such a polyphonic age; secondly, he claims that he did not want to be like an extra in comedy, without any words to deliver. Lucian introduces an anecdote about the philosopher Diogenes, who rolled his barrel up and down a hill in Corinth to avoid being the only idle man in Corinth, since he saw everyone else busying themselves with preparations to ward off Philip of Macedon (3). These metaphors compound the sense of history as play and represent Lucian getting in on the act – extending his talent for parody to yet another genre, and demonstrating one of his recurrent contentions: that knowledge is as much about performance, rhetoric and presentation, as it is about *what* is known. If you as reader enact Lucian's precepts, then you too can write history.[30] Needless to say, this notion of a rhetoric of history that can be 'acted' out is utterly at odds with Thucydides' insistence on the toil (*ponos*) that needs to be expended in establishing the truth. Lucian is well aware of this; in section 47 he expresses the requirement for strenuous historical research in terms that recall Thucydides' own views on the subject (he uses the adverbs *philoponôs* ('embracing hard work') and *talaipôrôs* ('painstaking')). This wording recalls 1.20.3, where Thucydides criticizes the majority for being satisfied with an investigation into the truth conducted *atalaipôros* ('sloppily') and 1.22.3, where he states that discovering what had taken place in the war involved 'a lot of hard work' (*epiponôs*). This is yet another example of Lucian reading Thucydides two ways in the same treatise: both as a 'straight' historian and against the grain.

True Stories

The parody of history becomes yet more sophistical in the serious play of *True Stories*, where the narrator teases his audience by flitting between the poles of truth and fiction. Lucian presents this as a relatively light-weight work and contrasts it with more serious reading (1.1-2). However, this statement is immediately qualified by the claim that this work, as well as providing a light *psuchagôgia* ('entertainment' – lit. 'leading of the soul') based on charming wit, can also offer the reader an opportunity for exploration (*theôria*) that is not without culture (*ouk amouson*). The Greek noun *theôria* has a variety of meanings, ranging from the cultural tourism undertaken by the sage Solon in Herodotus' *Histories*,[31] to the travels undertaken by envoys in order to consult oracles, participate as observers in religious festivals, or conduct diplomatic negotiations. It can also refer to the study of the heavens.[32] I have chosen to translate it as 'exploration', since this noun can have connotations of research, travel (including space travel) and tourism. What is striking about the phrase *theôria ouk amouson* is that it brings two different discourses into contact. The term *theôria* occurs predominantly in prose texts and suggests independent exploration and observation guided by human intelligence, whereas the adjective *amousos* conjures up the mediation of the muses and the sphere of poetry.[33] This juxtaposition is in keeping with Lucian's focus on history and myth in his critique of historiography, and serves an early warning that they are going to be difficult for the reader to separate in this work. Furthermore, Lucian claims that this work will prove enticing (*epagôgos*) for the reader on several fronts: because of the strangeness of the subject, the charm of the arrangement, the fact that he tells spangled lies (*pseusmata poikila*)[34] in a persuasive manner (*pithanôs*), after the fashion of truth (*enalêthôs*), and because the work is full of allusions to ancient poets, historians and philosophers (1.2). The adjective *epagôgos* is part of the vocabulary used by hostile critics of rhetoric. We have already encountered this adjective in Thucydides at 6.8.2, where it was used to describe the misleading speech made to the Athenian assembly by the Egestaean envoys (see Chapter 4 n. 49, p. 148 below). The Greek etymology of this adjective literally means 'leading on', and reinforces the noun *psuchagôgia* in the previous clause, which was also part of the terminology of rhetorical theory in classical Greek texts. Lucian makes no pretence of the fact that *True Stories* will draw on rhetorical devices to persuade the reader, and it will do so through true-seeming falsehoods.[35] This tactic harks all the way back to Hesiod's *Theogony* (27-8) and the problematic, age-old intertwining of truth and falsehood in Greek literature.[36]

This knowing emphasis on rhetorical technique could be said to undermine Lucian's truth-telling confession about the fact that he is lying right from the start. In one sense it does not matter what he tells the reader about the truth or falsehood of his account, since he intends to *persuade* them anyway. This is serious play that invites the reader to reflect on the interrelationship of truth and lies, and the genres of history and fiction, while the narrator is in the process of manipulating these very categories.[37] Unlike the approach in *How to Write History*, where Lucian, as an up-front narrator, appears to police the boundaries between truth and history on the one hand, and lies and fiction on the other, *True Stories* demonstrates how difficult it is to keep them apart. This intellectual challenge is compounded in the subsequent chapters, where Lucian expresses amazement at all the writers who have written lies under the banner of truth:

> Well, on reading all these authors, I did not find much fault with them for their lying, as I saw that this was already a common practice even among men who profess philosophy. I did wonder, though, that they thought that they could write untruths and not get caught at it. Therefore, as I myself, thanks to my vanity, was eager to hand something down to posterity, that I might not be the only one excluded from the privileges of poetic licence (*muthologia*), and as I had nothing true to tell, not having had any adventures of significance, I took to lying. But my lying is far more honest than theirs, for though I tell the truth in nothing else, I shall at least be truthful in saying that I am a liar. I think I can escape the accusation of the world by my own admission that I am not telling a word of truth. Be it understood, then, that I am writing about things which I have neither seen nor experienced (*epathon*) nor learned from others – which, in fact, do not exist at all and, in the nature of things, cannot exist. Therefore my readers should on no account trust them.
>
> *True Stories* 1.4[38]

As several scholars have pointed out, Lucian's argument in this passage employs a version of what is known in logic as the 'Cretan liar' paradox: Lucian claims that he resorted to lying, and that the only truthful statement that he makes is the statement that he is a liar. However, if the statement that 'Lucian is a liar' is true, then we cannot believe the truth of even this statement, since it is the utterance of a liar. Scholars who take Lucian at his word and read *True Stories* as a lie miss the subtlety of this passage.[39] Through this ambiguity Lucian deliberately leaves open the possibility that *True Stories* may contain truth, and covers himself with the disavowal that it's all a lie – a claim that we cannot wholly believe.

This riddling preface clears the way for Lucian's critique of the discourses of veracity and fiction in *True Stories*: does all fictional discourse have to be 'untrue', and what kind of 'truth' can fiction lay claim to? Conversely, is 'accurate' history invariably 'true', or invariably 'non-fictional'? These are questions that arise in scholarship on Thucydides. Recall, for example, the discussion on the question of the truthfulness of

Thucydides' speeches in Chapter 4. I remarked on the tendency of scholars to posit different modalities of truth in Thucydides' text. This idea has been stated explicitly by John Moles, who distinguishes between truth (lower case) and Truth (upper case) in the *History*. The latter Truth involves insight into realities, the expression of which may involve considerable invention and techniques commonly associated with fictional writing.[40] Lucian's paradoxical posturing forces us to rethink the relationship between truth and history, and lies and fiction. He exposes his own 'travelogue' as an imaginary journey that he invented because he wanted to be read by posterity (1.4); accordingly, it encompasses people and places that do not (and cannot) exist. However, when he embarks on the narrative of the journey, Lucian claims that his motives for his period away from home (*apodêmia* – 1.5) were 'intellectual curiosity and a desire for new experiences'. Already there is a blurring between the external narrative frame and the internal narrator: is this Lucian *qua* intellectual telling us of his travel lust and intellectual curiosity, or Lucian as lying travel-writer already resorting to conventional, 'literary' motives for travel? While Lucian freely admits that he has not undertaken the literal survey of other lands and cultures associated with *theôria*, the *True Stories* assume an extensive survey of the existing literature in this field. It is an overview of literature as opposed to physical territory. The journey narrative with which Lucian presents the reader effectively amounts to a voyage of exploration in different literary genres.

The ironic critique of historical narrative in *True Stories* anticipates some of the main lines of intellectual debate that have characterized postmodern historiography. As we have seen, after setting himself up as an 'honest' liar, Lucian's narrator then proceeds to approach the narrative as though writing a veridical account, and exploits historiographical techniques to promote its credibility. Lucian's serious play with historiography calls to mind twentieth-century debates about the 'narrativist-rhetorical conception of historiography':[41] the idea that there is a 'rhetoric' of history, to use Hayden White's formulation. Hayden White's challenge to history-writing was to highlight the problem of narrativity: the fact that history is always narrated, and that narration uses narrative structures and processes that are shared with 'imaginative discourses' (White cites epic, folk tale, myth, romance, tragedy, comedy and farce).[42] Consequently, White's work challenged historians to reconsider their conception of historical truth, given that there are no absolute *formal* distinctions between historical and fictional narratives. The historian typically gives the reader a commitment that he intends to narrate the truth, but this intentional commitment to the truth co-exists with so-called formal fictions, such as plot, that are shared with the very fictional works from which history as a discipline distinguishes itself.[43]

In *True Stories* Lucian mimics historiographical techniques that are used by authors to persuade the reader of the accuracy of the details of their accounts, and hence their overall veracity.[44] Within a narrative that indulges in blatantly imaginary events, he also assumes the historian's disdain towards fictional accounts that fall short of the truth; history emerges as both a compromised discourse and a corrective methodology. Although the primary object of parody is not always Thucydides, many of these tropes do occur in Thucydides' *History*. In what follows I examine Lucian's use of these tropes to comment on their presence in Thucydides' *History*.

Parodying the rhetoric of historiography

Numbers as a tool in the 'rhetoric of accuracy'

I start with Lucian's parody of the 'rhetoric of numbers', which may be considered as part of the broader field of the 'rhetoric of accuracy'. Our understanding of the rhetorical significance of numbers in Greek historiography is indebted to the work of Catherine Rubincam, who has studied the frequency of the citation of numbers in the works of ancient Greek historians. She has focused both on the rhetorical spin that can be put on numbers by various 'qualifying expressions' (e.g. *approximately* thirty triremes),[45] and on the use of so-called 'typical' or 'formulaic' numbers.[46] Rubincam defines a 'typical' / 'formulaic' number as follows: 'a typical or formulaic number is one that is not 'real' (that is, does not represent the result of a real attempt to count or measure the phenomenon in question)'.[47] In the case of Thucydides, Rubincam has argued that the casualty numbers that Thucydides cites in the *History* are subject to patterning, which tells against the idea that they represent actual 'body-counts'.[48] The point of highlighting the 'rhetoric' of numbers in ancient historiography is not to suggest that statistics were deliberately falsified in bad faith, hence undermining the reliability of the narratives. Instead, Rubincam explains the significance of her research in terms of the shortcomings of 'data collection' in the fifth century BC. The rhetoric of numbers and the rhetorical patterning of numerical data compensate for the lack of accurate data: 'even the most conscientious historian would have had to make do often with numbers that were mere approximations'.[49] Simon Hornblower offers a slightly different perspective on numbers in Thucydides' war narrative, citing Thucydides' use of numbers as one of the historian's virtues and commenting on his general avoidance of 'inflated figures'.[50]

In *How to Write History*, Lucian identifies the use of numbers as a truth-effect that can be abused by historians (20), citing the example of a contemporary historian of the Parthian Wars who allegedly made up false figures; according to this historian the number of enemy dead after a given battle was 70,236 and the number of Roman dead only two. This is a naked example of an incredible statistic, with no credible rhetoric to commend it to the reader. In *True Stories* Lucian himself employs some incredible statistics, but frames them with a credible rhetoric, challenging the reader to consider some of the ways in which fiction can ape the truth, and demonstrating that we often rely on rhetorical markers to indicate the presence or absence of truth. At 1.6 Lucian comments that he and his crew were buffeted across the ocean by a gale for seventy-nine days, arriving at an island on the eightieth day.[51] Although readers have been warned that this voyage never took place, psychologically the number seventy-nine gives us pause: who would invent a number like that? In their commentary on *True Stories* (ad loc.), Georgiadou and Larmour observe that Lucian has borrowed this detail from Iambulus, and that this passage is typical of Lucian's strategy of pretending numerical accuracy in order to make his narrative sound plausible. But if we accept the view that Lucian does not allow the reader to dismiss his entire account as 'mere lies', then this use of the rhetoric of numerical accuracy in *True Stories* stands as a critique of hard and fast notions of true and false in narrative discourse. Fictional, made-up accounts, such as the journey to the moon or the battles inside the whale, can be narrated plausibly using a rhetoric of accuracy and other 'truth-effects'. Conversely, there is no guarantee that events that actually happened will be plausible in the narration. This irony can itself be exploited in historical accounts to improve the historian's credibility by indicating his reluctance to discuss phenomena that will appear incredible. A good example is Herodotus *Histories* 1.193.4, where Herodotus states that he will not mention the size of the millet and sesame crops which grow in Babylonia, on the grounds that their huge dimensions will seem improbable to the less well travelled. Lucian's narrator draws on this credibility device when he declines to mention the number of the Cloud-centaurs (1.18) on the grounds that the number might not be believed because it is so large.[52]

When we come to Lucian's account of the battle between the Vulture-dragoons who inhabit the moon, and the army of Phaethon, king of the sun, Lucian again plays intricate tricks with the rhetoric of accuracy. At 1.13 he claims:

> The number of our army was a hundred thousand, apart from the porters, the engineers, the infantry and the foreign allies; of this total, eighty thousand were Vulture-dragoons and twenty thousand Grassplume riders.

First, in the Preface Lucian has thrown the veracity of his entire narrative into doubt and has made us very sceptical readers; secondly, these are manifestly make-believe creatures;[53] thirdly, the number 100,000 is suspiciously neat. However, Lucian then adds corroborating details. He qualifies the figure 100,000 by pointing out that this excludes porters, engineers, infantry and foreign allies, he then breaks the number for what is effectively the cavalry into 80,000 Vulture-dragoons and 20,000 Grassplume riders. Never mind that these creatures do not exist and have never existed, Lucian writes as though he has accurate information to convey and adds appropriate military detail.[54] Moving from one ludicrous battle-scene (the moon) to another, at 1.37 Lucian summarizes the outcome of a battle held inside the belly of the whale that has swallowed him and his travelling companions. The battle statistics are as follows: 'the slain on the side of the enemy were one hundred and seventy, on our side, one – the helmsman, who was run through the midriff with a mullet-rib'. Again, one hundred and seventy is another figure that is plausible because unlikely. Before we become too suspicious about the fact that there is only one casualty on Lucian's side, we are distracted by the significant detail: we are told how the helmsman died. The fatal weapon is absurd (a mullet-rib), but it could be said to be 'appropriate' technology, given that the battle took place inside a whale's belly.

A slightly different example of Lucian's deployment of the rhetoric of numbers occurs at 1.40, where the narrator dates an event (a strange sighting of huge men sailing on islands) according to a bizarre system of chronology which is an absurd take on the method of dating events in relation to months and annual seasons: 'For a year and eight months we lived in this way, but on the fifth day of the ninth month, about (*peri*) the second mouth-opening – for the whale did it once an hour …'. A factual sounding rhetoric and a plausible sounding system of chronology are applied to a blatant invention. If we scrutinize this passage more closely, we notice that Lucian is not just using numerical data to rhetorical effect,[55] but that he even qualifies his numbers for added plausibility. Lucian concludes the brief chronological sequence (a year and eight months [...] fifth day of the ninth month [...] second mouth opening) with an approximate figure: '*about* the second mouth opening' – a detail that is later repeated for emphasis. The preposition 'about' (*peri*) functions as what Catherine Rubincam calls an 'approximating' expression: the narrator adds credence to figures by voluntarily admitting a degree of approximation.[56] In this short passage Lucian pulls off a multi-faceted imitation of the rhetorical use of numbers in historical writing. Throughout *True Stories* there is a recurrent tension between apparent numerical accuracy and credible details, contrasting with blatantly fictional subject matter.

Lucian's practice in this passage is continuous with aspects of Thucydides' rhetoric of accuracy, but flouts the spirit of the latter's historiographical research. We can contrast Lucian's truly fictional approach to the rhetoric of numbers with Thucydides' strategy. In a well-known passage that concludes his account of the battle of Mantinea (418 BC), in which Spartan forces defeated the Argives and their allies (5.65-74), Thucydides employs a rhetoric of accuracy and manages to make a historiographical virtue out of areas of ignorance and the problematic gap between historical reality and its subsequent representation. At 5.68.2, Thucydides returns to the now familiar motif of misleading visual appearances, noting that the Spartan forces appeared greater than they were in reality. He also volunteers that he could not make an accurate record of the numbers involved, and attributes this to the covert nature of Spartan government, in the case of the Spartans, and to the human tendency for boastful exaggeration in the case of the other forces (see also Chapter 3, p. 48 above). However, next Thucydides introduces a subtle shift away from the misleading nature of appearances and the factors that obstructed the gathering of information about the battle, to an emphasis on reflection (*skopein*) and the insight to be gained from rational inference and calculation. Accordingly he proceeds to work out the numbers of the Spartan forces, presenting the reader with seemingly authoritative calculations about the numbers involved (5.68.3).[57] Through this process of insight, as opposed to actual sight, what was not clear is inferred.

In his post-mortem of the battle, Thucydides acknowledges the inevitable gap between the reality of the battle and his account of it, stating that the battle 'was of this nature and as close as is possible to the account given here' (5.74.1). He supplies round figures for the Argive, Ornean and Cleonaean casualties (700), the Mantinean casualties (200) and the Athenian and Aeginetan casualties (200). When it comes to the Spartan forces, the losses of their allies are dismissed as insignificant; they are not 'worthy of note' (*axiologon* – 5.74.3). The force of this adjective is presumably military: Thucydides writes up these casualty figures from a strategic point of view as one who had formerly been a general himself and who sees casualties in terms of their impact on the capacity of the forces that remain. Nevertheless, this authorial judgement circumvents the problem of the information gap by applying the vague criterion of significant / insignificant numbers. When it comes to the Spartan casualties, Thucydides again makes a virtue out of a poor set of data: 'about the Spartans themselves it was difficult to ascertain the real figure' (5.74.3). Having admitted this difficulty, Thucydides uses a passive verb as a distancing technique, absolving himself from responsibility for the figures that he does cite: 'about (*peri*) three hundred were said (*elegonto*) to have died' (5.74.3). Thucydides turns a shortfall in knowledge into a positive historiographical state that allows him to demonstrate his powers of analysis. He admits provisional, approximate figures but by subjecting them to a careful sequence of qualifying statements, he reassures the reader as to the trustworthiness of the narrator, if not the strict credibility of the numbers.

6. Reading Thucydides with Lucian

Rationalizing myth

In addition to Lucian's own fictions, which are redeemed or given a veneer of historicity by what I have called a rhetoric of accuracy, he also imports fictions from other authors and redeems them through a process of pseudo-rationalization. As before, Lucian deliberately merges the discourses of truth and fiction. Take, for example, Lucian's account of the aftermath of the first wave of battle between the Moon-people and the Sun-people (*True Stories* 1.17):

> It was a glorious victory, in which many were taken alive and many were slain; so much blood flowed on the clouds that they were dyed and looked red, as they do in our country when the sun is setting, and so much also dripped down on the earth as to lead me to conjecture (*eikazein*) whether something of the sort did not take place in the sky long ago, when Homer supposed that Zeus had sent a rain of blood on account of the death of Sarpedon.

The reader is required to envisage a battle in the heavens and the blood shed in this battle flowing downwards, dyeing the clouds and raining on the earth. Into this far-fetched scenario, Lucian interjects a comparison between the blood-stained clouds and the appearance of clouds at sunset 'in our country'. The inclusive first-person plural pronoun 'our' incorporates readers into the fiction, encouraging us, in the manner of an epic simile, to make the imaginative leap from something we know and are familiar with (sunset) to the image of clouds dyed with blood. Lucian then distracts the reader from his narrator's fiction by drawing our attention to the occurrence of the same motif (blood rain) in Homer (*Iliad* 16.458-61), where Zeus causes the clouds to rain blood in sympathy with the death of the young warrior Sarpedon. This shift in the narrative is framed in terms of a conjecture (the Greek verb *eikazein* means 'to conjecture', or 'to infer', and was frequently used as part of the language of proof in historical, scientific and philosophical argumentation)[58] and the narrator takes on a scholarly persona as a critic of Homer who rationalizes a patent fiction in the *Iliad*. But, perversely, the rationalization has recourse to another patent fiction: a battle in the heavens. The fictionality of the subject matter aside, this is a plausible parody of pseudo-historical/ philosophical/ literary, rational investigation. By juxtaposing his account with Homeric epic, Lucian is able to make his narrative sound more plausible. Compare the passage at 2.32 where Lucian introduces his account of the city on the Island of Dreams with the statement that 'no one else has written about it, and Homer, the only one to mention it at all, was not quite accurate (*ou panu akribôs*) in what he said'. This is not just Lucian presuming to 'correct' Homer in imitation of Alexandrian grammarians and allegorical interpreters, as Georgiadou and Larmour suggest in their commentary;[59] this is part of Lucian's ongoing play on the way in which different genres lay claim to truth and how they measure up to each other. Compare Thucydides' conclusion to his digression on the Pentekontaëtia, where he concedes that Hellanicus 'touched on' this period in his History of Attica, but that his coverage was brief and his record of the chronology was not accurate (*ouk akribôs* – 1.97.2).[60]

One of the hallmarks of early Greek historiography is the way in which authors such as Herodotus and Thucydides attempt to delineate between techniques of narration and subject matter that are appropriate for myth, and those which are suitable for factual genres.[61] The lines are never neat or absolute, since both authors sometimes treat subject matter that is blatantly 'mythical', but incorporate it into their historical methodology. Similarly, they also criticize authors who treat subject matter that properly belongs in the domain of rational inquiry in a mythical way, without due regard for accuracy or circumspection. In Herodotus and Thucydides the dialogue between history and myth is not surprising, given that they write in a tradition that is continuous with Homer, in which successive authors compare themselves to Homer.

Early Greek history attempted to define itself as a new form of knowledge by distancing itself from Homeric epic, primarily through an emphasis on different standards of truth. The mode of truth that operates in Homeric epic can be compared to the suspension of disbelief that is one of the distinguishing features of 'fiction'. Most readers do not approach Homer's poems in terms of historicity and veracity ('did these things actually happen; and did they happen in this way?'), but focus instead on the persuasiveness of the poetry as an account of human nature that rings true *to them*. There is an inter-subjective understanding between poet and audience. In contrast, readers apply – and are encouraged to expect – criteria of historicity and accuracy when reading Herodotus and Thucydides.

However, one problem with this antithesis between the domain of history and the domain of epic poetry is that it overlooks the extent to which epic poetry *was* and *is* history: it 'was' history for ancient Greek audiences, and it 'is' history for modern audiences.[62] For ancient Greek audiences and readers in the fifth and fourth centuries BC, Homer could be used as a source for military values and leadership (if a source of outmoded, not entirely practical advice),[63] 'civic' values such as patriotism, conceptions of the Gods, and geography and ethnography. Scholars treat Achilles, Hector and Odysseus as fictional characters, but we take Homer seriously as a source for archaic Greek attitudes to cunning, early ethnography, early Greek 'thought' broadly construed (ranging from constructions of gender to protocols and ideals of friendship), and embedded networks of exchange – to mention only a few areas of research.

In their various ways, both Herodotus and Thucydides rationalized Homeric epic in order to draw on the wealth of cultural, geographical, ethnographic and 'historical' information that it contained about the past.

Hence, in a fascinating passage in Book 2 of the *Histories*, Herodotus 'corrects' Homer's account of Paris' abduction of Helen in the *Iliad*. He rejects the version of the myth offered by Homer (2.116), but draws on passages from Homer (*Iliad* 6.289-92; *Odyssey* 4.227-30 and 351-2), in order to corroborate the version that he favours – a version that allegedly derives from oral interviews with priests at Memphis in Egypt (*Histories* 2.113-20). Herodotus engages with Homer as a source who manipulates the truth in order to satisfy the generic expectations of epic for the best story. However, he detects traces of the true account in Homer's poems, which he concludes that Homer has deliberately planted so as to signal that he was aware of the true account. Herodotus' complaint with epic is not, therefore, that it is 'fictional' in the way in which we typically use the term 'fiction', but rather that the account of the past which it provides is unreliable, because the genre of epic operates according to different truth conventions and because 'Homer' adapts his narrative to meet the audience's expectations of what an epic tale should sound like. In using the Homeric versions of the abduction of Helen, Herodotus makes the epic source compliant to his historiographical methodology.

Another approximation of historiography in *True Stories* consists in the peace treaty between the Moon-people and the Sun-people at 1.20. Scholars have detected parallels between the terms of this treaty and the treaty to cement the so-called 'Peace of Nicias' in 422-421 BC, which Thucydides records in Book 5 of the *History* (chapters 18-19). There certainly does seem to be a Thucydidean intertext in this passage, since Lucian builds up to the treaty with the information that Phaethon (the victorious Sun-King) and his people held two assemblies: 'on the first day they did not lay aside a particle of their anger, but on the second day they softened, and the peace was made on these terms:'. The detail of the two assemblies, the one ruled by anger and the other in a spirit of remorse, evokes Thucydides' account of the Mytilene debate. At 3.36.2-4, Thucydides recounts how the Athenians held two assemblies: at the first assembly the Athenians voted to put all the adult male citizens of Mytilene to death under the influence of anger, but on the next day they relented and reconsidered and had another assembly. If Lucian's description of the treaty does indeed allude to two separate passages in Thucydides simultaneously, then this passage (*True Stories* 1.20) is a good example of Lucian drawing indiscriminately on Thucydides in order to give his work a legitimate 'historical' texture.

Omniscient narrative point of view

In Chapter 2, I examined the significance of the vantage point from which Thucydides narrates the *History* and how this perspective is illustrated within the narrative by a focus on raised ground from which generals and their troops have a superior view over their enemies. The historical narrator sees even better than the participants, and has a complete overview of events. In *How to Write History* (49) Lucian equates the ideal perspective for the historian with the description of Zeus at the beginning of *Iliad* 13, where Zeus is depicted viewing several different regions simultaneously.[64]

In *True Stories*, Lucian goes yet one better and conceives of the ultimate viewpoint: the view from the moon, which enables him to see events from a higher vantage point than all other writers. Elsewhere in Lucian's corpus – in the *Icaromenippus*, for example – the journey to the moon and the view from the moon is used to up-stage philosophers.[65] As Georgiadou and Larmour note, the notion of being *meteôros* 'up in the air' / 'up on high' was typically associated with philosophers.[66] For instance, in his first appearance in Aristophanes' comedy *Clouds*, the philosopher Socrates is depicted hanging in a basket, observing heavenly phenomena (*ta meteôra* – line 228).[67] Again and again, Lucian exploits this idea of the view from above which is also an overview of a literary vista encompassing all Greek literature and stretching back to Homer. A corollary of the motif of omniscience is that, as a result of knowing everything, Lucian will be known to all and will be immortal.

Conclusion

In *How to Write History* (41), Lucian prescribes that the good historian, among other traits, should be a 'stranger' in his books (*xenos en tois bibliois*) and stateless (*apolis*). I take the phrase 'stranger in his books' to mean that the historian should be anonymous and disinterested, suppressing his identity and personal interests. Thucydides embodies both of these qualities: he held out his period of exile from Athens (424-404 BC) as an experience that improved his historical research (5.26.5-6), and he went to great lengths to suppress his presence in his own *History*. However, there is more to Lucian's Thucydides than exemplary historiography. Although Lucian's reading of Thucydides is anything but straight, and is certainly not straightforward, Lucian plays a subtle game, purporting to uphold Thucydides for the analytical qualities that made his *History* timeless, but ultimately fixating on the fame of Thucydides' work, onto which Lucian grafts his own name. In Lucian's reading Thucydides' intellectual rigour and detachment emerge as traits that enable him to leave the competition behind, and to leave his mark on the marketplace of ideas.

It is all too easy to dismiss Lucian's critique of ancient historians as a comedic parody and, consequently, to conclude that the critique is not meant to be taken seriously, which is to confuse the presence of humour and amusement with the absence of seriousness.[68] Moreover, as I stressed above, parody is never merely a one-way literary engagement (see above, pp. 112-13). Admittedly, Thucydides becomes disfigured and greatly reduced in Lucian's reading, but Lucian's work is equally transfigured by Thucydides in the process. The presence of Thucydides in *How to Write History* and, less obviously, in *True Stories* exercises a powerful force over the discourses of truth and fiction in those works, showing the extent to which to write and think about truthful discourse and the limits of historiography in Greco-Roman antiquity was to enter into dialogue with Thucydides' *History*.[69]

If we turn back to Thucydides' statement about the ambitions that he harboured for his work, then Lucian's parodic readings fulfil the *History*'s potential to appeal to future readers. Writing at the end of the fifth century BC, Thucydides threw down a serious challenge about the appropriate conditions and methodology for writing a factual narrative about contemporary events. Almost six hundred years later, Lucian's highly sophisticated critique of the interrelationship between truth in history and fictional invention shows what a vast intellectual frontier Thucydides had opened up, building on Herodotus' *Histories*. In the twenty-first century the philosophy of history is still exploring the borders of this frontier.

Notes

Preface

1. To date the first two volumes of this commentary have appeared: vol. I (Books I-III) and vol. II (Books IV-V.24). See the Bibliography for further details.

2. The projected publication date for Dewald's study is November 2005 (University of California Press).

3. H. Sonnabend (2004) *Thukydides*. Studienbücher Antike, 13 (Hildesheim: Olms).

1. Whose Contemporary?

1. C.L.R. James in Hall 1996, 39.

2. The debate about the importance of context in intellectual history centres on the work of Quentin Skinner, who originally advanced his ideas in relation to political texts from the European Early Modern period. For a discussion of Skinner's ideas on context and historical interpretation, see the collection of essays edited by Tully 1988.

3. See Crane 1996, chs 3-6. For further discussion of the suppression of religion in Thucydides, see Hornblower 1992, *passim*. On the suppression of women, see Cartledge 1993. Another example of Thucydides' counter-cultural thought is his economic theory: Kallet-Marx 1993 and Kallet 2001 explore the way in which Thucydides' understanding of the themes of finance and power overturn traditional ways of thinking about and assessing power.

4. In the twentieth century the work that posed the most fundamental challenge to the ideal of Thucydides as an objective historian was Francis Cornford's *Thucydides Mythistoricus* (first published in 1907). Virginia's Hunter's study *Thucydides: The Artful Reporter* (1973) was also very important in demonstrating the extent to which Thucydides shapes our perception of events through artful presentation. For a review of the shift away from the idea of an 'objective' Thucydides to the realization that Thucydides' objectivity is, in part, rhetorical and stylistic, see Crane 1998, 261-2 with n. 8.

5. Crane 1998, 4-5.

6. On the relationship between Thucydides and Herodotus, see Hornblower 1996, 19-38 (with 122-45); and Rood 1998b (4.2) and 1999.

7. Thomas 2000.

8. This is not to deny that the thought experiment 'was there a Herodotus before Herodotus?' (Fowler 1996, 68) can yield important insights about Herodotus' relationship to different intellectual traditions.

9. Connor 1984, 233.

10. Loraux bases this claim on the fact that in his first appearance as general in his own history, Thucydides introduces himself with his patronymic 'Thucydides the son of Olorus who wrote these things down' (4.104.4), which is his standard practice for introducing persons in the *History*. Conversely, with the other sixteen instances of his name he is simply 'Thucydides' (excluding the very first mention of his name at the beginning of the work where, following Herodotus, he mentions his place of origin). See Loraux 1986, 144 and *passim*.

11. Writing on the subject of Thucydides' *History* as a source for Athens' 'political unconscious', Wohl 2002, x counters the idiosyncrasy of Thucydides' account with the argument that 'idiosyncrasy occurs within culturally determined bounds, and even as Thucydides offers his unique and often critical views on the democracy, he also (perhaps unwittingly) reproduces its underlying assumptions'.

12. Diggins 1984, 159.

13. Moles 2001, 206.

14. The phrase in quotation marks is taken from Tully 1988, 4.

15. Dionysius mentions Thucydides in many of his surviving works on literary criticism. However, the most important source for Dionysius' interpretation of Thucydides is the essay entitled *On Thucydides*, which is framed in the form of a letter to the Roman historian Quintus Aelius Tubero. Dionysius also discusses Thucydides in the *Second Letter to Ammaeus* (also known by the title *On the Characteristics of Thucydides' Style*) and in chs 3-6 of the *Letter to Gnaeus Pompeius* (in this last work Dionysius constructs a comparison between Thucydides and Herodotus). All three works can be found in the Loeb edition of Dionysius' *Critical Essays*, translated by Stephen Usher. All quotations from Dionysius in this book are taken from Usher's translation, with a few adaptations.

16. *On Thucydides* 24. These adjectives are repeated elsewhere in the treatise. To give just one example: the adjectives *glôttêmatikê* (full of obscure words), *apêrchaiômenê* (archaic) and *xenê* (outlandish) recur in section 52.

17. For a discussion of Dionysius' treatment of Thucydides' predecessors and contemporaries (from the perspective of Herodotus), see Fowler 1996, 62-3.

18. Compare *On Thucydides* 42, discussed on p. 59.

19. For a brief discussion of Dionysius' criticism of Thucydides' style, see Dover 1973, 9.

20. Woodman 1988, 45-7 discusses judgements on Thucydides' style by both ancient and modern readers.

21. Moles 1993, 103.

22. Crane 1998, 57.

23. Dewald 1999, 233 and 237 respectively.

24. Allison 1997a, 20-1. Allison adds the important proviso that our view of the evolution of Greek work usage is contingent upon accidents of survival: we can base such statistics only on the texts that have come down to us. Cf. Hornblower 2004, 369 for a similar observation.

25. In a later work Allison (2001) has offered an interpretation of the language of value in Pericles' funeral speech (2.35-46), arguing that Thucydides made innovative, metaphorical use of technical language from the realms of banking and finance in a way which is not paralleled in contemporary sources (ibid., 54).

26. I offer two different translations here because there is a debate over the precise meaning of the adjective *exitêlos* at Herodotus 1.1. The adjective has a range of meanings, including 'extinct' and 'faded'. Moles 1999, section 5 has an excellent discussion of the interpretation of this passage. On Herodotus' concern with the afterlife of his work, see Rösler 2002 and Moles 1999 (sections 8-10). For a description of faded lettering on an inscription in Thucydides, see 6.54.7 where he describes the dedication that Peisistratus, son of Hippias, had inscribed on the altar to Apollo in the Pythian precinct. See Immerwahr 1960.

27. On the prefaces of Hecataeus, Herodotus and Thucydides as 'imaging' inscriptions, see Moles 1999, *passim*. Although I formulated my discussion independently, I note that Moles makes the same argumentative move at section 10, conceding that Herodotus and Hecataeus draw on the idea of inscriptions to symbolize their works as 'monuments', but that Thucydides trumps them with his explicit projection of his work into the future. As Moles points out, although Herodotus evidently envisaged that his work would have scope for the future, he does not state this in direct terms in the preface to the *Histories*.

28. 1993, 837. Compare ibid., 837-42. Edmunds argues that, by manipulating grammatical tenses when he speaks about his writing, Thucydides is able to split himself between a historical figure 'Thucydides', who is referred to in the third person and inhabits the past, and, on the other hand, 'Thucydides-narrator', who is always present to the reader through his work.

29. Thucydidean scholarship has shifted substantially since Woodman wrote: 'when we think of classical authors, we normally think about them in relation to their literary traditions, which in Thucydides' case would mean in relation to Herodotus and (as we have just seen) Homer' (1988, 6-7).

30. See Laird 1999, 49.

31. Rood 1998b (section 5).

32. Loraux 1980, *passim*.

33. See, e.g., Woodman 1988, 16.

34. See Crane 1998, 38-61 on Thucydides' 'ideological realism', which he defines as 'using your claim to privileged knowledge to beat your opponents' (38).

35. Hunter 2004, 240 comments: 'for Thucydides, the Homeric poems merely provide evidence about the past which requires (like all testimony) evaluation, whereas the size and importance of the Trojan War itself are easily surpassed by the contemporary war which Thucydides narrates. In making Pericles proclaim that Athens does not need a Homer to celebrate it (2.41.4), Thucydides offers himself and his history as a replacement for Homer and epic.'

36. Ober 1998, 62-3; on p. 62 Ober cites 1.23.5 where Thucydides states that he will go through the 'overt precipitating factors (*aitiai*) of the war' so that 'no one need ever again search for (*zêtêsai*) the sources of this war that fell upon the Hellenes'. Cf. also Nicolai 2001, 263.

37. Moles 1999, section 5 (cf. also Moles 2001, 218). See further Moles 1999, section 10, commenting on the authority conferred by the written-ness of Thucydides' text: 'Thucydides can still say: "my work is the only work you need to understand political life and to engage in it competently, no matter what your own context or time, hence it will be immortal" '. Compare Moles 2001, 207: 'Thucydides' *History* is *the* work, which "synthesizes" (*xunethesan*) and "compounds" (*xugkeitai*) all other relevant works.'

38. Ober 1998, 46-7. Hornblower 1994b, 29 (with n. 65) suggests that sections of Thucydides' work – he volunteers the account of civil unrest in Corcyra (3.81.4-3.84.3) – may have been read out at actual symposia – occasions for communal dining, drinking and entertainment among the city's élite. Cf. Hornblower 2004, 33.

39. It is important to point out that Ober does not attempt to account for the works of these authors in their entirety, but instead focuses on their shared dialogue on the subject of political criticism and theory.

40. For discussion of the phrase 'according to the human condition' (*kata to anthrôpinon*) see Stahl 2003, 28-30.

41. See Raaflaub 2002, 179, with n. 94: 'Thucydides lets the future begin with the present: his observations and insights would be important for audiences at any time, including not least his contemporaries.'

42. Crane 1998, 52.

43. Moles 1998, section 2. This interpretation has been contested by Charles Hedrick in an on-line exchange on Moles' paper (see http://www.dur.ac.uk/Classics/histos/1999/molesexchange.html, with Moles' defence). I accept Moles' interpretation; however, I note that he does not comment on the future tense of *boulêsontai* at 1.22.4, even though it plays into the thesis that he develops in Moles 2001 about Thucydides' focus on the temporal range of the *History*. If the inscription is indeed a strong model, then Thucydides' shift in tense from a general, universal present to the future tense is surely pointed.

44. See Ober 1998, 116 on Thucydides' critique of the performative nature of language in the Athenian Assembly. See also Debnar 2001, 20: 'Thucydides transformed an essentially oral genre – deliberative oratory – into a literary one, and it would seem from his own words that the history as a whole was not intended to be recited in a performative context (1.22.4).'

45. See Rösler 1991 and 2002 on the 'self-historicizing' authorial strategy of Herodotus. In the latter work Rösler compares the strategies of Herodotus and Thucydides.

46. For a critique of the interpretation of Thucydides by International Relations scholars see Bagby 1994. Contemporary studies of Thucydides in International Relations tend to concentrate on Thucydides as an analyst of foreign policy and power relations. Some of this work has a critical edge which successfully translates Thucydides' political criticism of imperial power, even though it domesticates Thucydides and makes the *History* speak to an anachronistic set of concerns from the twenty-first century; see e.g. Lebow and Kelly 2001. Crane 1998, *passim*, explores Thucydidean realism in terms of tensions between archaic and 'modern' world views. On 'Cold-War' readings of Thucydides in an American context, see Lebow and Strauss 1991, *passim* and Ober 2001, 273-5. Ober criticizes much scholarship on political realism in Thucydides for treating the *History* as a univocal text. He argues that there is a 'strong-realist' element in Thucydides' text, but that Thucydides, *qua* historian, undermines this element.

47. For this distinction between 'literary' history and 'history' see Perkins 1992, 172. On the assumptions contained in the terminology of the 'classic' work of literature, see the fourteen witty definitions offered by Calvino 2000, 3-9.

48. Feeney 1995, 310.

49. Connor 1984, 13. I note, however, that Connor does discuss Thucydides' contemporary audience in the conclusion to this work, defining this audience as a socio-political group: 'Thucydides' audience, moreover, was no representative cross-section of the Athenian citizenry or of Greeks in general. It was enlightened, well educated and affluent – not disposed to revert to aristocratic patterns of the archaic age, but distrustful of the populist strain in contemporary democracy' (ibid., 239).

50. Yunis 2003, 198.

51. Rood 1998a, 19.

52. The first comprehensive discussion of the 'history as text' debate in ancient history was the volume of essays *History as Text* (1989), edited by Averil Cameron. On the idea of Thucydides' *History* 'as text', see the qualification stipulated by Moles 2001, 219: 'not "history as text" in the sense of "merely text", but "history as text" in the sense that Thucydides has textualized the war in such a way as to incorporate rigorous historical method and suggest comprehensive treatment (the war "becomes" the text)'.

53. See Munz 1997, 852: 'while we are quite certain that the past has taken place and that we stand at the end of it, the past does not lie out there or back there, for us to look at. If we want to know it and talk about it, it first has to be written up and turned into a story. It has to be made ready for inspection'. Although the 'textualization' of history is characteristic of postmodernist historiography, the basic insight into the role of the historian in constructing history is not new.

54. Hornblower 1994b, 133 with n. 5. See also the controversial tone of Woodman 1988, ch. 1, on rhetoric and literary devices in Thucydides' *History*.

55. Rood 1998, 9.

56. For a discussion of the tensions between Thucydides 'as history' and 'as literature', see Dover 1983, especially pp. 55-6. Happily, within the disciplines of ancient history and classics these tensions have relaxed considerably.

57. It is not practicable to offer a representative discussion of recent studies on Thucydides here, but for the sake of example 'thematic' studies would include Crane 1998, Kallet 2001 and Hornblower 2004; 'linguistic' studies would include Allison 1989 and 1997a, and studies that focus on narrative structure would include Hornblower 1994a, Rood 1998a and Dewald 1999. However, as I note above, although these works exhibit a specific focus, they combine all three approaches.

58. Kallet 2001, 285.

59. See Connor 1984, 232: 'If the text makes the reader, then how does the reader preserve autonomy in evaluating the text?'

60. See Chapter 2, p. 40.

61. Connor 1984, 1-19 charts shifts in American readings of Thucydides – including his own – from the 1950s to the mid-1980s. Stahl 2003 (originally published in 1966), 13-35 gives a retrospective on the state of Thucydidean studies from the nineteenth century to the 1960s. Going further back, there is the question of how Thucydides was read in classical antiquity; see, for example, Hornblower 1995 on the fourth-century and Hellenistic reception of Thucydides. Moles 1999 (especially sections 11-13) urges scholars to re-examine the views of Thucydides' ancient readers.

62. See Segal 1999, 12: 'with the increasing globalization of all areas of academic life, we would do well to remember too that there are national, as well as personal, styles of doing classics'.

63. The quotation comes from L.E. Lord, *Thucydides and the World War* (Harvard University Press, 1945), 216 [*non vidi*] and is cited by Stahl as an example of the tendency in scholarship to give Thucydides a 'modern air' (2003, 13). The full quotation reads: 'in his [sc. Thucydides'] conception of what is required the writer of history he is nearer to the twentieth century AD than he is to the fifth BC'. Woodman 1988, pp. ix and 5, also quotes Lord's comment.

64. Debnar 2001, 21.

65. Yunis 2003, 201.

66. The theme of political education is discussed extensively in Yunis 1996.

67. See Moles 1999, section 10 for the argument that the reading experience would have offered more than the listening experience.

68. See Allison 1997, 239 on writing allowing a 'contemplative style'. See also Nieddu 1993, 153 on writing preserving the thoughts in the text and enabling them to be re-read.

69. Dover 1997, 187.

70. The quotation is from Edmunds 1993, 831. For the argument that writing is fundamental to Thucydides' conception and presentation of his work, see Loraux 1986; Edmunds 1993; Crane 1996; Allison 1997a, 227 and 239; Debnar 2001, 20; and Yunis 2003.

71. Loraux 1986.

72. Edmunds 1993, 834.

73. ibid., 837. For further discussion see Chapter 4 with n. 33, p. 67.

74. See Pelling 2000, 2: 'even historians will probably have had oral performance in mind as at least their primary mode of communication: they would very
likely give readings themselves to a contemporary audience, and they might expect
even posterity to hear their texts more often than read them silently'. See also the
accompanying note (ibid., 254, n. 2).

75. See Moles 2001, 207.

76. Thomas 2003, 163.

77. See Usener 1994, 228-9 on Plato's *Theaetetus*, where the reception of the
dialogue is an explicit theme in the text.

78. Thomas 2000, especially chs 7-8.

79. ibid., 260. See also Munson 2001, 14-17.

80. The term 'defamiliarization' was used originally by Russian formalist critics
to refer to the way in which literary language – poetic language in particular –
adapts ordinary, everyday language, as a means of gaining readers' attention and
prompting them to reconsider the familiar. When I use the term here, I have a
broad usage in mind, whereby not just language, but also social and cultural institutions are presented to the reader in unfamiliar ways.

2. Point of View and Vantage Point

1. See Brothers 1997, 210 on the first Gulf War as the world's 'first live tele-
vised war'. This is not a new phenomenon; the propagandist value of front-line
photography was mobilized in the two World Wars and the Spanish Civil War.
However, the 'cinema of war' was first fully realized in the Vietnam War, and the
'live' cinema of war in the first Gulf War. See Moeller 1989 and Brothers 1997,
passim, esp. ch. 10.

2. For example, see the soldiers interviewed in Michael Moore's documentary
Fahrenheit 9/11 (released June 2004).

3. The scandal of these photos (both real and fake) depicting the abuse of Iraqi
prisoners at Abu Ghraib prison broke in May-June 2004. I am aware that such
'contemporary' allusions date this work, but they are also an honest reflection of
the fact that history and studies of historical works are informed by the historical
contexts in which they are written.

4. On the 'natural' connection between the historical narrative and the visual
image see Ankersmit 1995, *passim* and Fox 2001, 77. Fox comments: 'The historian is a viewer, the past a matter of images. Even in the form of an impossible
ideal – the true picture – the reality of the past, its essence, is most naturally
described in the form of an image' (ibid.). Curiously, although Hunter 1973 applies
the motif of reportage to Thucydides' *History*, she does not consider analogies with
photo-reportage or the filmic.

5. Hornblower 1994b, 191.

6. ibid., 192: 'this is graphic and exciting; like much else in Thucydides it would
make an excellent piece of cinema'.

7. Debnar 2001, 20-2.

8. Allison 1997a, 85-6: 'A general texture is observable in much of the narrative
dealing with earlier events in the war; it is characterized by a framing technique,
by which the frames often overlap to varying degrees and narrow or intensify like
the expanded lens of a camera. Events after the Sicilian expedition, in the latter
years of the war, did move rapidly, both internal political events in Athens as well

as the military action in the Aegean. A less complex and hence a faster-moving narrative style could capture this quickened pace, punctuated as it was with changing treaties and alliances among enemies and political foes'. I discuss the narrative style of Book 8 in Chapter 5, pp. 83-6.

9. See Winkler 2001, 13 on envisaging certain Greek and Roman and narrative texts as 'precursors' of film, or 'le précinéma'. Mench 2001 has studied the narrative of Virgil's *Aeneid* in terms of techniques used by film directors: 'the literary critic should study not only philosophy or comparative literature but also the techniques employed by the filmmaker if he wishes to appreciate those literary works that utilize a kinetic visual approach: montage, variation of viewing angle, alternation of close-up and distance shot, and the like' (219).

10. Compare the 'scene' at 8.33.2-3 where the Spartan naval commander Astyochus anchors off the promontory of Corycus in Ionia (Map 1: 29) and the Athenian forces are at anchor in the same location, but on the other side of a hill, so that neither side detects the other. The fact that the reader can 'see' both sides creates a sense of tension at the potential (but unrealised) conflict.

11. On sight as a weapon in combat, see Brothers 1997, 1.

12. I use the term 'reader' here to refer to Thucydides' implied audience. See the discussion above at pp. 16-17. In cases where the *History* was read aloud to small audiences, this reading would have been non-dramatic. Although we can entertain the idea of a reader animating a reading of the text with non-verbal gestures and dramatic delivery, there is no evidence to suggest that performance of prose texts such as Thucydides' *History* involved dramatic performance and enactment.

13. On the centrality of *to saphes* ('clarity') in Thucydides' *History* see Edmunds 1975a, 155-63.

14. Rood 1998a, 62-9. Rood draws on James Davidson's idea of history as a 'didactic arena' in the work of Polybius (1991, 15). See also Walker 1993, who also draws on Davidson's article (see n. 30 below). For the idea that Thucydides' *History* offers the reader both visual lessons and lessons in the visual, see Kallet 2001, 21-2: 'Like other fifth century writers, Thucydides displays an intense interest in the relationship between vision and knowledge. [...] *Opsis* [appearance, sight, vision, viewing] is fundamentally ambiguous: it can be illusory or real, but even in the latter case, it must be interpreted correctly. The interpretive difficulty inherent in *opsis* relates to Thucydides' didactic approach in treating the problems of *opsis*: his narrative is constructed in such a way as to provide lessons in how to read and interpret visual signs.'

15. See Vernant 1988, 42-3 and *passim*.

16. On the 'privileged perspective' of the audience in Greek tragedy, see Segal 1995, 200-1: 'we sit above the action and look down upon it from quasi-Olympian distance, if not Olympian detachment'.

17. See Goldhill 2002a, 21-2 on the criterion of 'wonder' as one of the audience-friendly aspects of Herodotus' account: 'Herodotus too is keen to turn an analytic gaze at what he sees, and to stake a position in the competitive market of explanation. Yet when the prologue of the *History* promises *erga thaumasta*, "wondrous", "amazing deeds", he is also looking back towards the epic achievements of the heroes of the Trojan War, and promising stories and facts to amaze the reader' (21). See also Moles 1993, 93.

18. A number of scholars have rightly observed that, although Thucydides disdains the rhetoric of competition up-front, he nevertheless frames the *History* in extremely competitive terms. The claim that the work is 'not a competition-piece' is itself competitive. See, e.g., Ober 1998, 56.

19. Trans. Usher, adapted.

20. Elsewhere in the essay (e.g. chs 24 and 29) Dionysius uses the adjective *theatrikos* in a different sense, when he accuses Thucydides of employing *theatrika schêmata* (showy figures of speech).

21. See Chapter 1, n. 4 (p. 130).

22. Finley's article was first published in 1938/9 and reprinted in 1967. Curiously, Finley does not refer to Cornford's work.

23. Macleod 1983, ch. 13.

24. Pelling (ed.) 1997 and Pelling 2000.

25. Pelling 2000 and Ludwig 2002. D'Angour 1998 makes interesting points about the discourse of novelty and innovation in Thucydides in relation to the treatment of this theme in Aristophanes.

26. Goldhill 1998, 105-9. For an excellent discussion of the relationship between Thucydides' emphasis on sight and the visual as channels of knowledge (and misinformation), and the centrality of 'visual' knowledge in Athenian drama, see Kallet 2001, ch. 1 (cited at n. 14 above). See also Jordan (2000).

27. See the famous remarks about the confusion between political deliberation and spectatorship that Thucydides attributes to the Athenian politician Cleon (3.38.4 and 38.7). On the 'isomorphism' between law court and theatre in Athens see Hall 1995 and Cartledge 1997, 14-15. On oratory as entertainment, see Schloemann 2002; see also Halliwell 1997 for parallels and overlaps between theatrical and rhetorical culture.

28. See Segal 1995, 191: 'the knowing subject is construed as one who sees'. See also Allison 1997a, 195; Kallet 2001, 211-22 with n. 2, for further bibliography; and Rehm 2002, 3.

29. Goldhill 1998, 109. See now Nightingale 2004, *passim*.

30. See Walker 1993, 363: 'the spectators in Thucydides' text serve as an emblem for the reader, promoting our visualization of the events'. Cf. also the more general point at p. 354: 'the representation of spectators in ancient Greek historical narratives enhances the "visibility" of the larger narrative scene and comments implicitly on the processes of reading and representation'.

31. On *didaskalia* see Calame 1999, 150 with n. 49 for further bibliography.

32. I follow Hornblower 1994b, 106 in translating *paradeigma* as 'proof'. However, I think that he overstates the distinction between 'proof' and 'example'. On the use of *paradeigma* here, see Morrison 2000, 138 with n. 61. More generally, Morrison provides an excellent discussion of the Melian episode as a historical lesson: 'the Athenian-Melian exchange has become a kind of test case for the reader, asking how much the reader has learned by the end of five books' (119). Kallet 2001, 9-20 argues that the Melian dialogue challenges conventional assumptions about the assessment of power and the display of power. See ibid., 17-18 for comment on the current passage.

33. On the significance of the verb *sphallô* in Thucydides, see Hornblower 2004, 351-2.

34. See p. 91.

35. Plutarch claims that some of the Athenian captives in Sicily were saved by their ability to recite choruses from Euripides' tragedies (*Life of Nicias* 29).

36. Edmunds 1975a, 147. See also Debnar 2001, 22, who cites Edmunds.

37. Hornblower 1994a; Rood 1998a, *passim*, but especially 9-14; Dewald 1999.

38. See Davidson 1991, 11 on preferring 'gaze' over 'focalization'. Rood 1998, 11-13 discusses problems with the concept of 'point of view' from a narratological perspective.

39. On the adjective *meteôros*, see Chapter 6, p. 128.

40. Warner 1972, 351.

41. The translation of *huperoraô* as 'overlook' removes the need to account for the discrepancy between 5.6.3 (Brasidas thinking that Cleon would feel contempt for the size of the former's forces) and 5.8.2, where Thucydides comments that the numbers were more or less equal. See Hornblower 1996, 437 (ad loc.): 'Contrast 8.2, where we are told that numbers were equal, but Brasidas is the focalizer of the present passage, which merely purports to tells us what, at this early point in the episode, Brasidas thought Kleon would be thinking.'

42. Hornblower 1996, 439 (ad loc.) notes that the phrase *'kata thean'* is repeated from Cleon's reported speech 'exactly as if Brasidas had heard Cleon'.

43. Crane 1996, 238. Konstan 1987, 69 (with n. 21) has a brief comment on the nuances of the verb *theaomai* in Herodotus.

44. Hornblower 1996, 443 (ad loc.) quotes Leimbach 1985, 87 for the view that Brasidas makes out that the Athenians are behaving collectively like a group of tourists.

45. Ludwig 2002, 366.

46. Robbins 1993, 59. Compare Woodman 1988, 20 on the American reporter Theodore H. White, who reported on the Second World War in Asia. Woodman points out the contradiction between White's statement that war reporters should be 'as close to the sounds of guns as possible' and his concession that the reporter who is so close to the action does not have a clear picture of the narrative of events. More generally, see ibid., 17-22 on the poor reliability of eyewitness accounts in warfare.

47. I use David Whitehead's excellent translation and commentary (Whitehead 1990).

48. On Aineias' knowledge of Thucydides, see Hornblower 1995, 53 and Whitehead 1990, 102 (with further bibliography). In the present context it is interesting that one of the allusions to Thucydides that scholars have detected in Aineias is to Brasidas' speech to his troops before the second battle of Amphipolis (5.9.8). See Whitehead 1990, 201.

49. Whitehead 1990, 99 (ad loc.) notes the literal translation 'higher ground on the right'.

50. Whitehead 1990, 50-1.

51. On the intended readers of Aineias' work, see Whitehead 1990, 31-42.

52. Hesk 2000 discusses some instances of military deception in Thucydides' *History* and concludes that, while the stereotype of Spartan trickery prevails, Thucydides undercuts this ideal by recounting examples of Athenian generals resorting to trickery in warfare. Commenting on Pericles' funeral oration, Hesk writes: 'Within Thucydides' own writing as a whole then, Pericles' ideal image of military *apatê* as an unAthenian quality is contested by accounts of "real" Athenian military conduct during the war' (ibid., 99; see also pp. 26-9 on military values in Pericles' funeral oration).

53. See Hunter 1973, 25, on the connection in Thucydides' *History* between what people see and what they think.

54. Hornblower 1996, 46 and 165 (ad loc.) points out that the verb *epespcrche* has an epic and poetic flavour and suggests that Thucydides deliberately worked Homeric resonances into his account of Brasidas' brief but significant performance at Pylos. See ibid., pp. 38-61 for a discussion of the heroization of Brasidas, on the model of the Homeric Achilles.

55. *How to Write History* 40: 'In the engagement himself, let him not look at a single part or a single cavalryman or foot soldier – unless it be a Brasidas leaping forward or a Demosthenes beating off his attempt to land.' In the Greek Lucian simply uses the verb 'to look', the cinematic term 'zoom in' is my addition.

56. On Brasidas' awareness of 'the importance of being seen', see Rood 1998a, 66.

57. Price 2001, 254 (on Thucydides' comment about Brasidas' seductive rhetoric at 4.108): 'The fact that Brasidas used false and seductive rhetoric to achieve his ends does not necessarily taint this "intelligence": Theseus, Themistocles and Pericles, for instance, also find the right words to manipulate others.'

58. Hunter 1988, 25.

59. Rood 1998a and Price 2001. See especially Rood 1998a, 80 on Brasidas 'basing his strategy on an awareness of the gaze of others'.

60. Price 2001, 250. However, Price thinks that the second pair of qualities (excellence and intelligence) that are attributed to Brasidas are endorsed by Thucydides (ibid., 250-1). Hornblower 1996, 54-6 discusses the participle *paraschôn*, which Price translates as 'showed himself to be' / 'gave the impression of being', and argues that Thucydides' choice of expression is not cynical (i.e. Thucydides is affirming Brasidas' justice and moderation), opting instead for the translation 'showed himself'. However, Hornblower does concede that *paraschôn* places a 'subtle emphasis on the perception of others'.

61. Rood 1998a, 80.

62. ibid., 67.

63. On the term 'didactic arena' in Davidson 1991, see n. 14 above (p. 136).

64. On Thucydides' language in this passage see Crane 1996, 227-8.

65. Rood 1998a, 74 draws attention to the narrative device of *prolepsis:* Thucydides looks ahead in the narrative and the reader is consequently able to contrast his 'foresight' with the allies' lack of foresight (*pronoia*) in the context of 424/3 BC.

66. See Crane 1996, 227-8.

67. 'Blind wishing' is Crawley's neat translation for *boulêsis asaphês* at 4.108.4 (Strassler (ed.) 1996, 282). (Strassler (ed.) 1996 contains a revised version of Crawley's translation.) Warner translates this phrase as 'wishful thinking' (1972, 330).

68. The clearest and most ironic example of this pattern occurs at 6.60.4, where the Athenian *dêmos* settles for judicial verdicts that are not secure, because it *appears* to serve the interests of the majority. Compare Stahl 2003, 103 on the Athenians' wishful thinking in response to reports that Mytilene was planning to revolt from them (3.1.1): 'what they wish to be true wins out over a reality vouched for by informants'.

69. Williams 2001, 125.

70. Allison 1989, 61 argues that the narrative at 5.6-5.11 rehearses, at the level of the contest between Cleon and Brasidas, the struggle for greater preparedness at an interstate level in Books 6-8.

71. Kallet 2001, 77 and 292, points out that precious metal objects and other forms of non-monetary wealth are at the bottom of the inventory of resources for both Pericles and Thucydides. Moreover, this kind of wealth misleads viewers because its impressive appearance is at odds with its usefulness.

72. Wilson 1979, 10 points out that the fire would also have improved the perspectives of the Athenian triremes, which were waiting for an opportunity to land on Sphacteria.

73. Compare the advantages that accrue to Brasidas when he occupies the elevated position (*epi meteôrou*) of Cerdylium and subsequently enjoys a good vantage point over the movements of the Athenians (5.6.3). See above, p. 26.

74. Compare Davidson 1991, 21 on the 'reflexive gaze' – the gaze directed at oneself or one's own side – in Polybius.

75. 7.59.2: *agônisma*; 7.66.1: *agôn* x 2; 7.70.3: *agônisma*. The noun *agôn* could also describe an athletic contest. For a discussion of the connections between the theme of the *agôn* in Thucydides Books 6 and 7 and Pindar's epinician poetry, see Hornblower 2004, 336-42 (esp. pp. 337-8).

76. In his *Life of Nicias*, 21.1, Plutarch develops the dramatic potential of this scene, describing Demosthenes as 'most brilliant to behold' (*lamprotatos*), mentioning the fancy arrangement (*kosmos*) of the weapons, the insignia of the triremes, and concluding that Demosthenes acquitted himself theatrically (*theatrikôs*). Roisman 1993, 56 has a brief comment on this passage.

77. Hornblower 1994a, 134-5 (following Dover 1988), argues that this is Thucydides' reasoning. Moles 2001, 213-14 argues that this is a case of 'deviant focalization' and that both Thucydides, *qua* narrator, and Demosthenes 'see' in this passage.

78. The *kataplêxis* (7.42.2) and *ekplêxis* (7.42.4) of the Syracusans are soon reversed; at 7.69.2 Nicias is struck with fear at the situation the Athenians are in.

79. Some scholars have suggested that Thucydides conceives of the labour involved in writing his *History* as a quasi-military undertaking requiring *ponos* and perseverance. See Connor 1984, 28; and Crane 1996, 36.

80. Cf. Marincola 1997, 69.

81. Compare 2.64.6 where Pericles instructs the Athenians not to send heralds to Sparta and not to show any signs (*mête endêloi este*) that they are weighed down by present sufferings.

82. See also 7.50.3, where Nicias, having agreed to a retreat, is still of the opinion that they should not vote for the retreat 'in the open' (*mê **phanerôs** ge axiôn psêphizesthai*), and wants them to sail away 'as invisibly as possible' (*hôs adêlotata*).

83. See Padel 1990, 337 on the conflict between the visible exterior and the unseen interior in Greek tragedy: 'One cannot see into another person's feelings. No external mark can tell us what people are inside. We infer what is in them from how they look and what they say.'

84. The use of the superlative adjective is a clever circumspect touch here. Instead of making insupportable claims to absolute truth, Thucydides speaks in terms of the 'truest' reason for the war, conceding the objection that there was no one, single definitive reason. Thucydides is very reluctant to use the adjective '*alêthês*' in his own narrative voice, but the use of the superlative form here actually serves to reinforce his commitment to *akribeia* (precision). See pp. 64 and 78.

85. See, e.g., *Iliad* 9.312-13.

86. I am drawing on the reasons that Thucydides cites at 7.14.2 for Nicias' decision to send a letter containing a written report of the situation in Sicily, rather than entrusting an oral version to messengers. I discuss Nicias' letter in Chapter 4, pp. 76-81.

87. On the agonistic vocabulary, see above, n. 75. For excellent discussions of the visual and theatrical qualities of this section of narrative see Walker 1993, 355ff.; Jordan 2000; and Kallet 2001, 163-5. All three scholars highlight the ironic verbal echoes and inversions of the visual in the account of the send-off of the expedition from Piraeus (6.31). As Hornblower (1994a, 164) notes, Davidson 1991, 24 underestimates this passage when he comments that 'Thucydides' account is straightforward', and compares it unfavourably with Polybius' 'complex treatment of perception'.

88. Scholars have interpreted this passage in different ways. Lateiner 1985 relates Nicias' rhetoric either to the heroic age or a bygone political era: 'He retreats to an earlier world, in which a gentleman dealt with the rich only (trierarchs), swayed them by recalling their genealogy and tribe, their own exploits and their own ancestors' *aretê*' (ibid., 205). Zadorojnyi 1998, 301 sees an analogy between Nicias' appeal to ancestral virtues and families, and the terms of Nestor's exhortation at *Iliad* 15.661-6: 'Thucydides leaves the reader with the impression that Nicias' harangues and, generally, his command prove inefficient precisely because they are too Homeric, that is, anachronistic.' For criticism of Lateiner's and Zadorojnyi's arguments, see Rood 1998b (section 1); Rood interprets the Homeric resonances in this passage as reinforcing the seriousness of Nicias' appeals, rather than implying that Nicias' rhetoric is obsolete / anachronistic.

89. See Jordan 2000, 78 on the vocabulary of brilliance in this passage as a repetition of similar language at 6.31. Jordan argues that this repetition underscores the tragic irony of the end of the Sicilian expedition. On the ambiguity of the term *lamprotês* (brilliance / illustriousness) see Macleod 1983, 153, for the use of the term in Pericles' funeral speech (2.64.5).

90. See Kallet 2001, 37-8; Kallet argues that Alcibiades shows himself to be aware of the distinction between 'symbolic' capital and real capital.

91. On the fleet as 'spectacle', see Jordan 2000, 68: 'The chapters represent a spectacle, as at Olympia, or a scene, as in the theatre, in which the civilians are the spectators and the military the actors.' See also Hornblower 2004, 330-6, on Thucydides' description of the launching of the expedition.

92. 6.8.2; 6.23.1; 6.46. On the deceit of the Egestaeans, see Mader 1993 and Kallet 2001, 27-31 and 69-75.

93. Jordan 2000, 71 notes that *periboêtos* can have the more negative connotation 'notorious' or 'scandalous' and that *tolmê* can mean 'recklessness'.

94. On the motif of competition throughout the Sicilian expedition, see Jordan 2000, 63-5 and 77; see also Kallet 2001, 54.

95. In addition to the 'sight' vocabulary that I discuss in this paragraph, the following words also occur in 7.71.3: *horaô* ('I see'); *blepô* ('I look'); *opsis* ('sight'); and *aphoraô* ('to look in another direction').

96. See Davidson 1991, 16 for the idea of Polybius' *Histories* as 'a series of concentric circles of spectators, from the combatants in the centre to the remote reader in the twentieth century'.

97. I refer to this passage above, Chapter 1, p. 13.

98. Walker 1993, 355-6 discusses the harbour scenes in Piraeus and Syracuse in terms of the psychology of viewing and the disproportional impact of sight on the emotions.

99. See p. 48.

100. Crane 1996, 241-2 records that *skopeô* and the cognate verb *skeptomai* are Thucydides' favourite words for vision, and are used 38 times in the *History*.

101. See 5.1 where Thucydides refers to an episode in the preceding narrative with the phrase 'which I have revealed in my previous narrative' (*hê proteron moi dedêlôtai*). See also the plague narrative; especially 2.48.3 *tauta dêlôsô* ('I will reveal these things').

102. See Hedrick, Jr. 1993, 21 with n. 14 on the ambiguous status of writing as both visual and verbal.

103. Segal 1995, 214. For Thucydides' written text as a mimetic spectacle, see Moles 2001, 213: 'the historian also "looks" (1.1.3, 1.22.2-3), and then constructs his *mimesis*, at which the reader "looks" '.

104. Moles 1993, 110.

3. Temporal and Spatial Perspectives

1. See LSJ s.v. III, 2. Warner 1972, 349 translates this phrase as 'at about this same time'; similarly Crawley translates 'about the same time' (in Strassler (ed.) 1996, 303).

2. Allison 1997a, 55 writes of 'view[ing] the narrative at a distance, as a landscape'.

3. On linearity and its avoidance in Thucydides' narrative, see Rood 1998a, 109-11 ('Telling it Straight'). See also Hunter 1982, 166-9 on the pointlessness of linearity in Thucydides' conception of his *History*.

4. The most important work is Rood 1998a, ch. 5. Rood examines how the displacement of material from its chronological place ('anachrony') reflects Thucydides' judgement of its historical significance. Compare De Jong 2001 on anachrony in Herodotus' *Histories*.

5. Cf. Edmunds 1975a, 4, 'It is just this difference between the actor in history, facing the unknown future, and the historian, looking back on the better known past, on which the *History* is constructed'. See the discussion at pp. 15-16 above.

6. Stahl 2003 contains many judicious comments about the way in which repetitions within Thucydides' *History* establish patterns of recognition and prediction. See, e.g., the following comment (219): 'the work would fulfil the author's intention if today's readers, when being acquainted with the events and vicissitudes of Greek history as detailed by him, could likewise, in an act of recognition, gain clarity about constitutive elements of the history of their own time – elements which, though recurring with inescapable constancy, nevertheless, since being variables, cannot be completely calculated beforehand'. See also Moles 2001, 205 on the history's 'predictive power', which he differentiates from cyclical history.

7. See above, pp. 6 and 9.

8. On 'self-historicization' in Thucydides (and Herodotus), see above, Chapter 1, p. 10 with n. 45.

9. See Moles 2002, 214: 'The time frames of the narrative evoke future contexts. Foresight, commended within the text, is promoted by its very existence.'

10. See Macleod 1983, 58 who refers to Diodotus' remark that the assembly should deliberate about the future, rather than the present, and cites Aristotle *Rhetoric* 1358b13-15 for the view that the future is the proper sphere for political deliberation.

11. Cf. Hunter 1982, *passim*. Cf. also Hartog 1982, 25.

12. The adjective *palaios* and the adverbial phrase *to palai* occur 18 times in 1.1-21: 1.1.3; 1.2.1; 1.2.6; 1.3.1; 1.4.1; 1.5.1; 1.5.2; 1.6.5; 1.6.6; 1.7.1; 1.10.2; 1.13.4; 1.13.5 (*bis*); 1.15.1; 1.18.1; 1.20.1; and 1.21.1. For further chronological references in 1.1-12, see Hunter 1982, 43 with n. 45.

13. For a discussion of the chronology and Thucydides' motives in this passage, see Hornblower 1991, 236-9 (ad loc.); at p. 236 Hornblower cites the desire for solemnity as a motive for using six different chronological indicators, but also suggests the polemical, pedantic motive of wanting to 'correct' Hellanicus' chronology.

14. See Carson 2001, 3-4: 'Thucydides sets us on a high vantage point above such facts, so we look down as if at a map of the Greek states and see lives churning forward there – each in its own time zone, its own system of measures, its own local names. Soon this manifold will fuse into one time and system, under the name of war. But first we see it as hard separate facts.'

15. Cf. Konishi 1970, 116, on the *dêmos*' mistaken understanding of Athenian history and the repercussions of this misunderstanding in terms of their response to the alleged tyrannical plot in 415 BC. Cf. also ibid., 65-6, for the narrative parallels between the 'Archaeology' at the beginning of Book 1 and the 'Archaeology' at the beginning of Book 6 of the *History*.

16. On the catholic scope of the *History* and Thucydides' avoidance of parochialism, cf. Ridley 1981, 26. However, there are definite limits to the catholicity of the *History*. This is particularly evident when we contrast the cosmopolitan scope of Herodotus' *Histories* with the restricted perspective of Thucydides' *History*. See Dewald 1999, 248.

17. For clarification of this passage see Thomas 1989, 242-3.

18. Note the use of this adjective in the speech of the Spartan envoys (addressing the Athenian assembly) at 4.17.2; they describe their 'national' character with the phrase *epichôrion on hêmin* ('being "local" to us').

19. The noun *chôrion* denoting a 'passage' in a text occurs at Herodotus 2.117.1, in relation to the *Odyssey*, but some editors delete this word. In later writers this use is well established, cf. e.g. Lucian *How to Write History* 12: *to chôrion tês graphês* (a passage in a work). In ch. 33 of the same work, Lucian constructs an extensive territorial metaphor for the historian's *field* of research.

20. See pp. 62-3.

21. Herodotus also uses the motif of the 'reach of knowledge' in the following passages: 1.171.2 (on the Carians as subjects of Minos); 2.29.1 (on the source of the Nile); 2.34.1 (on the current of the Nile); and 4.31.2 (on the snow which the Scythians mistake for feathers).

22. See Moles 2001, 208 for a brief but excellent discussion of this phrase in the context of the spatial and temporal dimensions of Thucydides' statement about the scope of his work at 1.22.1-4. See also Luraghi 2001, 145.

23. On *kinêsis* as novelty or change, cf. D'Angour 1998, 11-12, who cites Aristotle's *Politics* (1268b26-1269a28). The superlative *megistê* gestures towards the 'inferior' themes of two of Thucydides' chief rivals – Homer and Herodotus.

24. Crane 1996, 140-6 argues that, although Thucydides suppresses discussion of individual, private households (*oikos, oikia* – see ibid., 126-7), the language of the family resurfaces in the way in which he discusses the relationship between the individual and the *polis* in the *History*. For example, whereas the ratio of household vocabulary in Thucydides' text in comparison to Herodotus' *Histories* is 46:100, Thucydides uses the adjective *oikeios* 2.93 times as often as Herodotus (ibid., pp. 127 and 141). Crane points out that 62 per cent of the instances of *oikeios* refer to one's homeland or ethnic group as a whole (145) and concludes: 'Thucydidean usage is thus pointed and polemical, for he uses the term *oikeios* to appropriate the traditional language of the *oikos* for the ideology of the *polis*, constructing a system in which state exercises domination over family' (146).

25. The adjective *akinêtos* (unchanged / unmoved) also has political connotations. The noun *kinêsis* is sometimes used to denote political turmoil, or radical political action. See Chapter 5, p. 86.

26. Edmunds 1975b does not comment on this motif.

27. Where *atopia* signifies 'having no place' on any existing intellectual, social or moral map.

28. Macleod 1983, 70 connects the Corinthians' critique to the criticism which Cleon levels at the Athenian assembly audience at 3.37-8.

29. Cf. Demosthenes 19.184. Macleod 1983, 69 comments, 'though Cleon is seen to be at fault, his view of the assembly, like Thersites' of Agamemnon, is allowed to contain some truth'.

30. 3.38.5. Cleon's language echoes Pericles' statement at 2.61.3, that what is sudden, unexpected and unlikely enslaves judgement (*douloi phronêma*). Hornblower 1991 cites Macleod's discussion of Cleon's use of the novelty motif: Macleod 1983, 70.

31. While the noun *huperoptai* is usually translated as 'disdainers', the verb from which it derives (*huperoraô*) means both to overlook / take no notice of and to despise [Warner mistakenly translates as 'are suspicious of', as though from *huphoraô*]; I have tried to span both senses with 'have no time for'. At one level, Cleon clearly does mean that the Athenians 'look down on' the familiar, but it also suits the Thucydidean motif of popular oversight (particularly in relation to past experience and how to respond to it), to retain the sense of 'overlook'. See Chapter 2, p. 26.

32. Compare Nicias' implied reasoning at 7.8.2 (see Chapter 4, p. 78). On this passage and the repudiation of memory cf. Edmunds 1993, 85. Cf. also Shrimpton 1997, 16.

33. On 'time' as a critico-ideological mechanism that can upset current régimes of knowledge, see Vidal-Naquet 1995, 26.

34. Cf. Connor 1984, 116 on the public reaction after the mutilation of the Herms: 'The *dêmos* thought it had the clear truth of the matter, just as it thought it understood the truth about the tyrants, the tyrannicide and its effects. Indeed, it was this belief in its knowledge of the murder of 514 that led it to act so harshly in the affairs of 415. It thought it saw a parallel between the two events.' More generally cf. Rutherford 1994, *passim* and Ober 1998, 54 with n. 4. Cf. also Loraux 1980, 145.

35. Macleod 1983, 70. Macleod refers to Nicias' warning to the assembly at 6.13.1, not to indulge in an 'ill desire for what lies in distant lands'. Cf. Hornblower 2004, 73. Both Macleod and Hornblower refer to Young 1968, who has an appendix on the theme of 'the Near and Far in Greek literature'. Cf. also Rood 1998, 177 (with n. 68) on the theme of 'longing for the remote'.

36. This is the very failure of vision that the Athenian envoys criticize in the Melian dialogue (5.103.1-2).

37. Rood 1998a, 161 with n. 10.

38. On thematic continuities between the Melian Dialogue and the Sicilian expedition, see Kallet 2001, 9-20.

39. *HCT* IV, 197 (ad loc.).

40. Kagan 1981, 165.

41. Hornblower 1994b, 147-8.

42. Pericles' authority is arguably undermined by an intratextual echo of his ancestor Cylon, who botched his attempt at a tyrannical take-over of Athens, 'thinking that he understood things correctly' (1.126.7).

43. Cf. also 2.65.1, where Pericles' speech distracts the Athenians from their 'present dire straits' (*paronta deina*), discussed on p. 70.

44. See further the discussion of Pericles' final speech, Chapter 4, pp. 70-1.

45. However, see Hornblower 1991, 341 (on 2.65.5) on Thucydides' misjudgement in crediting Pericles with foresight in the calculation of Athenian resources.

46. Cf. Hunter 1973, 28-9.

47. Cf. Ober 1998, 79-80. Wheeler 1988, 47 attributes the invention of *pronoia* as a military skill to Thucydides.

48. For illustrations of 'foresight in action', see the passages discussed by Hunter 1973: see her index under *pronoia*, *prognôsis*, prediction, forecast, prognostication, foresight and forewarning.

49. Hornblower 1994b, 132 discusses the connection between Thucydidean *pronoia* and the Hippocratic treatise *Prognostic*.

50. Compare Macleod 1983, 54-6 on the corruption of *krisis* in the Melian dialogue.

51. Compare Morrison 2000 on the historical lessons in the Melian dialogue, especially p. 137: 'From the reader's perspective at this point in the *History*, saying that the past is irrelevant goes against the entire spirit of Thucydides' work:

history is useful, similar sorts of things may happen in the future, study of the past may lead to learning.'

52. See p. 15 on Thucydides' new intellectual economy.

53. Contrast 8.1.1, where Thucydides observes sardonically that, when they heard about the failure of the Sicilian expedition, the Athenians grew angry at the *rhêtores* who had spoken in favour of the expedition, 'as if they themselves had not cast the vote'.

54. I am thinking of the contract between élite speakers and mass audiences described by Ober 1989.

55. Macleod 1983, 69 (cited at n. 29 above) argues that Cleon's rhetoric, although it contains some truth, is as flawed in contrast to that of Pericles.

56. See Kurke 2000, 154: 'Exile produced very different effects on the first great practitioners of *historiê*. For Herodotus, it was perhaps what inspired the "global vision" that informs his work, while for Thoukydides, it seems to have enabled the carving-out of a private space for meticulous writing and effortful reading.'

4. Speaking the Truth

1. In translating Gorgias' subtle and polysemous Greek, I risk simplifying the layered meaning of this passage. I have borrowed the phrase 'good quality in its men' as a translation for *euandria* from Wardy 1996, 29, whereas I have followed MacDowell 1982, 20 in translating *pragma* as 'action', while acknowledging that its range may be even vaguer (i.e. 'thing').

2. See Hornblower 1991, 59 (ad loc.): 'essentially *logographoi* were men who wrote about the past in prose'. For a discussion of the intellectual overlap between Thucydides and Gorgias, see Crane 1996, 217-20. See also Finley 1967, ch. 2.

3. Although Gorgias' *Encomium* emphasizes the psychology of the *spoken* word, *logos* has a broad range of meanings, including verbal account, verbal argument and spoken discourse (where verbal can imply either 'spoken' or 'written'). It is notable that Gorgias speaks of his motives for 'writing the speech' at the end of the text (21); however, since written texts were generally read out loud in the fifth century BC and silent reading was extremely rare, written works had a strong oral dimension. See above, pp. 16-17.

4. On Gorgias' visit, see Hornblower 1991, 427 (on 3.38.7).

5. On *kosmos* in Gorgias' *Encomium*, see the excellent discussion in Wardy 1996, 30. See also Cartledge 1998, 3-4: 'From the Cosmetic to the Cosmic'.

6. See above, pp. 4 and 21.

7. Section 42, trans. Usher (adapted).

8. See Crane 1998, 49 for a comparison between what he calls Thucydides' 'ideological realism' and Mark Twain's literary realism: 'He [sc. Twain] understood the Hesiodic trick of mixing true things with false (cf. Hes. *Theog.* 26-8), so that he could blur the realistic and the fantastic, making each reinforce the other. His procedural realism was fundamental to his success at creating idealized characters or situations that were at once incredible and convincing, and hence powerful.' Crane defines procedural realism as 'getting the facts straight' (ibid., 38). See above, Chapter 1, p. 7 with n. 34.

9. Trans. MacDowell 1982, 23-5 (adapted).

10. For comment on *sumboulos* and the theme of the insecurity of decision-making guided by belief, see Yunis 1996, 133.

11. See e.g. *Histories* 1.5.3; 1.95.1; 2.3.2; 2.18.1; 2.35.1; 4.82.

12. Dionysius of Halicarnassus reads Thucydides on these terms. See, for example, *On Thucydides* ch. 6, where he states that Thucydides 'did not give his writing over to deceit (*apatê*) and sorcery (*goêteia*)', contrasted with his predecessors. At section 10 of the *Encomium of Helen*, Gorgias refers to incantations that use speech as a medium for enchantment.

13. Hornblower 1991, 133 (ad loc.). For a recent discussion of the historical force of the Pentekontaëtia and its role in Thucydides' narrative, see the discussion of Rood 1998, ch. 10.

14. See, e.g., 2.103.2.

15. e.g. Herodotus *Histories* 2.123.1 and 4.30.1. On metanarrative in Herodotus, see now Munson 2001, ch. 1, especially pp. 20-4.

16. Hellanicus of Lesbos (*c.* 480-395 BC) is the earliest author known to have written a local history of Attica known as *Atthis*. See Hornblower 1991, 147 (ad loc.).

17. Although Thucydides does not mention Herodotus by name in this passage, or anywhere else in his *History* for that matter, he may be deliberately suppressing the extent to which the latter five books of Herodotus' *Histories* (Books 5-9) constitute a commentary on events in Herodotus' own time. In particular, scholars are increasingly inclined to read the last five books of Herodotus as an implicit analysis of the rise of Athenian imperialism. See Munson 2001, 3-4 and Moles 2002, *passim*, both with further bibliography.

18. Hornblower 1991, 148 (ad loc.) notes the Herodotean echo and observes that *apodeixis* is used only one other time in the *History* (2.13.9).

19. See Boedeker 2000, 98. See also Boedeker 2002, 109 on Herodotus' use of the noun *muthos*: 'for Herodotus, as for Aristotle, *muthos* is someone else's fabulous and incredible story'.

20. Boedeker 2000, 104.

21. For example, see Stesichorus' 'Palinode' (Stesichorus fr. 192), in which he revoked an earlier version that he had sung about the presence of Helen at Troy with the words 'that story (*logos*) is not true (*etumos*)'.

22. An example of such an exception are the admissions of uncertainty about the precise nature of events and the motives of individuals in Book 8, on which see Chapter 5, p. 90 with n. 33.

23. I have translated the Greek phrase '*hosa logôi eipon*' as 'the things that they said by way of argument' in order to get away from the idea that this passage refers only to speeches in direct discourse. As Wilson (1982, 101) and Laird (1999, 144) point out, there is nothing in the Greek text that suggests that *logos* should be understood as referring exclusively to speeches in direct discourse. Rather, it also incorporates the arguments that Thucydides renders in indirect discourse.

24. In making my translation, I have drawn on the interpretation of specific words put forward by the following scholars: *hosa logôi eipon* – 'the things that they said in argument' (Wilson 1982, 101; Laird 1999, 144); *akribeia* – 'precision' / 'precise details' (Crane 1996, 35); *diamnêmoneusai* – 'to carry word for word in one's memory' (Crane 1996, 71); *malista* – 'more or less' (Rusten 1989, 13 n. 44); *hê xumpasê gnômê* – 'ideas behind' (Wilson 1982, 99); *hôs emoi edokei* – 'according to ideas of my own' (Hornblower 1991, 60); *epexelthôn* – 'going in pursuit' (Connor 1984, 28; Crane 1996, 36). I have also found the literal translation of Moles 2001, 199 very helpful.

25. See Hornblower 1994b, 19 (with n. 13) and 1991, 58 (on 1.20.3). Allison 1997a, 231-2 and 236, makes this point in greater detail, drawing on the discussions of Nagy (1990, 58-9) and other scholars. At pp. 206-37, Allison offers a thorough and instructive discussion of the use of *alêtheia* in Thucydides, in which she argues that, in Thucydides, *alêtheia* is properly used of verbal accounts, not of 'what exists'.

26. Wilson 1982, 102; Allison 1997a, 223; Crane 1996.

27. On the technology of writing and its impact on cognitive processes in ancient Greece and Rome see Small 1997, *passim*. Small discusses the concept of 'accuracy as gist' on p.193. Compare Moles 2001, 209: 'the licence claimed by Thucydides for his speeches reflects the information deficit of a predominantly oral society'.

28. The use of modern recording technology is not without *ponos*; Small 1997, 192 cites Michael Agar for the statistic that it takes him eight hours to transcribe one hour of tape, and that further runs / drafts are required.

29. Compare Potter 1999, 79: 'Even with the aid of modern technologies like the videotape, we must realize that factors such as camera angle, light or timing may (and do) prevent the production of a record that is "completely accurate". And even if one could obtain a flawless visual record of some moment in time, it would need to be supplemented with material to assist the other senses: what was heard, felt, smelled, thought or tasted as something happened.'

30. See Partner 1995, 33 on 'primary' and 'secondary' categories of fiction, where the primary category ('the creation of form in language') is distinguished from the secondary category ('the invention of imaginary descriptions of events and persons'). See also the discussion of Hornblower 1994a, 131-3 on fiction and the rhetoric of history, from the perspective of narratology; and Rood 1998a, 9-10 on fiction in history (also from the perspective of narratology). Laird 1999, ch. 4 offers a rigorous discussion of speeches in historical narrative and distinguishes between the presentation of speeches in fiction and the presentation of speeches in factual narrative.

31. 'Improvisation' is the term suggested by Laird 1999, 152 in order to side-step the problematic associations of 'invention'.

32. On narrative history as a 'transcription' of reality, see Dewald 1999, 222.

33. Edmunds 1993, 835-6. See also Dover 1973, 3 who lists contexts in which this verb was used.

34. Loraux 1986; Edmunds 1993. Cf. also Crane 1996, 28, who discusses the role of the verb *xungraphô* in constructing the authority that Thucydides claims for his text.

35. Ober 1998, 56 offers a good discussion of this passage, concluding that, 'The truth of the war is no longer a matter of verbal persuasion or interpretation. It has become a self-evident matter of visual perception.'

36. See Pelling 2000, 115.

37. Macleod 1983, 52; Connor 1984, 273; Hornblower 1987, 46 (with n. 7); Zadorojnyi 1998, 299.

38. Debnar 2001, 2.

39. See Ober 1989, *passim*. See also Chapter 1, p. 4 above.

40. This point is made by Yunis 2003, 202: 'Are the speeches meant to be effective for the original audience being addressed by the speaker, as the formal commitment to the narrative suggests, or are they meant to be effective for Thucydides' audience, the person reading the text?'

41. Williams 2002, 165.

42. Many scholars have remarked that Thucydides kills Pericles off 'prematurely', in that he gives him his final speech in the year 430 BC, whereas Pericles did not die until late in 429 BC. See, e.g., Woodman 1988, 35. Halliwell 2002, 76 argues that Thucydides omits a discussion of Pericles' death quite deliberately, in order to avoid the emotional overtones that it would introduce into the work. In this way he is able to preserve the image that he has constructed of Pericles as a dispassionate, rational leader who transcends the emotional weaknesses and vulnerabilities of the Athenian demos. Cf. especially ibid., 76.

43. Good discussions of this speech include: Edmunds 1975, 70-5; Yunis 1996, 83-5; Ober 1998, 89-94.

44. On learning from history and Thucydides' *History*, see Rutherford 1993, *passim* and Morrison 2000 (on historical lessons in the Melian dialogue).

45. The speeches of Cleon and Diodotus in the Mytilene debate would also be close contenders. See the discussions of Ober 1998, 94-104; and Hesk 2000, 248-55.

46. For the idea of a 'turning point', compare Yunis 1996, 67: 'Thucydides declares a turning point in Athens' fortunes after Pericles' death (2.65.5-7): Athens reached the height of her greatness under Pericles' leadership; his policy for conducting the war was sound, but after his death the Athenians abandoned that policy and, pursuing private goals rather than the public good, they endangered the *polis*'.

47. Ober 1998, 81 notes that Pericles' are the only speeches by an Athenian politician not countered or paired with opposing speeches.

48. See Westlake 1968, 37: 'This is the speech of a brave man. Only a brave man would have refused to appease the assembly, and indeed have adopted a most unconciliatory attitude, when he well knew that, in theory at least, he might have been condemned to death.' However, we need to ask to what extent the bravery is a feature of the Thucydidean, as opposed to the historical, Pericles. On the construction of Pericles' 'heroic rationalism', see below, n. 63.

49. See 6.8.2 where Thucydides uses this adjective in a comment on a speech delivered by Egestaean ambassadors in front of the Athenian assembly: 'they said many other things that were seductive (*epagôgos*) and not true'. Compare the adjective *prosagôgos* (enticing) at 1.21.1 (see pp. 21 and 37 above).

50. On the contrast between the changeability of the demos and the resolution of Pericles see Edmunds 1975, 70 and Rusten 1989, 198.

51. 'Each situation' is Rex Warner's translation of *ta aiei paronta* (p. 47).

52. *Contra* Macleod 1983, 52, who distinguishes between *ta deonta* in this passage (2.60.5), which he interprets as 'necessary advice', and the same phrase at 1.22.1, where he interprets it as referring to 'those elements of a speech which make it coherent or persuasive, the valid presentation of a "case" '.

53. Hornblower 1991, 333 (ad loc.) comments: 'Thucydides here gives Pericles a slightly softened, and more rhetorically appropriate, version of the more usual charge that the Athenian assembly preferred to blame anybody *except* themselves.'

54. See 7.48.4 where Nicias refuses to put the proposal to retreat from Sicily to the vote, on the grounds that, if the Athenians were to vote for a retreat, they would turn on the generals when they got back to Athens and suppress their own role in voting for the retreat. Rood 1998, 190 n. 33 compares Nicias' views about the Athenian assembly with observations by 'Pericles' at 1.140.1, 2.61.2, 2.64.1, and by Diodotus at 3.43.5. Hornblower 1991, 330 (on 2.59.2 and 8.1.1) refers to Ps.-Xenophon, *Constitution of the Athenians* 2.17.

55. *On Thucydides* 44-5.

56. Cf. Cole 1991, 81-9, on Thucydides' speeches as paradigms of political rhetoric (I was alerted to Cole's argument by Zadorojnyi 1998, 298).

57. There is some debate about the meaning of the adverb *eleutherôs* in this passage. Following Edmunds and Martin 1977 and Rusten 1989, 210, I interpret the phrase to mean that 'Pericles exercised complete independence in controlling the mass'. Cf. Greenwood 2004, 184-5, with n. 29.

58. For a careful discussion of the potential relationship between Socrates, Socratic literature and Thucydides, see Hornblower 1994b, 122-6.

59. See the argument of Ober 1998, cited above at p. 8.

60. On the ideology behind Thucydides' obituary for Themistocles, see Ober 1998, 79-81.

61. Macleod 1983, 145 and Rusten 1989 (ad loc.) point out that the claim 'better to be envied than to be pitied' is a commonplace of Greek aristocratic thought. However, the reader should also be alert to the way in which Thucydides makes this conventional sentiment jar in the context of a speech to the Athenian assembly, particularly in view of the disconcerting analogies between Athens' imperial subjects and the Athenian demos.

62. On the distinction between metaphorical and literal medical language, see Swain 1994, 308.

63. Edmunds 1975, 72-3 comments that 'Pericles puts the whole matter of the Athenians' misfortunes [...] in terms of their effect upon the minds of the Athenians'. Edmunds puts forward a convincing argument for Pericles' 'heroic rationalism' in Thucydides' *History*, and argues that Pericles' reliance on intelligence and judgement in the face of all eventualities would have been blatantly counter-cultural.

64. Halliwell 2002, 70-2.

65. Halliwell 2002, 70-1.

66. See Swain 1994, 305.

67. Kallet-Marx 1993 and Kallet 2001.

68. I have argued elsewhere that the substitution of the written word for the spoken word is an integral part of Thucydides' historiography and is reflected, primarily, in the speeches (Greenwood 2004).

69. See Allison 1997a, 227: 'It is another way by which Thucydides can examine the relationship of words to events. This further accounts for the complex arrangements or effort at verisimilitude surrounding the presentation of the letter.'

70. The secretary (*grammateus*) referred to here was employed to read documents aloud to the citizen body in the Assembly. See *HCT* IV ad loc. (p. 387).

71. Westlake 1968, 190.

72. Lang 1995.

73. Allison 1997a, 210: there is a full discussion of the connotations of *alêtheia* in Thucydides at ibid., pp. 206-37.

74. I cite the Greek text from the Oxford Classical Text edition of Thucydides, where the editor prints *mnêmês*, following an eleventh-century manuscript (Vaticanus 126); however, the remaining medieval manuscripts have *gnômês*. If the latter is the correct reading, then it would serve to strengthen the emphasis on Nicias' anxiety about getting his considered view and arguments across to the Athenians.

75. See above, p. 64.

76. Edmunds' antithesis between Pericles as the embodiment of *gnômê* and Nicias as the embodiment of *tuchê* overlooks the role of *gnômê* in the characterization of Nicias (1975, 139-42).

77. See Kallet 2001, 151-9.

78. On Homeric patterns and allusions to Homer in the narrative of the Sicilian expedition, see Avery 1973, Lateiner 1985, Zadorojnyi 1998, Mackie 1996, Allison 1997b and Rood (1998b), who qualifies all of these studies; Rood's article stresses that the heavy focus on allusions to Homeric epic in previous scholarship risks obscuring the range of different inter-generic allusions in Books 6 and 7, which encompass epic (not just Homeric epic), tragedy, historiography (especially Herodotus) and – Rood suggests – lyric and epigram as well. Kallet 2001, 97-120 also discusses allusions to Homeric epic in Books 6 and 7, but rightly stresses the close inter-dependence of allusions to Homer and Herodotus and counsels that Thucydides' use of Homer is multi-faceted (see p. 98). See further p. 151 n. 23 below.

79. 1998, 298: 'The detail about decaying timbers in the context of Nicias' letter could not help striking educated Greek readers, who, like Thucydides himself, had Homer at their fingertips, as an echo of Agamemnon's words in *Iliad* 2.135. I argue that Thucydides intends the reminiscence to be perceived and, moreover, uses it to trigger our understanding that the figure of Nicias should be read against that of the Homeric Agamemnon'. See Rood's criticism of this argument in the article referred to in n. 78 above.

80. I note Kallet's tentative suggestion that this statement alludes to a passage in Herodotus *Histories* (6.12) where Herodotus comments, in the style of ethnographic writing, that the Ionians were too undisciplined and unaccustomed to toil to submit to the full training programme laid out for them by the Phocaian commander Dionysius (2001, 93). However, I think that Nicias' comment is better explained in terms of a provocative rhetorical topos about the potential ungovernability of the Athenian demos and its capacity for poor government.

81. 1994b, 39-40.

82. Several scholars have observed the militaristic overtones of the participle *epexelthôn*, which I have translated as 'going in pursuit of'. Crane 1996, 36 notes that Thucydides uses this term to describe an army launching itself into an assault on the enemy. More generally, Crane has an excellent discussion on Thucydides' self-depiction as a 'heroic researcher' in this passage. See above, Chapter 2, n. 79.

83. Loraux 1980. See ibid., 68: 'the omissions, the silences, the gaps are only there in our minds, since we do not think of history in the same terms as him' (my translation).

5. New Theatres of War: Book 8 and Sophocles' *Philoctetes*

1. Crane 1996, 256.

2. Contrast Herodotus' *Histories* where scholars have argued, convincingly, that the ending that we have is deliberate. See Dewald 1997, *passim*.

3. See Rawlings 1981, ch. 5 ('Books "IX" and "X": Thucydides' plan').

4. Cf. Pelling 2000, 93: 'our methodology must still be to begin by addressing the text as we have it, and provisionally expect it to make literary and interpretative sense'.

5. See *HCT* V, 374. Drawing an analogy with the political climate of modern Greece in the early 1970s, Hammond suggests that in 404 BC, when Thucydides returned to Athens, it may have been too dangerous, from a political standpoint, to write up the period of events from 410 BC to the present (1973, 59).

6. Flory 1993, *passim*.

7. Ober 1998, 120.

8. On innovations in Thucydides' narrative technique in Book 8 see Connor 1984, 215-17; Rood 1998a, ch. 11 (esp. pp. 251-3); and Kallet 2001, 227-8.

9. See McCoy 1973 on the 'non-speeches' in Book 8.

10. See Gribble 1998, 63-6: ' "Casual" narrator interventions and book 8'.

11. Connor 1984, 217: 'The omniscient narrator is replaced by a fellow inquirer who, at least from time to time, stops to look more closely at motives, admits his uncertainties and explains his reasoning.'

12. Allison 1997a, 85-100: 'Book 8: the strategy of composition'.

13. See, for example Rawlings 1981, 177-8: 'Thus book VIII seems both incomplete and unpolished, a truncated first draft.' More generally, see *HCT* V, 361-83 on 'Indications of Incompleteness' in the *History*. Dover surveys apparent indications of incompleteness in Book 8 in relation to the other books of the *History* (for Book 8 in particular, see pp. 369-75).

14. See, e.g., Rawlings 1981, 211 on Phrynichus' speech at 8.48.4-7: 'Thucydides clearly found Phrynichus' remarks to the conspirators percipient. Did he intend to raise them to the level of a direct speech in a final draft?' However, Dionysius of Halicarnassus cites Cratippus, who was a contemporary of Thucydides and was allegedly entrusted with the task of editing the *History*, for the view that Thucydides had come to realize that speeches impede the action, and consequently excluded speeches from the last parts of the *History* (*On Thucydides* 16).

15. Macleod 1983, 141: 'If Book 8 is in some ways odd and exceptional, that is partly because the historian has to find a way of beginning again after so triumphantly concluding his work; and its more tentative and less dramatic style may indicate not so much that he had not thought through his material, as that he was seeking new ways of presenting it, and felt he had a different kind of material to present.' Compare Gribble 1998, 66: 'But the greater fragmentation of Book 8, and the increased use of narratorial voice to mediate between focalizations on relatively unimportant points, seem to me more likely to represent a conscious decision for a different type of narrative than evidence of a first draft.' See also Connor 1984, 217.

16. Connor 1984, 201-11.

17. ibid., 210.

18. On 'fragmentation' see Rood 1998a, 253 and Kallet 2001, 228; on 'disintegration' see Connor 1984, 215.

19. See 8.66.5, where Thucydides observes that among those who participated in the oligarchic revolution were those whom one would never have thought capable of resorting to oligarchy. Cf. also 8.68.4, where Thucydides comments on the difficulty of engineering an oligarchic coup in Athens, of all places.

20. *Kinêsis* is an important motif for Thucydides; it is introduced in the opening chapter of the *History*. See p. 48.

21. See 6.11.7, where Nicias tells the Athenian assembly that the Egestaeans, who are supposedly their allies, and who have appealed to them to intervene in Sicily, are 'barbarians'.

22. On Thucydides' instruction to the reader in the Melian dialogue, see Morrison 2000. See above, Chapter 2, p. 24 with n. 32.

23. In recent years there has been much discussion about the 'generic' echoes at the close of Thucydides' account of the Sicilian expedition. It is broadly agreed that he echoes both Herodotus (Athenian expedition to Sicily: Xerxes' invasion of Greece) and Homer (Athenian expedition to Sicily: Achaean expedition to Troy), as well as Homer *through* Herodotus, but the precise nature of these echoes and their implications are debated. For the idea of the Sicilian expedition as an Odyssean quest, see Mackie 1996. Allison 1997b, *passim*, esp. p. 515, links Thucydides' account of the close of the Sicilian expedition to the (Homeric) epic theme of return and survival. Rood 1998b (section 3) criticizes Mackie's 'implausibly detailed correspondences', and argues that Allison distorts Thucydides by insisting on allusions that are too specific, yet at the same time allowing these allusions to apply to several different passages in Homer. Cf. also p. 149 n. 78 above.

24. In the Greek text, the phrase 'for those who were destroyed it was the most wretched' is an iambic trimeter – echoing the iambic trimeter (a line of three iambic units) that was typically used for dialogue in Greek tragedy. See Rood 1998b, 4.3 with n. 86 and Hornblower 2004, 351 and 366.

25. Several scholars have read the noun *panôlethria* as a double reference: first to Herodotus, and ultimately to Homer, since the noun occurs in a context where Herodotus refers to the fall of Troy (2.120.5) as an act of divine retribution. Marinatos Kopff and Rawlings 1978 argue that the use of this Herodotean phrase implies that Thucydides also wanted to import the theology implicit in Herodotus' passage, too. For discussion see Hornblower 1994b, 148 with n. 8; Connor 1984, 208-9 with n. 57; Rood 1998a, 163; and Kallet 2001, 114.

26. See Price 2001, 360. On the use of comparative and superlative adjectives in the characterization of Alcibiades in Book 6, see Jordan 2000, 64 with n. 3. On the ring composition see Hornblower 1994b, 148.

27. Price 2001, 361. Rood 1998b, 4.2 discusses the fact that Thucydides defines the Sicilian expedition as *'ergon touto hellênikon'* at 7.87.5 and argues that this phrase, combined with the phrase *'megiston ergon'* (greatest action) has a Herodotean feel to it. Accordingly, Rood argues that Thucydides' summary of the Sicilian expedition echoes patterns of commemoration that we find in Herodotus.

28. On *apenostêsan* see Allison 1997, 512-14, with the criticism of Rood 1998b (section 4.1).

29. Cf. Rood 1998b, 4.1.

30. See Hornblower 2004, 349-52 for a discussion of *apenostêsan* and the *nostos* of the athlete in Pindar.

31. Avery 1973 argues that Thucydides characterizes the Athenians in terms of *elpis* and optimism. Thus this passage marks a shift in character – the Spartans take on characteristics that were previously associated with the Athenians. 'They [sc. the Athenians] now experience the same sense of helplessness (8.1.2: *anelpistoi*) that the troops in the field had felt. But if we read further we feel that the shift has been complete, for one result of the Syracusan victory is that the Lacedaimonians are now – *euelpides*! (8.2.4), ready to prosecute the war vigorously, thinking that they will win easily'. See also Stahl 2003, 198. Hornblower 2004, 347-8 discusses the theme of the reversal of Athenian hopes in Thucydides' description of the beginning and end of the Sicilian expedition.

32. Dover *HCT* V, p. 6 (ad loc.), argues that there are muted oligarchic overtones in the language that Thucydides uses to describe the election of the *probouloi*, but no indication of explicit oligarchic intentions at this stage.

33. See Gribble 1998, 65.

34. The suspicion that he arouses is an important part of the characterization of Alcibiades in the *History*. See 6.61.4 ('Alcibiades was surrounded by suspicion on all sides') and 6.89.1 and 6.92.2, where Alcibiades acknowledges and attempts to refute the Spartans' suspicions of him.

35. See the discussion of *didaskalia* (2.42.1) above, Chapter 2, p. 24 with n. 31.

36. Plutarch uses the same verb (as a substantive) in relation to Theramenes – the double conspirator – in his *Life of Nicias* 2.1-2.

37. See Gribble 1998, 66: 'The action Thucydides chooses to describe in this book (the complex Greek-Persian diplomacy, the revolution of 411) is more minute than in any previous section of narrative, the general themes less clear.'

38. Compare Thucydides' exposure of Brasidas' false speeches at 4.108.5 and 4.122.6.

39. Steiner 1994, 221 connects this secret exchange of letters with the substitution of the written word for the spoken word, which is a defining feature of Thucydides' account of the oligarchic coup.

40. The claim that Astyochus colluded with Tissaphernes with a view to private gain is repeated at 8.83.3.

41. On Peisander's speech see McCoy 1973, 80-2; Yunis 1996, 114-15; and Taylor 2002, 96-100.

42. Monoson 2000, 16.

43. On the negative associations of *ochlos* in the *History* see Hunter 1988, 17.

44. See Kallet 2001, 263 with n. 112: 'The phrase "abundance of hope of pay" is a nice touch: hope will be what is abundant, not pay.' Cf. 6.24.3, where Thucydides cites the desire for a source of 'ongoing pay' as one of the chief factors that motivated the mass of poorer Athenians to vote for the Sicilian campaign in 415 BC.

45. LSJ s.v. II, 3.

46. Aristophanes, *Acharnians* 162-3.

47. Taylor 2002, 95: 'Thucydides crafts the episode to highlight the men's love of money and to suggest that they have little love for anything else. No one opposes the oligarchic proposals for longer than a moment. The crowd of *thêtes* themselves (*ho men ochlos*) those men almost certainly to be disenfranchised by any oligarchic movement – are upset only for the moment, so long as they can be assured of money from the King. The implication is that this mass of men cares little about ideology, office-holding or voting rights in the assembly, but only about pay.'

48. In addition, the Four Hundred introduce specious terms, such as the government of the 'Five Thousand' – which have no basis in reality. At 8.92.11 the hoplites who are attempting to overthrow the Four Hundred 'concealed themselves behind the name of the Five Thousand', afraid to use the term 'democracy' outright.

49. Cf. Hunter 1988, 20 in relation to Thuc. 6.17.4.

50. See Loraux 1991, *passim* and 1997, ch. 4.

51. The status of the deme Colonus in relation to the civic space of the city is explored in Sophocles' late tragedy *Oedipus at Colonus*, cf. Allison 1984. Edmunds 1996, 100-1 argues that the play rewrites the existing politico-geographical code of the *polis*.

52. Cf. Connor 1994, 38. Cf. also Croally 1994, 205-6 for the way in which war has a tendency to change spatial organisation (in reference to the *Troades*); and Goldhill 1996, 246.

53. Cf. Xenophon, *Anabasis* V.6.15-16.

54. Furthermore, as Paul Cartledge pointed out to me, the 'ideal' of the troops in Sicily as a movable *polis* is further fractured by the fact that the troops are a diverse community of Athenians and allies.

55. Raaflaub 1996, 157: 'As long as the *thêtes* did not serve as hoplites, they were *a priori* excluded from the training and rituals that prepared the Athenian males for their function as citizens [...]. As far as the social and institutional recognition of their military role was concerned, not all citizens were equal. In status and prestige the *nautai* clearly were considered inferior to the hoplites and horsemen.'

56. Cf. Amit 1965, 63-4. The close identification of the fleet with democracy is seen in the tradition of naming triremes after democratic slogans. See Hansen 1996, 92 and Strauss 1996, 318.

57. Cf. Aristotle, *Politics* 1340a122-4. Cf. also Loraux 1973a, 39.

58. For the logistics cf. *HCT* V, ad loc. (pp. 269-70). The fleet at Samos, *qua* substitute *dêmos*, even minted Athenian coins. Cf. Amit, 1965, 66-7.

59. The idea of tangible, physical buildings, and of a circuit wall, was central to traditional conceptions of the *polis*. These criteria can be traced back to the image of the *polis* in Homeric epic (see Scully 1990). The notion of a movable *polis* cuts across deeply entrenched ideas.

60. See Gabrielsen 1994, 39 for comment.

61. See the discussion of Ober 2001, 285-7.

62. Kallet-Marx 1993, Kallet 2001.

63. For the election of the emergency *probouloi* after the Sicilian expedition see Thuc. 8.1.3 (see p. 89 above). Ps.-Aristotle, *Constitution of the Athenians* 29.2

states that twenty additional special advisers were appointed in 411 BC. Aristotle (*Rhetoric* 1419a25ff.) cites the case of Sophocles who voted for the Four Hundred as *proboulos* (Jameson 1971, *passim*). Calder 1971, 174 has suggested that *Philoctetes* is Sophocles' *apologia*, in hindsight, for having endorsed the régime of the Four Hundred. In the same vein, Edmunds 1996, 10 and 92 argues that *Oedipius at Colonus* apologises for events in Colonus (Sophocles' deme) in 411 BC.

64. Commenting on the historical allusions in Euripides' *Orestes*, Pelling remarks: 'The audience's memories of these events and of their own reactions to these events will affect the way they respond to what they see on stage' (2000, 186). Hesk 2003, 32 conceives of the overlapping historical and epic frames of reference for Sophocles' *Ajax* as a 'dialectic between Homeric intertext and Athenian context'. Rose's 1995 study of Sophocles' *Ajax* attempts to reconstruct contemporary debates through the images of social and political relations in the tragedy.

65. See Jameson 1956. On the limitations of one-to-one allegories, see Pelling 2000, 166 (discussing allegorising readings of Euripides' *Orestes*).

66. Bowie 1997, 61.

67. Hesk 2000, 189; Hesk analyses *Philoctetes* as a critique of the idea of the 'noble lie' (ibid., 188-201).

68. I have found Easterling's approach to the difficulty of reconciling what she terms 'heroic vagueness' with historical context particularly useful. Easterling identifies 'images of the community' in Greek tragedy as one point of entry in trying to identify allusions to the political community of the audience (1997, 28-9).

69. In the opening lines of Sophocles' *Ajax* (3-4), Ajax occupies the frontier land between sea and inhabited space. See Buxton 1994, 103 on the shore as a boundary where opposites meet, and 106 for the withdrawal of the marginalized hero to the shore. See also Rehm 2002, 138 on Sophocles' Lemnos as an 'eremetic space'. At pp. 139-40 Rehm discusses different hypotheses about the significance of this 'eremetic' space.

70. 1987, 72. According to this interpretation of the play's staging, it is not clear how to account for the initial entrance of Philoctetes at line 218. Cf. more recently, Craik 1990, 83. For my argument, all that is important is that the audience's attention is focused on one *eisodos* as the route to and from the sea.

71. This anxiety over orientation may also be construed as a personal dilemma about how to orientate one's conduct and whether to uphold or betray one's inner convictions (cf. Goldhill 1990, 121-2). This is an aspect of the play that I am unable to treat in detail, although it has some bearing on the crisis of civic conscience about the relation of the city to the *patrios politeia* that surfaced in 411 BC. See p. 104 with n. 94.

72. Translation taken from Schein 2003 (in the following text I indicate wherever I use Schein's translation).

73. See Rehm 2000, 142, who discusses Sopchocles' 'layering of language onto landscape'.

74. LSJ s.v. IV, 2.

75. For on-stage and off-stage geography in the play, see Taplin 1987.

76. On the relevance of myths and cults connected with the setting, see Segal 1981, 307 and Rehm 2000, 138-9. Sophocles also wrote a (lost) play, the *Lemnian Women*.

77. Cf. Meiggs 1972, 424-25. A 'cleruchy' was a special sort of colony where the settlers preserved their original citizenship and maintained close ties with the *polis* from which they had come.

78. See Budelmann 2000, 97-8.

79. On the introduction of other places apart from the scene into the imagination of the audience, see Croally 1994, 175-6. Easterling 1983, 226-7 discusses the 'double significance' of Troy in *Philoctetes*. Budelmann 2000, 107 sees Philoctetes' desire to go to Malis as a potentially disruptive counterplot that plays with the audience's expectations based on previous versions of the myth.

80. However, as Easterling notes (1983, 218), the role of the prophecy in the plot is highly ambiguous and does not lead to rigid determinism. For further discussion of the prophecy see ibid., 221-4.

81. Gould 1996, 220. Cf. Goldhill 1996, 247 (response to Gould 1996) on the need to say more about the choice of identity and role for any given tragic chorus.

82. See Cartledge 1997, 16-17. For socio-economic and political tensions between the Athenian 'centre' and its harbour, see von Reden 1995, *passim*.

83. Pelling 1997, 1 (with n. 1) gives an overview of these studies.

84. Budelmann 2000, 232. See also Rose (1995, 69-70), who sees in the portrayal of Sophocles' *Ajax* the contemporary image of a navy-orientated military commander and discusses the play's representation of a military hierarchy.

85. Nautical vocabulary pervades the play: *naustolein* (to sail), *nautês* (sailor), *naus* (ship), *plous* (voyage), *nautilos* (sailor), *nauklêros* (sea-merchant), *naubatês* (seafarer), *stolos* (fleet) and *nautikon strateuma* (naval force).

86. Trans. Schein 2003, 88.

87. Taplin 1987, 75: the *nostos* is the return to Greece, not the immediate return to Troy. Cf. Rehm 2002, 149.

88. Croally 1994, 206.

89. Andrewes 1953, 2. Although the fleet was based in Samos it did operate as far North as the Hellespont.

90. Vidal-Naquet 1988a, *passim*; Winkler 1990, *passim*; Goldhill 1990, 118-23; and Hesk 2000, 188-99.

91. Taplin 1987, 73 and Easterling 1997, 33 n. 47, highlight the Greek army at Troy as the only image of a community within the play.

92. On the distortion of the assembly see Finley 1975, 35, and on the exclusion of *nautai* from political decision-making owing to occupational absences see Rosivach 1985, 51-3.

93. See Plutarch, *Life of Pericles* 24.5.

94. On the '*patrios politeia*' cf. Finley 1975, ch. 2: 'The Ancestral Constitution'), who reconstructs the late fifth-century debate. See also Strauss 1993, 25.

95. Trans. Schein 2003, 26.

96. Schein's note on these lines is helpful: 'Odysseus, in his intrigue against Philoktetes, is made, as it were, a representative not only of the Greek army but of contemporary Athens.' Cf. also Vidal-Naquet 1988, 171 on Sophocles' deliberate casting of Odysseus as an Athenian politician in these lines.

97. Trans. Schein 2003, 36.

98. LSJ s.v. 3.

99. We find this topos in the Mytilene debate, where Diodotus draws a contrast between the accountability that falls on political advisers, contrasted with the *dêmos* which is an 'unaccountable audience' (Thucydides 3.43.4-5). See *HCT* V, p. 5 (ad loc.), where Dover refers to Pericles' speech at 2.60.4 and 64.1. See also p. 55 above.

100. See, e.g., Neoptolemus' statement at lines 925-6: 'both what is right and / what is expedient make me heed those in authority'. In Sophocles' *Ajax* Agamemnon asserts his authority with a similar dictum: 'the noble man must listen to those in authority' (1352). Perhaps the most vivid example of the individual clashing with the hierarchy of militarized human power is Antigone in Sophocles' play of that name.

101. Cf. King 1987, 67: 'As we examine Neoptolemus' actions we shall find that our attention is directed to *Iliad* 9, the quarrel with Agamemnon and the rejection of the embassy.'

102. Bowie 1997, 59 n. 154 gives additional references.

103. He is addressed fourteen times with circumlocutions involving Achilles – cf. King 1987, 67 and Bowie 1997, 60.

104. The idea of the changed circumstances of the war and the changed policies of the post-Periclean generals are prominent features of Thucydides' account. Cf. Strauss 1993, 14-15 on father-son conflict as an ideological motif in the later stages of the Atheno-Peloponnesian War: 'it was a theme perfectly suited to symbolize conflicts between generations, between tradition and novelty, between the differing conceptions of authority among oligarchs and democrats, and between go-slow "mature" war policies and "youthful" gung-ho adventurism'.

105. *Politics* 1304b10.

106. Wilson 1996, 321 even suggests that the concept of 'politics as theatre' was a factor in the decision of the pro-democratic hoplites to hold an assembly to discuss the overthrow of the Four Hundred in the Theatre of Dionysus at Mounychia (*History* 8.93): 'as though there was a connection between this site of heightened dramatic action, especially of tragedy, and the drama of such politics'. Cartledge 1997, 14 points out the connection between theatre and war in 403 BC when the democratic forces who rose up against the Oligarchic junta met for battle in the theatre of Piraeus.

107. Xenophon, *Hellenica* 2.3.31. Plutarch, *Life of Nicias* 2.1-2 also states this nick-name.

108. Wilson 1996, 320-4.

109. See Rehm 2002, 154-5.

110. Worman 2002, 140 observes that: '[Odysseus] trains others to deploy the misrepresentational techniques that constitute his typical style [...] The lying hero thus serves as a stage manager who masks his presence by using Neoptolemus and the merchant to trick Philoctetes into relinquishing his bow.' More generally on the theme of acting, disguise and deception, see ibid., 139-44.

111. Budelmann 2000, 101.

112. Stahl 2003, 135-6.

6. Reading Thucydides with Lucian

1. For Dionysius of Halicarnassus, see Chapters 1, 2 and 4 above. For Aineias Tacticus, see Chapter 2, pp. 28-9 above.

2. See above, p. 3 with n. 10.

3. For the idea that Thucydides encourages the reader to envisage his text as an inscribed monument, see Moles 1999, cited above, Chapter 1, p. 9.

4. See above, Chapter 1, p. 7.

5. On Thucydides' bias, see Roberts 1982, ch. 7, for the view that, as a general who had himself been impeached, Thucydides was biased against the *dêmos* in his representation of the impeachment trials of Athenian generals. For another aspect of Thucydides' bias, see Badian 1993, ch. 4. Badian argues that Thucydides distorted the motives surrounding the outbreak of the Atheno-Peloponnesian War in order to blame the origins of the conflict on Spartan expansionism. See also Dionysius of Halicarnassus' criticism of Thucydides' allegedly anti-Athenian bias in the *Letter to Gnaeus Pompeius* 3 (Usher, pp. 372-3) and *On Thucydides* 41. However, as Matthew Fox notes (2001, 81), the fact that Thucydides frequently represents the Athenians in a bad light, which Dionysius interprets as evidence of unpatriotic bias, is taken by Lucian as a sign of Thucydides' impartiality and lack of bias on the grounds that he is able to transcend loyalty to his native *polis* (*How to Write History*, 38).

6. *How to Write History*, ch. 42.

7. On cultural identity in Lucian, see Saïd 1994, Whitmarsh 2001, Elsner 2001 and Goldhill 2002b. On Lucian and historiography, see primarily Georgiadou and Larmour 1994 and 1998; see also Anderson 1994 and Bartley 2003.

8. The title *True Stories* is a pointed oxymoron. Most scholars use the Latin title *Verae Historiae* (abbreviated to *VH*), and translate it as '*True Histories*'; however, I prefer *True Stories* as a translation of the Greek title (*alêthê diêgêmata*), since *diêgêma* is a general term for a narrative / account – not necessarily a historical account – and the combination of the adjective 'true' with 'story' is more provocative than the combination of 'true' and 'history'. However, Georgiadou and Larmour note that the historian Polybius defines *diêgêma* as 'history without truth' (1998, 1 with n. 1).

9. See Georgiadou and Larmour 1994, 1478-82 with a survey of previous scholarship on this question. At p. 1480 they observe: 'the value of juxtaposing the two works lies in the fact that the "Hist. Conscr." [*How to Write History*] appears to provide the material for the parody and criticism of sensationalist historians in the "Ver. Hist.".' And at p. 1481: 'The "Ver. Hist." serves as an outstanding example of the kind of historiography which Lucian criticizes in his treatise.' Cf. also Georgiadou and Larmour 1998, 2.

10. 1994, 1480.

11. See Goldhill 2002b, 69-70. The noun *diaphônia* occurs at ch. 65.1 of *The Apology*.

12. Georgiadou and Larmour 1998, 44: 'The *VH* is driven by the force of parody, a force which appropriates and delegitimizes other texts, while, at the same time, guaranteeing their continued existence.'

13. See Nightingale 1995, 6-8 on differing models of parody in relation to the Platonic dialogues.

14. For a recent discussion of the reception of Thucydides in *True Stories*, see Bartley 2003; at pp. 227-8 Bartley provides an overview of Thucydidean influences noted by other scholars. The passages that are thought to draw on Thucydides most directly are the battle between the Sun- and Moon-men and the resultant peace treaty (1.13-21); the battle between Lucian's crew and the inhabitants of the whale (1.35-9); and the naval battle of the giants sailing on the islands (1.40-2). See also Georgiadou and Larmour 1998, 28-9.

15. For *True Stories* as an (allegorical) journey narrative, see Georgiadou and Larmour 1998, 13-22.

16. See Anderson 1976, 117-18; and Whitmarsh 2001, 33 with n. 140, who cites Anderson.

17. Westlake 1977 argued that *legetai* in Thucydides is used to signal information whose reliability is not known. Fowler 1996, 76, with n. 106 points out that there is a high concentration of the use of *legetai* / *legontai* in the 'Archaeological' sections of the work (1.1-21; 2.15-16; 6.1-5), and associates this vocabulary with a Herodotean mode of historiography.

18. See Branham 1989, 57 on *How to Write History* (3-4): 'The disarming ambivalence, in this case the irony, is typical of the author. He hesitates to let us take even his own serious efforts with unqualified seriousness.'

19. Trans. Kilburn, 1959. All translations of *How to Write History* are taken from the Loeb Classical Library edition of Lucian's works, vol. 6, translated by K. Kilburn (1959).

20. The prologues (*prolaliai* in Greek) are short works that are thought to have been delivered as prefaces / frames for the performance of longer works. See Branham 1985, who argues that the prologues encapsulate the main themes and strategies of Lucian's self-presentation and function as examples of his art in miniature (*passim*, esp. 237). For a discussion of the *Herodotus* in the context of Lucian's prologues, see Nesselrath 1990, 117-22.

21. Lucian depicts the historians of the Parthian War being engaged in a battle (*hamilla*) with Thucydides.

22. Fox 2001, 79.

23. Wheeldon 1989, 48.

24. Williams 2002, 165, cited above, Chapter 4, p. 68.

25. The verb *oikodomêo* is used at 62, connecting this passage to Lucian's earlier metaphor of 'history as a building'.

26. Georgiadou and Larmour 1998, 30 point out that shipwrecked sailors are guided by a lighthouse at the end of *True Stories* (2.47), and identify this lighthouse with Sostratus' lighthouse at the end of *How to Write History*: 'The Architect of the lighthouse is perhaps Lucian himself, and it is a construction which guides other historians.'

27. Moles 1999, sections 2-7. See above, Chapter 1, p. 9.

28. Rotella 2004, 20.

29. Thucydides contends that the conflicts that occurred between Athens and Sparta and their respective allies in the years 431-404 BC should properly be regarded as a single war. Contrary to Thucydides, it is possible to subdivide the Atheno-Peloponnesian War into an Archidamian War (431-421 BC) and an 'Ionian' or 'Decelean' War (414-404 BC), with a patchy intervening peace. See Strauss 1997, *passim* for a discussion of Thucydides' construction of a monumental war.

30. It is instructive to compare Lucian's rhetorical enactment of history-writing, selectively mimicking Thucydides (a classical Greek paradigm), with the emphasis on acting out or imitating (but not possessing) culture (*paideia*) elsewhere in his corpus. Whitmarsh 2001, 262 calls attention to Lucian's satirical critique of contemporary philosophy in *The Fisherman*, where philosophers merely 'act' or 'play' at being philosophers. Whitmarsh ibid., ch. 5 offers an excellent discussion of Lucian's sustained criticism of the theatricalization and phoniness of knowledge among contemporary intellectuals. As is evident from *How to Write History* and *True Stories*, Lucian's own parody is not exempt from this very criticism.

31. Herodotus *Histories* 1.29.2 and 1.30.1.

32. For more on the use of the term *theôria*, see Monoson 2000, 206 and 229. See also Nightingale 2001 (especially pp. 29-31) and 2004, *passim*.

33. See *How to Write History* 14, where Lucian exposes an example of bad historical writing which he alleges to have heard in Ionia: the writer's fault was to begin his account with an invocation to the muses.

34. On the rhetorical significance of the Greek adjective *poikilos* ('spangled', 'embroidered', 'variegated') see Hesk 2000, 36-9. Hesk emphasizes the associations, beginning in Homer, between *poikilia* / *poikilos* and the arts of fabrication and cunning typically practised by women (see esp. p. 36).

35. Wheeldon 1989, *passim* and 41. Wheeldon draws an analogy between 'persuasive authority' in oratory and historiography: 'In historiography [...] much depended on a writer's ability to establish the kind of authority to which readers were accustomed; unless a writer fulfilled this condition of the genre, an audience would be less able to believe his version of events' (41).

36. See Moles 1993, 116.

37. Georgiadou and Larmour stress the significance of the divided voices (the authorial voice and the narratorial voice) for the theme of the interplay between truth and fiction (1998, 3): 'The authorial voice, speaking in the Introduction, emphasizes the untruthfulness of what follows, while the narratorial voice which tells the story strives to make it seem believable.' Compare Hartog 2001, 38.

38. Trans. Harmon 1913, adapted. All translations of *True Stories* are taken from the Loeb Classical Library edition of Lucian's works, vol. 1, translated by A.M. Harmon (1913).

39. See Whitmarsh 2001, 253 n. 25: '*True Stories* at any rate is explicitly marked as an unadulterated lie (1.4)!' Whitmarsh acknowledges the echo of the Cretan liar paradox at p. 252, n. 24, but does not apply it to his reading of this passage. Cf. also Anderson 1994, 1428, with n. 19: 'How far can one be prepared to trust an author who will confide in the reader as a self-confessed liar?'

40. Moles 2001, 211.

41. This phrase is quoted from Zagorin 1990, 263. This article is a hostile critique of current tendencies in postmodernist historiography, focusing chiefly on Ankersmit's endorsement of Hayden White's theories of historiography and narrative.

42. White 1984, 2. White's seminal works on form and narrativity in history-writing are *Metahistory* (1973), *Tropics of Discourse* (1978), and *The Content of the Form* (1987). For a discussion of the evolution of White's theories of historiography, see Kansteiner 1993. Cameron 1989, 34 discusses the productive dialogue between the emphasis on 'narrativity' in twentieth-century theory and rhetorical *topoi* in ancient historical works.

43. Partner 1995, 30-3, cited above, Chapter 4, p. 66 with n. 30.

44. See Georgiadou and Larmour 1998, 32 on markers of a 'reliable historical methodology' in *True Stories*.

45. Rubincam 1979.

46. Runbincam 2003. Rubincam's focus on 'typical' / 'formulaic' numbers is a response to Detlev Fehling's study of the use of 'typical numbers' in Herodotus (Fehling 1989).

47. Rubincam 2003, 449.

48. Rubincam 1991, summarized at Rubincam 2003, 457-8.

49. 2003, 462.

50. Hornblower 1994b, 202-4.

51. *True Stories* 1.6: 'Committing ourselves to the gale and giving up, we drove for seventy-nine days. On the eightieth day, however, the sun came out suddenly and at no great distance we saw a high, wooded island ringed about with sounding surf [...].'

52. See Georgiadou and Larmour 1998, 32; however, their conclusion that 'this suggests that the narrator is fully aware that his numbers may not be believed' misses the sophistication of the manipulation of numbers in *True Stories*.

53. At ch. 11 Lucian informs the reader that the Vulture-dragoons are men who ride on large vultures, in place of horses, and that many of these vultures have three heads.

54. See Georgiadou and Larmour 1998, 102: 'The composition of those military forces which accompany the 100,000 is presented in a realistic manner which makes them seem analogous to those in the human world.' Compare Bartley 2003, 223 on the 'realistic language' in the report of the battles in Book 1 of *True Stories*.

For the view that the would-be historian should have a knowledge of military matters, see *How to Write History* 37.

55. Note how the narrator combines cardinal numbers (e.g. eight) with ordinal numbers (fifth, ninth, second).

56. See Rubincam 1979 and 2003, 451 with n. 8.

57. 'Seemingly', because there is a debate about the reliability of Thucydides' calculations in this passage: see Hornblower 1994b, 203 with n. 23.

58. Compare *True Stories* 1.10, where this rationalizing vocabulary is used to add credibility to the narrator's claim that they saw earth from the moon: 'We also saw another country below, with cities in it and rivers and seas and forests and mountains. This we inferred (*eikazein*) to be our own world.' The technical language and the tentative argument from inference add momentary plausibility to the lie that the narrator has seen the earth from the moon.

59. Georgiadou and Larmour 1998, 218.

60. See above, p. 62.

61. Ankersmit 1989, 142: 'Historical interpretations of the past first become recognizable, they first acquire their identity, through the contrast with other interpretation, they are what they are only on the basis of what they are *not*.'

62. See Woodman 1988, 4.

63. See the discussion of Homeric warfare in Plato's *Laches*.

64. *Iliad* 13.3-6: 'and he turned his shining eyes away, looking far out over the land of the horse-herding Thracians, and the Mysians, fighters at close quarters, and the proud Hippemolgoi, who live on mares' milk, and the Abioi, most civilized of all men' (trans. M. Hammond 1987, 225). Lucian quotes only lines 4-5. For comment on this passage, see Walker 1993, 373 and Fox 2001, 85.

65. On the motif of being *meteôros* and the significance of the 'view from above' in Lucian, see Whitmarsh 2001, 258, 270, 271, 274.

66. Georgiadou and Larmour 1998, 87.

67. *Clouds* 218-28. For Lucian's knowledge of Aristophanes' *Clouds* across his corpus, see Georgiadou and Larmour 1998, 25 with n. 73. For affinities between *True Stories* and Aristophanes' *Birds*, *Clouds* and *Peace*, see ibid., 24-5.

68. See Branham 1989, 7-8 on the description of Lucian's art as 'seriocomic'.

69. The phrase 'the limits of historiography' is the title of a collection of essays on historiography in the ancient world, edited by C.S. Kraus (1999).

Appendix 1. Timeline

From 480 BC to the death of Thucydides

Year (BC)	Political / military	Literary / intellectual
480	Battle of Salamis; Athenian fleet defeats the Persian fleet	(approx.) Birth of Euripides
479	A coalition of Greek states defeat the Persians at the Battle of Plataea: end of the 'Persian Wars'	
478/7	Delian league formed ('defensive' league of Greek states against Persia); Athens is elected leader of the league	
476		(?)Phrynichus' *Phoenician Women*
472		Aeschylus' *Persian Women*
467	The Athenians defeat the Persians in a battle at the river Eurymedon	Aeschylus' *Seven Against Thebes*
465	The Athenians and their allies suffer a major defeat at Drabescus at the hands of the Thracians	
465-464	Thasos revolts from Athens, the Athenians crush the revolt	
460-454	Athenian expedition to Egypt to provide support for an Egyptian revolt against Persia; the expedition ends in failure in 454	
460-446	First Atheno-Peloponnesian War	
c. 459/8.	Birth of Thucydides	458 Aeschylus' *Oresteia*
456		Death of Aeschylus
454	Treasury of the Delian league is transferred from Delos to Athens; creation of the Athenian empire with the other states in the league paying tribute / contributing ships to Athens	
451	Five-year truce between Athens and Sparta	
451	Athenian victory over the Persians in Cyprus	
450-449	Peace of Callias between Athens and Persia	
447-446	Spartan army, led by King Pleistoanax, invades Attica (turns back at Eleusis)	
446	Euboea and Megara revolt from Athens	
446	Thirty Years' Peace between Athens and Sparta	

Year (BC)	Political / military	Literary / intellectual
445		(approx.) Birth of Aristophanes
442		(?) Sophocles' *Antigone*
440	Samos revolts from the Athenian empire; the revolt is put down by Pericles. Byzantium also revolts	
435	Outbreak of war between Corcyra and Corinth	
433	Athens enters into an alliance with Corcyra	
432	Potidaea revolts from Athens; the Athenians besiege the town	
431	Theban invasion of Plataea initiates outright war; beginning of the second Atheno-Peloponnesian War	Euripides' *Medea*
431-421	The Archidamian War (the first phase of the second Atheno-Peloponnesian War as we know it)	
430	Peloponnesian forces invade Attica	
430	First outbreak of the plague in Athens	
430-429	Potidaea falls to Athens, ending the siege begun in 432	
429	Death of Pericles	
429	Peloponnesian forces attack Plataea	
428	Lesbos revolts from the Athenian empire; the Athenians besiege Mytilene	Euripides' *Hippolytus*
427	Two emergency debates about Mytilene in the Athenian assembly; Thucydides gives an account of the debate at the second assembly meeting (the so-called 'Mytilene debate'); the outcome is that one thousand ringleaders of the revolt are put to death	
427	Plataea surrenders to Sparta; the Spartans execute the men and enslave the women	
427	Civil war in Corcyra	
427	Athens sends forces to Sicily	The orator Gorgias visits Athens as part of an embassy from Leontini in Sicily
427/6	Recurrence of the plague in Athens	
425	The Athenians send reinforcements to Sicily – the fleet delays and is deployed against the Spartans at Pylos	
425	Pylos Campaign; under the command of Cleon the Athenians defeat the Spartans at Pylos and take Spartan prisoners	Aristophanes' *Acharnians*
424	Athenian forces return from Sicily; the generals are put on trial	Aristophanes' *Knights*
424	The Spartan general Brasidas takes the strategic city of Amphipolis in Northern Thrace; Thucydides fails to prevent him and is sent into exile	

Year (BC)	Political / military	Literary / intellectual
423	One-year truce between Sparta and Athens	Aristophanes' *Clouds*
422	Truce ends	Aristophanes' *Wasps*
422	Athenian expedition to Thrace; Cleon and Brasidas fight for Amphipolis: the Peloponnesians are victorious, but both Brasidas and Cleon are killed in the battle	
422	Athenian embassy to Sicily	
422-421	Peace of Nicias ends ten years of war between Athens and Sparta; Athens and Sparta enter into an alliance	421: Aristophanes' *Peace*
420	Alliance between Athens, Argos, Elis and Mantinea, orchestrated by Alcibiades	
416	The Athenians besiege Melos	
416-415	Negotiations between the Athenians and Melians fail; the adult males are put to death and the women and children are enslaved	
416-415	Egesta in Sicily sends envoys to Athens to request support in their war against Selinus	
415	Athenian assembly debates a proposal to send an expedition to Sicily	Euripides' *Trojan Women*
415	Scandal of the mutilation of the Herms, and the profanation of the Mysteries; the Athenian expedition sails for Sicily	
415	Alcibiades is recalled to strand trial in Athens on suspicion of involvement in the profanation of the Mysteries and the mutilation of the Herms Alcibiades ignores his recall and escapes to Sparta; he is condemned to death in his absence	
415-413	Athenian expedition to Sicily	
414		Aristophanes' *Birds*
414-413	The Spartans invade Decelea in Attica and fortify it	Euripides' *Iphigeneia among the Taurians* (?) Sophocles' *Electra*
413	Athenian navy defeated in Syracuse; the Athenian forces surrender at the river Assinarus	
412		Euripides' *Helen*
412	Both the Spartans and Athenians vie for the support of Tissaphernes, the Persian Governor of Sardis	
412-411	Negotiations between Tissaphernes and the Spartans. After two preliminary treaties of alliance, a final treaty is concluded in the winter of 412	
411	Oligarchic revolution in Athens; the régime of the Four Hundred assumes government	Aristophanes' *Lysistrata* Aristophanes' *Thesmophoriazousae*
411	Democratic counter-revolution; government of the Five Thousand established	

Year (BC)	Political / military	Literary / intellectual
411	The Athenians win a naval battle against the Spartans at Cynossema	
Thucydides' narrative breaks off at this point (8.11)		
411	The Athenians defeat the Peloponnesians at Abydos	
410	Government of the Five Thousand dissolved; restoration of democracy; Athenian naval victory over the Peloponnesians at Cyzicus	
409		Sophocles' *Philoctetes*
408	Under Alcibiades, the Athenians take back Byzantium on the Hellespont (a crucial city for trade)	Euripides' *Orestes*
407	Alcibiades returns to Athens	
407	Cyrus the younger, son of the Persian King Darius II, becomes Persian commander and supports the Spartans	
406	Athenian fleet defeated at Notium; Alcibiades goes into exile	
406	Athenian naval victory at Arginousae; however, Athenian generals were subsequently put to death on account of negligence (many Athenian lives were lost in a storm after the naval battle)	406-5 Death of Euripides
405	Battle of Aegospotami – the Spartan commander Lysander destroys the Athenian fleet	Death of Sophocles Aristophanes' *Frogs*
404	The Athenians surrender to the Spartans, who set up a garrison on the Acropolis of Athens	
404	End of the Atheno-Peloponnesian War	
404	The régime of the 'Thirty Tyrants': a junta led by Critias and backed by Sparta	
404	Alcibiades is killed	Thucydides returns to Athens
403	The Athenian Thrasybulus leads a democratic uprising against the Thirty Tyrants. The democratic forces kill Critias and occupy Piraeus; Eventually the Spartan King Pausanias intervenes and an amnesty is declared	
401		Sophocles' *Oedipus at Colonus*
c. 400-399		Thucydides dies (precise year unknown)

Appendix 2. Structure of the *History*

Book 1	
1.1-20	The 'Archaeology' (overview of the growth of Greek civilization, and commentary on earlier wars)
1.24-30	Civil war in Epidamnus precipitates war between Corcyra and Corinth
1.31-44	Assembly at Athens; speeches by the Corcyraeans (32-6), and the Corinthians (37-43)
1.59-65	Revolt of Potidaea; the Athenians besiege the city
1.67-88	Conference of the Peloponnesian league at Sparta; speeches by the Corinthians (68-71), the Athenians (73-8), and the Spartan King Archidamus (80-85.2), and Sthenelaïdas (86)
1.89-118	The Pentekontaëtia (50 year period covering Athens' expansion from 479 onwards)
1.90-3	Description of Themistocles rebuilding the city walls of Athens and fortifying Piraeus
1.114-15	Revolt of Megara
1.119-125.2	Conference of the Peloponnesian league at Sparta; speech by the Corinthians (120-4)
1.126	The Cylonian affair
1.128-35	The Medism of the Spartan king Pausanias
1.135-8	Exile of the Athenian Themistocles; obituary for Themistocles (138)
1.139.3-145	Assembly at Athens: Spartan ambassadors address the Assembly; Speech of Pericles (140-4)
Book 2	
2.2-6	The Thebans attack Plataea
2.10-11	The Peloponnesian army holds an assembly at the isthmus of Corinth; Speech of Archidamus (2.11)
2.12-17	The Athenians abandon Attica and move inside the city walls
2.18-21	Peloponnesian invasion of Attica
2.13	Archidamus addresses the Peloponnesian forces

2.13	Assembly at Athens; 2.13.2-9 – speech of Pericles (narrated in reported speech)
2.34-46	Description of the public burial at the end of the first year of the war
2.35-46	Pericles' Funeral Oration
2.47-54	Description of the Plague at Athens
2.60-4	Last speech of Pericles
2.65.5-9	Obituary for Pericles
2.65.10-13	Thucydides comments on the next generation of politicians and anticipates the disastrous Sicilian expedition and, ultimately, the end of the war.
2.71-8	Peloponnesian forces besiege Plataea
2.71.2-4	Speech of the Plataeans
2.72.1	Speech of Archidamus
2.86-9	The Spartan and Athenian generals prepare their respective forces for a naval battle between Rhium and Naupactus (Speeches by the Spartan generals Cnemus and Brasidas (2.87), and by the Athenian general Phormio (2.89))
2.90-2	Naval battle between Rhium and Naupactus; the Athenians win, but the Peloponnesians also erect a victory trophy

Book 3

3.2-6	Lesbos revolts from Athens
3.8-15	Conference of the Peloponnesians at Olympia
3.9-14	Speech of the Mytileneans
3.36-50	Assembly at Athens; 'Mytilene Debate': speech of Cleon (37-40); speech of Diodotus (41-8)
3.52-68	Plataea surrenders
3.53-60	Speech of the Plataeans
3.61-7	Speech of the Thebans
3.68	The Spartan judges condemn and execute the Plataean men; the Plataean women are enslaved
3.70-85	*Stasis* (civil war) in Corcyra
3.82-5	Thucydides' analysis of the *stasis* in Corcyra

Book 4

4.8-14	Spartans and Athenians fight over Pylos
4.15-16	A truce is arranged
4.16-22	Meeting of the Athenian Assembly to discuss the situation in Pylos

4.16-23	Spartan envoys address the Athenian assembly
4.27-9	Second Assembly meeting to discuss the situation in Pylos
4.27-8	Debate between Nicias and Cleon
4.29	Cleon is chosen to command the Athenian expedition against the Spartans at Pylos
4.31-8	The Athenians launch an attack on the island of Sphacteria (off Pylos)
4.38	The Spartans surrender
4.58-65.2	Assembly of Sicilian cities at Gela: speech of Hermocrates (4.59-64)
4.67-72	The Athenians attack Megara
4.85-7	Speech of Brasidas to the Assembly at Acanthus
4.102-6	Brasidas captures Amphipolis
4.107	Thucydides saves Eion
4.114	Speech of Brasidas to the Assembly at Torone (reported speech)
4.117-19	The Athenians and Spartans make a one-year truce
4.120.3	Speech of Brasidas to the Assembly at Scione (reported speech)

Book 5

5.6-11.1	Battle over Amphipolis with Cleon leading the Athenians and Brasidas leading the Peloponnesians
5.10.11-11.2	Description of the death and heroization of Brasidas
5.14-19	Peace of Nicias
5.20	Thucydides defends his system of dating
5.26	Thucydides makes a further statement about his system of dating and comments on the experiences of writing the war in exile
5.44.2-46.3	Assembly at Athens (speeches of Spartan ambassadors, Alcibiades, and Nicias); all reported speech
5.84.3-113	Melian Dialogue

Book 6

6.1-5	Digression on the Colonization of Sicily
6.8-26	Assembly at Athens to debate the Sicilian expedition
6.9-14	Speech of Nicias
6.16-18	Speech of Alcibiades
6.20-3	Response of Nicias
6.27-8	The Mutilation of the Herms in Athens and the subsequent outcry
6.30-2	Description of the departure of the Sicilian expedition

6.32.3-41	Assembly at Syracuse (Speeches by Hermocrates (33-4) and Athenagoras (36-40))
6.53-60	Digression about the tyranny of Hippias and the so-called tyrannicides, Harmodius and Aristogeiton
6.75.3-88	Assembly at Camarina (Speeches by Hermocrates (76-80) and the Athenian ambassador Euphemus (82-7))
6.88.9-93	Assembly at Sparta; speech by Alcibiades (89-92)

Book 7

7.11-15	Letter of Nicias to the Athenian Assembly
7.29	Thracian mercenaries, sent back from Athens, commit a massacre at Mycalessus
7.42	The Athenian general Demosthenes arrives in Sicily with reinforcements
7.43-4	Demosthenes launches a night attack on Epipolae; the attack fails
7.47-9	Council of Athenian generals (speeches by Demosthenes and Nicias, narrated in reported speech)
7.60.5-69.2	Speeches before the battle in the harbour of Syracuse (Speeches by Nicias (61-4) and Gylippus (66-8))
7.69-72	Description of the battle in the harbour of Syracuse; the Athenians are beaten
7.73-85	The Athenians army retreats
7.85	The Athenians surrender at the Assinarus river
7.87.5-6	Thucydides concludes his narrative of the Sicilian expedition

Book 8

8.1	News of the defeat in Sicily reaches Athens
8.14	Chios, Erythrae and Clazomenae revolt from Athens
8.18	First treaty between the Peloponnesians and the Persian King Darius II
8.36	Second treaty between the Peloponnesians and the Persian King
8.47-8	Alcibiades tells the Athenian fleet that they will secure the assistance of Persia if Athens establishes an oligarchic government
8.48.4-51	The Athenian general Phrynichus challenges Alcibiades and the two men try to discredit each other
8.53-4	Envoys from the oligarchs in Samos propose to the Athenian assembly that Athens should establish an oligarchic government
8.58	Third treaty between the Spartans and the Persian King

8.65-70	'The Oligarchic Revolution': Peisander reaches Athens and the Oligarch conspirators, led by Peisander abolish the democracy and establish an oligarchic régime known as the Four Hundred
8.68	Thucydides comments on the oligarchic conspirators and praises Antiphon
8.75-6	The Athenian fleet in Samos votes to preserve the democracy and to oppose oligarchy both in Samos and Athens
8.91-4	Counter-revolution against the Oligarchic conspirators, led by Theramenes
8.95	The Spartans defeat thirty-six Athenian ships in a battle off the coast of Eretria; Euboea revolts from Athens
8.97	The Athenian assembly convenes on the Pnyx and annuls the régime of the Four Hundred; the assembly votes to confirm the Government of the Five Thousand
8.104-6	Battle between the Athenians and Peloponnesians at Cynossema in the Hellespont; the Athenians are victorious
8.109	Thucydides' narrative of the war breaks off; at this point he has reached the summer of the twenty-first year of the war (411 BC)

Appendix 3. Maps

1. Map of Greece

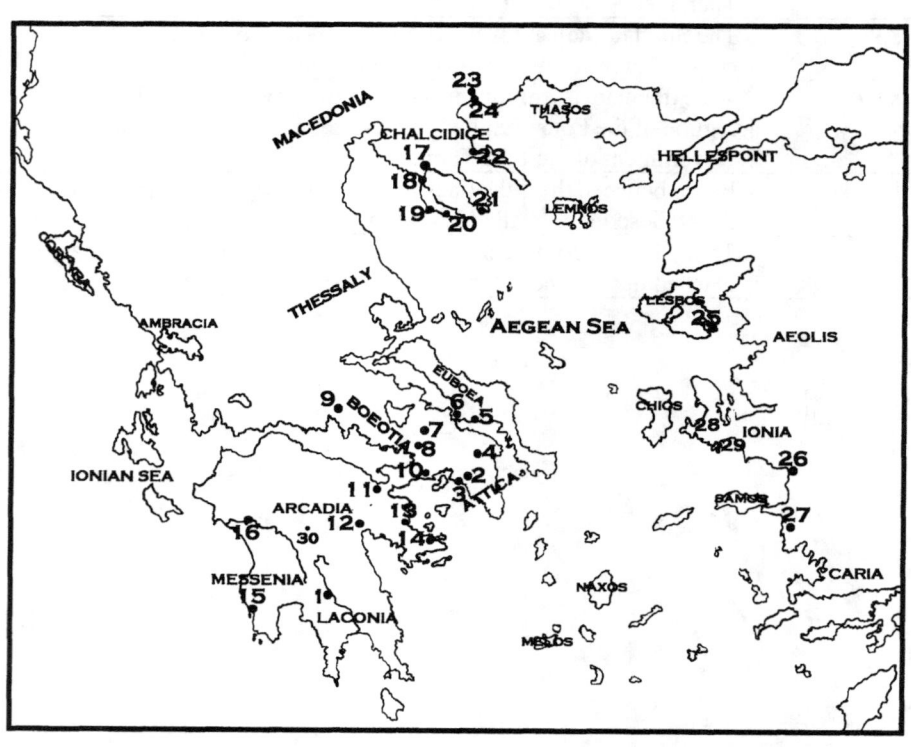

Key:

1 Sparta	**11** Corinth	**21** Torone
2 Athens	**12** Argos	**22** Acanthus
3 Piraeus	**13** Epidaurus	**23** Amphipolis
4 Decelea	**14** Troezen	**24** Eion
5 Eretria	**15** Pylos	**25** Mytilene
6 Chalcis	**16** Olympia	**26** Ephesus
7 Thebes	**17** Olynthus	**27** Miletus
8 Plataea	**18** Potidaea	**28** Erythrae
9 Delphi	**19** Mende	**29** Mt. Corycus
10 Megara	**20** Scione	**30** Mantinea

2. Southern Italy and Sicily

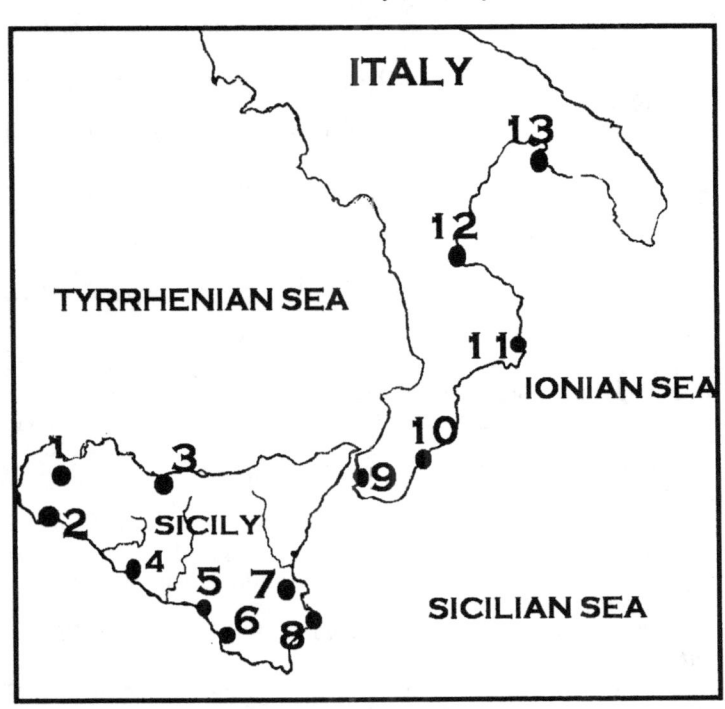

Key:

1 Egesta   2 Selinus
3 Himera   4 Agrigentum
5 Gela   6 Camarina
7 Leontini   8 Syracuse
9 Rhegium   10 Locri
11 Croton   12 Thurii
13 Tarentum

Bibliography

Allison, J.W. (1989), *Power and Preparedness in Thucydides* (Baltimore and London: Johns Hopkins University Press).
—— (1997a), *Word and Concept in Thucydides*. American Classical Studies 41 (Atlanta: Scholars Press).
—— (1997b), 'Homeric Allusions at the Close of Thucydides' Sicilian Narrative', *AJP* 118: 499-516.
—— (2001), '*Axiosis*, the New *aretê*: a Periclean Metaphor for Friendship', *CQ* 51: 53-64.
Allison, R.H. (1984), 'This is the Place: Why is Oidipous at Kolonos?', *Prudentia* 16: 67-91.
Amit, M. (1965), *Athens and the Sea (A Study in Athenian Sea-Power)*. Collection Latomus 74 (Brussels: Latomus).
Anderson, G. (1976), *Theme and Variation in the Second Sophistic*. Mnemosyne Supplement 41 (Leiden: E.J. Brill).
—— (1994), 'Lucian: Tradition Versus Reality', *ANRW* II.34.2: 1422-47.
Andrewes, A. (1953), 'The Generals in the Hellespont, 410-07 BC', *JHS* 73: 2-9.
Ankersmit, F.R. (1989), 'Historiography and Postmodernism', *HT* 28: 137-53.
—— (1995), 'Statements, Texts and Pictures', in F.R. Ankersmit and H. Kellner (eds): 212-40.
—— and H. Kellner (1995) (eds), *A New Philosophy of History* (London: Reaktion Books Ltd).
Austin, J.L. (1975), *How to do Things With Words*. William James Lectures, Harvard, 1955, J.O. Urmson and M. Sbisà (eds) (Oxford: Clarendon Press).
Avery, H.C. (1973), 'Themes in Thucydides' Account of the Sicilian Expedition', *Hermes* 101: 1-13.
Badian, E. (1993), *From Plataea to Potidaea: Studies in the History of the Pentecontaetia* (Baltimore: Johns Hopkins University Press).
Bagby, L.M.J. (1994), 'The Use and Abuse of Thucydides in International Relations', *International Organization* 48: 131-53.
Bakker, E.J., I.J.F. de Jong and H. van Wees (2002) (eds), *Brill's Companion to Herodotus* (Leiden, Boston, Köln: E.J. Brill).
Bartley, A. (2003), 'The Implications of the Reception of Thucydides within Lucian's *Vera Historia*', *Hermes* 131: 222-34.
Bedford, R. and T. Workman (2001), 'The Tragic Reading of the Thucydidean Tragedy', *RIS* 27: 51-67.
Bentley, M. (1997) (ed.), *Companion to Historiography* (London: Routledge).
Billault, A. (1994) (ed.), *Lucien de Samosate*. Actes du Colloque International de Lyon organisé au Centre d'Études Romaines et Gallo-Romaines (les 30 septembre – 1er octobre 1993) (Paris: de Boccard).
Boedeker, D. (2000), 'Herodotus's Genre(s)', in M. Depew and D. Obbink (eds): 97-114.
—— (2002), 'Epic Heritage and Mythical Patterns in Herodotus', in E.J. Bakker, I.J.F. de Jong and H. van Wees (eds): 97-116.
Boegehold, A.L. and A.C. Scafuro (1994) (eds), *Athenian Identity and Civic Ideology* (Baltimore: Johns Hopkins University Press).

Bowie, A.M. (1997), 'Tragic Filters for History: Euripides' *Supplices* and Sophocles' *Philoctetes*', in C.B.R. Pelling (ed.): 39-62.

Branham, R.B. (1985), 'Introducing a Sophist: Lucian's Prologues', *TAPA* 115: 237-43.

———— (1989), *Unruly Eloquence: Lucian and the Comedy of Traditions* (Cambridge, Mass.: Harvard University Press).

Brock, R. (2003), 'Authorial Voice and Narrative Management in Herodotus', in P. Derow and R. Parker (eds): 3-16.

Brothers, C. (1997), *War and Photography: a Cultural History* (London and New York: Routledge).

Budelmann, F. (2000), *The Language of Sophocles, Community, Communication and Involvement* (Cambridge: Cambridge University Press).

Buxton, R. (1994), *Imaginary Greece: The Contexts of Mythology* (Cambridge: Cambridge University Press).

Calame, C. (1999), 'Performative Aspects of the Choral Voice in Greek Tragedy: Civic Identity in Performance', in S. Goldhill and R. Osborne (eds): 125-53.

Calder, W.M. (1971), 'Sophoclean Apologia: *Philoctetes*', *GRBS* 12: 153-74.

Calvino, I. (2000), *Why Read the Classics?* (London: Vintage). [originally published in Milan in 1991 as *Perché leggere i classici*]

Cameron, A. (1989) (ed.), *History as Text: The Writing of Ancient History* (London: Duckworth).

Carson, A. (2001), 'Ordinary Time: Virginia Woolf and Thucydides on War', in A. Carson, *Men in the Off Hours* (London: Vintage): 3-8. [first published in 2000 by Alfred A. Knopf]

Cartledge, P.A. (1984), 'A New Lease of Life for Lichas Son of Arkesilas?', *LCM* 1984 vol. 9: 98-102.

———— (1993), 'The Silent Women of Thucydides: 2.45.2 Reviewed', in R.M. Rosen and J. Farrell (eds): 125-32.

———— (1997) ' "Deep Plays": Theatre as Process in Greek Civic Life', in P.E. Easterling (ed.): 3-35.

———— (1998), 'Introduction: Defining a *kosmos*', in P.A. Cartledge, P. Millett and S. von Reden (eds): 1-12.

————, P. Millett and S. von Reden (1998) (eds), *Kosmos: Essays in Order, Conflict and Community in Classical Athens* (Cambridge: Cambridge University Press).

Cole, T. (1991), *The Origins of Rhetoric in Ancient Greece* (Baltimore and London: Johns Hopkins University Press).

Connor, W.R. (1984), *Thucydides* (Princeton: Princeton University Press).

———— (1987), 'Tribes, Festivals and Processions; Civic Ceremonial and Political Manipulation in Archaic Greece', *JHS* 107: 40-50.

———— (1994), 'The Problem of Athenian Civic Identity', in A.L. Boegehold and A.C. Scafuro (eds): 34-44.

Cornford, F.M. (1907), *Thucydides Mythistoricus* (London: Edward Arnold).

Craik, E.M. (1990), 'The Staging of Sophocles' *Philoctetes* and Aristophanes' *Birds*', in E.M. Craik (ed.): 81-4.

———— (1990) (ed.), *'Owls to Athens': Essays on Classical Subjects Presented to Sir Kenneth Dover* (Oxford: Clarendon Press).

Crane, G. (1996), *The Blinded Eye: Thucydides and the New Written Word* (Lanham, MD, and London: Rowman & Littlefield).

———— (1998), *Thucydides and the Ancient Simplicity: The Limits of Political Realism* (Berkeley: University of California Press).

Croally, N.T. (1994), *Euripidean Polemic: The Trojan Women and the Function of Tragedy* (Cambridge: Cambridge University Press).

Bibliography

D'Angour, A. (1998), 'The Dynamics of Innovation. Newness and Novelty in the Athens of Aristophanes', unpublished PhD thesis (University of London).

Davidson, J. (1991), 'The Gaze in Polybius' *Histories'*, *JRS* 81: 10-24.

—— (1997), *Courtesans and Fishcakes. The Consuming Passions of Classical Athens* (London: Harper Collins).

De Jong, I.J.F. (2001), 'The Anachronical Structure of Herodotus' *Histories'*, in S.J. Harrison (ed.): 93-116.

Debnar, P. (2001), *Speaking the Same Language: Speech and Audience in Thucydides' Spartan Debates* (Ann Arbor: University of Michigan Press).

Depew, M. and D. Obbink (2000) (eds), *Matrices of Genre: Authors, Canons, and Society* (Cambridge, Mass.: Harvard University Press).

Derow, P. and R. Parker (2003) (eds), *Herodotus and His World: Essays from a Conference in Memory of George Forrest* (Oxford: Oxford University Press).

Dewald, C. (1997), 'Wanton Kings, Pickled Heroes, and Gnomic Founding Fathers: Strategies of Meaning at the End of Herodotus' *Histories'*, in D.H. Roberts, F.M. Dunn and D. Fowler (eds): 62-82.

—— (1999), 'The Figured Stage: Focalizing the Initial Narratives of Herodotus and Thucydides', in T.M. Falkner, N. Felson and D. Konstan (eds): 221-52.

Diggins, J.P. (1984), 'The Oyster and the Pearl: The Problem of Contextualism in Intellectual History', *HT* 23.2: 151-69.

Dover, K.J. (1973), *Thucydides. Greece and Rome New Surveys in the Classics No. 7* (Oxford: Clarendon Press).

—— (1983), 'Thucydides "As History" and "As Literature" ', *HT* 22: 54-63.

—— (1988), 'Thucydides' Historical Judgement: Athens and Sicily', in his *The Greeks and their Legacy*, vol. 2 (Oxford: Basil Blackwell): 74-82. [first published in 1981]

—— (1997), *The Evolution of Greek Prose Style* (Oxford: Clarendon Press).

Easterling, P.E. (1983), '*Philoctetes* and Modern Criticism', in E. Segal (ed.): 217-28.

—— (1985), 'Anachronism in Greek Tragedy', *JHS* 105: 1-10.

—— (1997), 'Constructing the Heroic', in C.B.R. Pelling (ed.): 21-37.

—— (1997) (ed.), *The Cambridge Companion to Greek Tragedy* (Cambridge: Cambridge University Press).

Edmunds, L. (1975a), *Chance and Intelligence in Thucydides* (Cambridge, Mass.: Harvard University Press).

—— (1975b), 'Thucydides' Ethics as Reflected in the Description of *stasis* (3.82-3)', *HSCP* 79: 73-92.

—— (1993), 'Thucydides in the Act of Writing', in R. Pretagostini (ed.): 831-52.

—— (1996), *Theatrical Space and Historical Place in Sophocles' Oedipus at Colonos* (Lanham, MD: Rowman & Littlefield).

—— and R. Martin (1977), 'Thucydides 2.65.8: *Eleutherôs'*, *HSCP* 81: 187-93.

Elsner, J. (2001), 'Describing Self in the Language of the Other: Pseudo(?) Lucian at the temple of Hierapolis', in S. Goldhill (ed.): 123-53.

Euben, J.P. (1986), 'Political Corruption in Euripides' *Orestes'*, in J.P. Euben (ed.): 222-51.

—— (1986) (ed.), *Greek Tragedy and Political Theory* (Berkeley: University of California Press).

Falkner, T.M., N. Felson and D. Konstan (1999) (eds), *Contextualizing Classics: Ideology, Performance, Dialogue* (Lanham, MD: Rowman & Littlefield).

Farred, G. (1996) (ed.), *Rethinking C.L.R. James* (Cambridge, Mass. and Oxford: Blackwell Publishers).

Feeney, D. (1995), 'Criticism Ancient and Modern', in D. Innes, H. Hine and C.B.R. Pelling (eds): 301-12.

Fehling, D. (1989), *Herodotus and His 'Sources': Citation, Invention, and Narrative Art*, translated by J.G. Howie (Liverpool: Cairns). [first published in 1971 as *Die Quellenangabben bei Herodot. Studien zur Erzählkunst Herodots* (Berlin)]

Finley, J.H., Jr. (1967), *Three Essays on Thucydides* (Cambridge, Mass.: Harvard University Press).

Finley, M.I. (1975), *The Use and Abuse of History* (New York: Viking Press). [revised edition published by Penguin in 1986]

Flory, S. (1993), 'The Death of Thucydides and the Motif of "Land on Sea" ', in R.M. Rosen and J. Farrell (eds): 113-23.

Fowler, D. (1997), 'Second Thoughts on Closure', in D.H. Roberts, F.M. Dunn and D. Fowler (eds): 3-22.

Fowler, R. (1996), 'Herodotus and his Contemporaries', *JHS* 116: 62-87.

—— (2004) (ed.), *The Cambridge Companion to Homer* (Cambridge: Cambridge University Press).

Fox, M. (1993), 'History and Rhetoric in Dionysius of Halicarnassus', *JRS* 83: 31-47.

—— (2001), 'Dionysius, Lucian and the Prejudice against Rhetoric in History', *JRS* 91: 76-93.

Gabrielsen, V. (1994), *Financing the Athenian Fleet: Public Taxation and Social Relations* (Baltimore: Johns Hopkins University Press).

Georgiadou, A. and D.H.J. Larmour (1994), 'Lucian and Historiography: "De Historia Conscribenda" and "Verae Historiae" ', *ANRW* 2.34.2: 1448-1509.

—— (1998), *Lucian's Science Fiction Novel True Histories. Interpretation and Commentary. Mnemosyne* Supplement 179 (Leiden, Boston, Köln: E.J. Brill).

Gill, C. and T.P. Wiseman (1993) (eds), *Lies and Fiction in the Ancient World* (Exeter: University of Exeter Press).

Goff, B. (1995) (ed.), *History, Tragedy, Theory: Dialogues on Athenian Drama* (Austin: University of Texas Press).

Golden, M. and P. Toohey (1997) (eds), *Inventing Ancient Culture: Historicism, Periodization, and the Ancient World* (London and New York: Routledge).

Goldhill, S.D. (1990), 'The Great Dionysia and Civic Ideology', in J.J. Winkler and F.I. Zeitlin (eds): 97-129.

—— (1996), 'Collectivity and Otherness – The Authority of the Tragic Chorus: Response to Gould', in M.S. Silk (ed.): 244-56.

—— (1998), 'The Seductions of the Gaze: Socrates and his Girlfriends', in P.A. Cartledge, P. Millett and S. von Reden (eds): 105-24.

—— (2002a), *The Invention of Prose. Greece and Rome New Surveys in the Classics No. 32* (Oxford: Oxford University Press for the Classical Association).

—— (2002b), *Who needs Greek? Contests in the Cultural History of Hellenism* (Cambridge: Cambridge University Press).

—— (2001) (ed.), *Being Greek Under Rome: Cultural Identity, the Second Sophistic and the Development of Empire* (Cambridge: Cambridge University Press).

—— and R. Osborne (1999) (eds), *Performance Culture and Athenian Democracy* (Cambridge: Cambridge University Press).

Gomme, A.W., A. Andrewes and K.J. Dover (1945-81), *A Historical Commentary on Thucydides*, 5 vols (Oxford: Clarendon Press).

Gould, J.P.A. (1996), 'Tragedy and the Collective Experience', in M.S. Silk (ed.): 217-43.

Greenwood, E. (2004), 'Making Words Count: Freedom of Speech and Narrative in Thucydides', in R.M. Rosen and I. Sluiter (eds): 175-95.

Gregory, J. (1991), *Euripides and the Instruction of the Athenians* (Ann Arbor: University of Michigan Press).

Gribble, D. (1998), 'Narrator Interventions in Thucydides', *JHS* 118: 41-67.

Hall, E. (1993), 'Political and Cosmic Turbulence in Euripides' *Orestes'*, in A.H. Sommerstein et al. (eds): 263-85.
—— (1995), 'Lawcourt Dramas: The Power of Performance in Greek Forensic Oratory', *BICS* 40: 39-58.
Hall, S. (1996), 'A Conversation with C.L.R. James', in G. Farred (ed.): 15-44.
Halliwell, S. (1997), 'Between Public and Private: Tragedy and Athenian Experience of Rhetoric', in C.B.R. Pelling (ed.): 121-41.
—— (2002), 'Thucydides, Pericles and Tragedy', *Dioniso* 1 (new series): 62-77.
Hammond, M. (1987), *Homer. The Iliad*. Translated with an Introduction (London: Penguin Books).
Hammond, N.G.L. (1973), 'The Particular and the Universal in the Speeches in Thucydides with Special Reference to that of Hermocrates at Gela', in P.A. Stadter (ed.): 49-59.
Hansen, M.H. (1996), 'The Ancient Athenian and the Modern Liberal View of Liberty as a Democratic Ideal', in J. Ober and C.W. Hedrick, Jr. (eds): 91-104.
Harrison, S.J. (2001) (ed.), *Texts, Ideas, and the Classics: Scholarship, Theory, and Classical Literature* (Oxford and New York: Oxford University Press).
Harrison, T. (2003), ' "Prophecy in Reverse"? Herodotus and the Origins of History', in P. Derow and R. Parker (eds): 237-55.
Hartog, F. (1982), 'L'oeil de Thucydide et l'histoire véritable', *Poétique* 49 (1982), 22-30.
—— (2001), *Memories of Odysseus: Frontier Tales from Ancient Greece*, translated by Janet Lloyd (Edinburgh: Edinburgh University Press). [first published in French in 1996 by Éditions Gallimard, Paris]
Hedrick, C.W., Jr. (1993), 'The Meaning of Material Culture: Herodotus, Thucydides, and their Sources', in R.M. Rosen and J. Farrell (eds): 17-37.
Hesk, J. (2000), *Deception and Democracy in Classical Athens* (Cambridge: Cambridge University Press).
—— (2003), *Sophocles: Ajax* (London: Duckworth).
Hornblower, S. (1991), *A Commentary on Thucydides*, vol. I: *Books I-III* (Oxford: Clarendon Press). [reprinted with additions and corrections, 1997]
—— (1992), 'The Religious Dimension to the Peloponnesian War, Or, What Thucydides Does not Tell Us', *HSCP* 94: 169-97.
—— (1994a), 'Narratology and Narrative Techniques in Thucydides', in his (1994) (ed.) *Greek Historiography* (Oxford: Clarendon Press): 131-66.
—— (1994b), *Thucydides²* (London: Duckworth). [first edition 1987]
—— (1995), 'The Fourth-century and Hellenistic Reception of Thucydides', *JHS* 115: 47-68.
—— (1996), *A Commentary on Thucydides*, vol. II: *Books IV-V.24* (Oxford: Clarendon Press). [reprinted with additions and corrections, 2004]
—— (2004), *Thucydides and Pindar: Historical Narrative and the World of Epinikian Poetry* (Oxford: Oxford University Press).
How, W.W. and J. Wells (1912), *A Commentary on Herodotus*, vol. 2 (Oxford: Clarendon Press).
Hunter, R. (2004), 'Homer and Greek Literature', in R. Fowler (ed.): 235-53.
Hunter, V.J. (1973), *Thucydides: The Artful Reporter* (Toronto: Hakkert).
—— (1982), *Past and Process in Herodotus and Thucydides* (Princeton: Princeton University Press).
—— (1988), 'Thucydides and the Sociology of the Crowd', *CJ* 84: 17-30.
Immerwahr, H.R. (1960), 'ERGON: History as Monument in Herodotus and Thucydides', *AJPh* 81: 261-90.
Innes, D., H. Hine and C.B.R. Pelling (1995) (eds), *Ethics and Rhetoric. Classical Essays for Donald Russell on his Seventy-Fifth Birthday* (Oxford: Clarendon Press).

Jameson, M.H. (1956), 'Politics and the Philoctetes', *CP* 51: 217-27.
—— (1971), 'Sophocles and the Four Hundred', *Historia* 20: 541-68.
Jebb, R. (1898), *Sophocles: Philoctetes*² (Cambridge: Cambridge University Press). [first published in 1890]
Johnson, W.A. (1994), 'Oral Performance and the Composition of Herodotus' *Histories*', *GRBS* 35: 229-54.
Jordan, B. (2000), 'The Sicilian Expedition was a Potemkin Fleet', *CQ* 50: 63-79.
Kagan, D. (1981), *The Peace of Nikias and the Sicilian Expedition* (Ithaca, NY: Cornell University Press).
—— (1987), *The Fall of the Athenian Empire* (Ithaca, NY: Cornell University Press).
Kallet-Marx, L. (1993), *Money, Expense and Naval Power in Thucydides' History 1-5.24* (Berkeley: University of California Press).
—— (as Kallet) (2001), *Money and the Corrosion of Power in Thucydides. The Sicilian Expedition and its Aftermath* (Berkeley: University of California Press).
Kansteiner, W. (1993), 'Hayden White's Critique of the Writing of History', *HT* 32: 273-95.
King, K.C. (1987), *Achilles: Paradigms of the War Hero from Homer to the Middle Ages* (Berkeley: University of California Press).
Knox, B. (1983) (ed.), *Sophocle*. Fondation Hardt Entretiens 29 (Vandoeuvres and Geneva: Fondation Hardt).
Konishi, H. (1970), 'Thucydides' Method in the Episodes of Pausanias and Themistocles', *AJP* 91: 52-69.
Konstan, D. (1987), 'Persians, Greeks and Empire', *Arethusa* 20: 59-73.
Kraus, C.S. (1999) (ed.), *The Limits of Historiography: Genre and Narrative in Ancient Historical Texts* (Leiden and Boston: E.J. Brill).
Kullmann, W. and J. Althoff (1993) (eds), *Vermittlung und Tradierung von Wissen in der griechischen Kultur* (Tübingen: G. Narr).
Kurke, L. (2000), 'Charting the Poles of History: Herodotus and Thucydides', in O.P. Taplin (ed.): 133-55.
Laird, A. (1999), *Powers of Expression, Expressions of Power: Speech Presentation and Latin Literature* (Oxford and New York: Oxford University Press).
Lang, M. (1995), 'Participial Motivation in Thucydides', *Mnemosyne* 48: 48-65.
Lateiner, D. (1985), 'Nicias' Inadequate Encouragement (Thucydides 7.69.2)', *CP* 80: 201-13.
Lebow, R.N. and B.S. Strauss (1991) (eds), *Hegemonic Rivalry. From Thucydides to the Nuclear Age* (Boulder: Westview Press).
—— and R. Kelly (2001), 'Thucydides and Hegemony: Athens and the United States', *RIS* 27: 593-609.
Leimbach, R. (1985), *Militärische Musterrhetorik: eine Untersuchung zu den Feldherrnreden des Thukydides* (Stuttgart: F. Steiner).
Longo, O. (1990), 'The Theater of the Polis', in J.J. Winkler and F.I. Zeitlin (eds): 12-19.
Loraux, N. (1973a), ' "Marathon", ou l'histoire idéologique', *Revue des Études Anciennes* 75: 13-42.
—— (1973b), 'L'interférence tragique', *Critique* 317: 908-25.
—— (1980), 'Thucydide n'est pas un collègue', *QS* 12: 55-81.
—— (1986), 'Thucydide a écrit la Guerre du Péloponnèse', *Métis* 1: 139-61.
—— (1991), 'Reflections of the Greek City on Unity and Division', in A. Molho, K.A. Raaflaub and T. Emlen (eds): 33-51.
—— (1997), *La cité divisée: l'oubli dans la mémoire d' Athènes* (Paris: Éditions Payot et Rivages). [English translation published in 2002: *The Divided City: On*

Memory and Forgetting in Ancient Athens, translated by C. Pache and J. Fort (New York: Zone Books)]

Ludwig, P. (2002), *Eros and Polis: Desire and Community in Greek Political Theory* (Cambridge: Cambridge University Press).

Luraghi, N. (2001), 'Local Knowledge in Herodotus' *Histories*', in his (ed.): 138-60.

────── (2001) (ed.), *The Historian's Craft in the Age of Herodotus* (Oxford and New York: Oxford University Press).

MacDowell, D.M. (1982) (ed.), *Gorgias. Encomium of Helen*. Edited with Introduction, Notes and Translation (Bristol: Bristol Classical Press).

Mackie, C.J. (1996), 'Homer and Thucydides: Corcyra and Sicily', *CQ* 46: 103-13.

Macleod, C. (1983), *Collected Essays*, O.P. Taplin (ed.) (Oxford: Clarendon Press).

Mader, G. (1993), 'Rogue's Comedy at Segesta (Thucydides 6.46): Alcibiades Exposed?', *Hermes* 121: 181-95.

Marinatos Kopff, N. and H.R. Rawlings III (1978), 'Panolethria and Divine Punishment: Thuc. 7.87.6 and Hdt. 2.120.5', *PP* 182: 331-7.

Marincola, J. (1997), *Authority and Tradition in Ancient Historiography* (Cambridge: Cambridge University Press).

Martin, R.P. (1987), 'Fire on the Mountain: *Lysistrata* and the Lemnian Women', *CA* 6: 77-105.

McCann, D.R. and B.S. Strauss (2001) (eds), *War and Democracy. A Comparative Study of the Korean War and the Peloponnesian War* (Armonk and London: M.E. Sharpe).

McCoy, W.J. (1973), 'The Non-Speeches of Pisander in Thucydides, Book Eight', in P.A. Stadter (ed.): 78-89.

Meiggs, R. (1972), *The Athenian Empire* (Oxford: Clarendon Press).

Mench, F. (2001), 'Film Sense in the *Aeneid*', in M.M. Winkler (ed.): 219-32.

Moeller, S.D. (1989), *Shooting War: Photography and the American Experience of Combat* (New York: Basic Books).

Moles, J. (1993), 'Truth and Untruth in Herodotus and Thucydides', in C. Gill and T.P. Wiseman (eds): 88-121.

────── (1999), 'Anathema kai Ktema: the Inscriptional Inheritance of Ancient Historiography', *Histos* 3 posted October 1999 (online journal): http://www.dur.ac.uk/Classics/histos/1999/moles.html.

────── (2001), 'A False Dilemma: Thucydides' *History* and Historicism', in S.J. Harrison (ed.): 195-219.

────── (2002), 'Herodotus and Athens', in E.J. Bakker, I.J.F. de Jong and H. van Wees (eds): 33-52.

Molho, A., K.A. Raaflaub and J. Emlen (1991) (eds), *Athens and Rome, Florence and Venice: City-States in Classical Antiquity and Medieval Italy* (Ann Arbor: University of Michigan Press).

Momigliano, A. (1978), 'The Historians of the Classical World and Their Audiences', *The American Scholar* 47: 193-204.

Monoson, S. S. (2000), *Plato's Democratic Entanglements: Athenian Politics and the Practice of Philosophy* (Princeton: Princeton University Press).

Morrison, J.V. (2000), 'Historical Lessons in the Melian Episode', *TAPA* 130: 119-48.

Mossman, J. (1995), *Wild Justice : A Study of Euripides' Hecuba* (Oxford: Oxford University Press).

Munson, R.V. (2001), *Telling Wonders: Ethnographic and Political Discourse in the Work of Herodotus* (Ann Arbor: University of Michigan Press).

Munz, P. (1997), 'The Historical Narrative', in M. Bentley (ed.): 851-72.

Nagy, G. (1990), *Pindar's Homer: The Lyric Possession of an Epic Past* (Baltimore: Johns Hopkins University Press).

Nesselrath, H.G. (1990), 'Lucian's Introductions', in D.A. Russell (ed.): 111-40.

Nicolai, R. (2001), 'Thucydides' Archaeology: Between Epic and Oral Traditions', in N. Luraghi (ed.): 263-85.

Nieddu, S.F. (1993), 'Neue Wissenformen, Kommunikationstechniken und schriftliche Ausdrucksformen in Griechenland im sechsten und fünften Jahrhundert V. Chr: Einige Beobachtungen', in W. Kullmann and J. Althoff (eds): 151-65.

Nightingale, A.W. (1995), *Genres in Dialogue: Plato and the Construct of Philosophy* (Cambridge: Cambridge University Press).

——— (2001), 'On Wandering and Wondering: Theôria in Greek Philosophy and Culture', *Arion* (3rd series) 9.2: 23-58.

——— (2004), *Spectacles of Truth in Classical Greek Philosophy: Theôria in its Cultural Context* (Cambridge: Cambridge University Press).

Ober, J. (1989), *Mass and Elite in Democratic Athens: Rhetoric, Ideology, and the Power of the People* (Princeton: Princeton University Press).

——— (1998), *Political Dissent in Democratic Athens: Intellectual Critics of Popular Rule* (Princeton: Princeton University Press)

——— (2001), 'Thucydides Theoretikos / Thucydides Histor: Realist Theory and the Challenge of History', in D.R. McCann and B.S. Strauss (eds): 273-306.

——— and Hedrick, C.W., Jr. (1996) (eds), *Dêmokratia: A Conversation on Democracies, Ancient and Modern* (Princeton: Princeton University Press).

Osborne, R. and S. Hornblower (1994) (eds), *Ritual, Finance, Politics. Athenian Democratic Accounts Presented to David Lewis* (Oxford: Clarendon Press).

Padel, R. (1990), 'Making Space Speak', in J.J. Winkler and F.I. Zeitlin (eds): 336-65.

Parry, A. (1981), *Logos and Ergon in Thucydides* (New York: Arno Press).

Partner, N. (1995), 'Historicity in an Age of Reality-Fictions', in F. Ankersmit and H. Kellner (eds): 21-39.

Pelling, C.B.R. (2000), *Literary Texts and the Greek Historian* (London and New York: Routledge).

——— (1997) (ed.), *Greek Tragedy and the Historian* (Oxford: Clarendon Press).

Perkins, D. (1992), *Is Literary History Possible?* (Baltimore: Johns Hopkins University Press).

Potter, D. (1999), *Literary Texts and the Roman Historian* (London and New York: Routledge).

Pozzi, D.C. and Wickersham, J.M. (1991) (eds), *Myth and the Polis*, (Ithaca, NY: Cornell University Press).

Pretagostini, R. (1993) (ed.), *Tradizione e Innovazione nella Cultura Greca. Da Omero All' Età Ellenistica. Scritti in Onore di Bruno Gentili* (Rome: GEI).

Price, J.J. (2001), *Thucydides and Internal War* (Cambridge: Cambridge University Press).

Proctor, D. (1980), *The Experience of Thucydides* (Warminster: Aris & Phillips).

Raaflaub, K.A. (1996), 'Equalities and Inequalities in Athenian Democracy', in J. Ober and C.W. Hedrick, Jr. (eds): 139-74.

——— (2002), 'Philosophy, Science, Politics: Herodotus and the Intellectual Trends of his Time', in E.J. Bakker, I.J.F. de Jong and H. van Wees (eds): 149-86.

Rawlings, H.R. (1981), *The Structure of Thucydides' History* (Princeton: Princeton University Press).

Rehm, R. (2002), *The Play of Space: Spatial Transformation in Greek Tragedy* (Princeton: Princeton University Ress).

Ridley, R.I. (1981), 'Exegesis and Audience in Thucydides', *Hermes* 109: 25-46.

Robbins, B. (1993), *Secular Vocations, Intellectuals, Professionalism, Culture* (New York and London: Verso).

Bibliography

Roberts, D.H., F.M. Dunn and D. Fowler (1997) (eds), *Classical Closure: Reading the End in Greek and Latin Literature* (Princeton: Princeton University Press).

Roberts, J.T. (1982), *Accountability in Athenian Government* (Madison, WI: University of Wisconsin Press).

Roisman, J. (1993), *The General Demosthenes and his Use of Military Surprise. Historia* Einzelschriften 78 (Stuttgart: Franz Steiner Verlag).

Rood, T.C.B. (1998a), *Thucydides: Narrative and Explanation* (Oxford: Clarendon Press).

—— (1998b), 'Thucydides and his Predecessors', *Histos* vol. 2 posted April 1999 (on-line journal): http://www.dur.ac.uk/Classics/histos/1998/rood.html.

—— (1999), 'Thucydides' Persian Wars', in C.S. Kraus 1999 (ed.): 141-68.

Rose, P.W. (1976), 'Sophocles' *Philoctetes* and the Teachings of the Sophists', in *HSCP* 80: 49-105.

—— (1992), *Sons of the Gods, Children of Earth: History and Ideology and Literary Form in Ancient Greece* (Ithaca, NY: University of Cornell Press).

—— (1995), 'Historicizing Sophocles' *Ajax*', in B. Goff (ed.): 59-90.

Rosen, R.M. and J. Farrell (1993) (eds), *Nomodeiktes: Greek Studies in Honour of Martin Ostwald* (Ann Arbor: University of Michigan Press).

—— and I. Sluiter (2004) (eds), *Free Speech in Classical Antiquity* (Leiden and Boston: E.J. Brill).

Rosivach, V. J. (1985), 'Manning the Athenian Fleet, 433-26 BC', *AJAH* 10: 41-66.

Rösler, W. (1991), 'Die "Selbshistorisierung" des Autors. Zur Stellung Herodots zwischen Mündlichkeit und Schriftlichkeit', *Philologus* 135: 215-20.

—— (2002), 'The *Histories* and Writing', in E.J. Bakker, I.J.F. de Jong and H. van Wees (eds): 79-94.

Rotella, G. (2004), *Castings: Monuments and Monumentality in Poems by Elizabeth Bishop, Robert Lowell, James Merrill, Derek Walcott, and Seamus Heaney* (Nashville: Vanderbilt University Press).

Rubincam, C.R. (1979), 'Qualification of Numerals in Thucydides,' *AJAH* 4 (1979): 77-95.

—— (1991), 'Casualty Figures in the Battle Descriptions of Thucydides', *TAPA* 121: 181-98.

—— (2003), 'Numbers in Greek Poetry and Historiography: Quantifying Fehling', *CQ* 53.2: 448-63.

Rutherford, R.B. (1994), 'Learning from History: Categories and Case-Histories', in R. Osborne and S. Hornblower (eds): 53-68.

Russell, D.A. (1990) (ed.), *Antonine Literature* (Oxford: Clarendon Press).

Saïd, S. (1994), 'Lucien Ethnographe', in A. Billault (ed.): 149-70.

Schein, S.L. (2003), *Sophokles: Philoktetes.* Translation with Notes, Introduction, and Interpretive Essay (Newburyport, MA: Focus Publishing).

Schloemann, J. (2002), 'Entertainment and Democratic Distrust: The Audience's Attitudes towards Oral and Written Oratory in Classical Athens', in I. Worthington and J.M. Foley (eds): 133-46.

Scully, S. (1990), *Homer and the Sacred City* (Ithaca, NY: Cornell University Press).

Segal, C. (1981), *Tragedy and Civilization (An Interpretation of Sophocles)* (Cambridge, Mass.: Harvard University Press).

—— (1995), 'Spectator and Listener', in J.-P. Vernant (ed.): 184-217.

—— (1999), 'Introduction: Retrospection on Classical Literary Criticism', in T.M. Falkner, N. Felson and D. Konstan (eds): 1-13.

Segal, E. (1983) (ed.), *Oxford Readings in Greek Tragedy* (Oxford: Clarendon Press).

Shapiro, H.A. (1989), *Art and Cult under the Tyrants in Athens* (Mainz: P. von Zabern).

Bibliography

Shrimpton, G.S. (1997), *History and Memory in Ancient Greece* (Montreal and London: McGill-Queen's University Press).

Silk, M.S. (1996) (ed.), *Tragedy and the Tragic: Greek Theatre and Beyond* (Oxford: Oxford University Press).

Skinner, Q. (1988), 'Meaning and Understanding in the History of Ideas', in J. Tully (ed.): 29-67. [first published in *HT* 8 (1969): 3-53]

Small, J.P. (1997), *Wax Tablets of the Mind: Cognitive Studies of Memory and Literacy in Classical Antiquity* (London and New York: Routledge).

Sommerstein, A.H. (1997), 'The Theatre Audience, the Demos, and the *Suppliants* of Aeschylus', in C.B.R. Pelling (ed.): 63-79.

———, S. Halliwell, J. Henderson and B. Zimmermann (1993) (eds), *Tragedy, Comedy and the Polis: Papers from the Greek Drama Conference* (Bari: Levante Editori).

Stadter, P.A. (1973) (ed.), *The Speeches in Thucydides: A Collection of Original Studies* (Chapel Hill: University of North Carolina Press).

Stahl, H.-P. (2003), *Thucydides: Man's Place in History* (Swansea: Classical Press of Wales). [first edition published in German in 1966]

Steiner, D.T. (1994), *The Tyrant's Writ: Myths and Images of Writing in Ancient Greece* (Princeton: Princeton University Press).

Strassler, R.B. (1996) (ed.), *The Landmark Thucydides: A Comprehensive Guide to the Peloponnesian War*, introduction by V.D. Hanson (New York: The Free Press).

Strauss, B.S. (1993), *Fathers and Sons in Athens: Ideology and Society in the Era of the Peloponnesian War* (Princeton: Princeton University Press).

——— (1996), 'The Athenian Trireme, School of Democracy', in J. Ober and C.W. Hedrick, Jr. (eds): 313-25.

——— (1997), 'The Problem of Periodization: The Case of the Peloponnesian War', in M. Golden and P. Toohey (eds): 165-75.

Swain, S. (1994), 'Man and Medicine in Thucydides', *Arethusa* 27: 303-27.

Taplin, O.P. (1983), 'Sophocles in his Theatre', in B. Knox (ed.): 155-74.

——— (1986), 'Fifth-century Tragedy and Comedy: A *synkrisis*', *JHS* 106: 163-74.

——— (1987), 'The Mapping of Sophocles' *Philoctetes*', *BICS* 34: 69-77.

——— (2000) (ed.), *Literature in the Greek and Roman Worlds: A New Perspective* (Oxford, New York: Oxford University Press).

Taylor, M.C. (2002), 'Implicating the *demos*: a reading of Thucydides on the rise of the Four Hundred', *JHS* 122: 91-108.

Thomas, R. (1989), *Oral Tradition and Written Record in Classical Athens* (Cambridge: Cambridge University Press).

——— (1993), 'Performance and Written Publication in Herodotus and the Sophistic Generation', in W. Kullmann and J. Althoff (eds): 225-44.

——— (2000), *Herodotus in Context* (Cambridge: Cambridge University Press).

——— (2003), 'Prose Performance Texts: *Epideixis* and Written Publication in the Late Fourth and Early Fourth Centuries', in H. Yunis (ed.): 162-88.

Tompkins, D.P. (1972), 'Stylistic Characterization in Thucydides: Nicias and Alcibiades', *YCS* 22: 181-214.

Tully, J. (1988) (ed.), *Meaning & Context: Quentin Skinner and his Critics* (Princeton: Princeton University Press).

Usener, S. (1994), *Isokrates, Platon und ihr Publikum. Hörer und Leser von Literatur in 4. Jahrhundert V. Chr.* (Tübingen).

Vernant, J.-P. (1988), 'Tensions and Ambiguities in Greek Tragedy', in J.-P. Vernant and P. Vidal-Naquet: 29-48. [first published in 1972]

——— (1995) (ed.), *The Greeks*, translated by C. Lambert and T.L. Fagan (Chicago: University of Chicago Press).

——— and P. Vidal-Naquet (1988), *Myth and Tragedy in Ancient Greece*, translated by Janet Lloyd (New York: Zone Books). [first published in French in two volumes (vol. 1, 1972; vol. 2, 1986)]

Vidal-Naquet, P. (1988a), 'Sophocles' Philoctetes and the Ephebeia', in J.-P. Vernant and P. Vidal-Naquet (eds): 161-79. [first published in 1972]

—— (1988b), 'Oedipus in Athens', in J.-P. Vernant and P. Vidal-Naquet (eds): 301-27. [first published in 1986]

—— (1995), *Politics Ancient and Modern*, translated by Janet Lloyd (Harvard University Press). [originally published in French in 1990]

von Reden, S. (1995), 'The Piraeus – A World Apart', *G&R* 42: 24-37.

Walker, A.D. (1993), 'Enargeia and the Spectator in Greek Historiography', *TAPA* 123: 353-77.

Wardy, R. (1996), *The Birth of Rhetoric: Gorgias, Plato and their Successors* (London and New York: Routledge).

West, W.C. III (1973), 'The Speeches in Thucydides: A Description and Listing', in P.A. Stadter (ed.): 3-15.

Westlake, H.D. (1960), 'Athenian Aims in Sicily, 427-424', *Historia* 9: 385-402.

—— (1968), *Individuals in Thucydides* (Cambridge: Cambridge University Press).

—— (1977), '*Legetai* in Thucydides', *Mnemosyne* 30: 345-62.

Wheeldon, M.J. (1989), ' "True Stories": the reception of historiography in antiquity', in A. Cameron (ed.): 36-63.

Wheeler, E.L. (1988), *Stratagem and the Vocabulary of Military Trickery. Mnemosyne* Supplement 108 (Leiden: E.J. Brill).

White, H. (1973), *Metahistory: The Historical Imagination in Nineteenth Century Europe* (Baltimore: Johns Hopkins University Press).

—— (1978), *Tropics of Discourse: Essays in Cultural Criticism* (Baltimore: Johns Hopkins University Press).

—— (1984), 'The Question of Narrative in Contemporary Historical Theory', *HT* 23: 1-33.

—— (1987), *The Content of the Form: Narrative Discourse and Historical Representation* (Baltimore: Johns Hopkins University Press).

Whitehead, D. (1990), *Aineias the Tactician: How to Survive Under Siege. Translation with an Introduction and Commentary* (Oxford: Clarendon Press).

Whitmarsh, T. (2001), *Greek Literature and the Roman Empire: The Politics of Imitation* (Oxford: Oxford University Press).

Williams, B. (2002), *Truth and Truthfulness: an Essay in Genealogy* (Princeton: Princeton University Press).

Wilson, J. (1982), 'What does Thucydides Claim for his Speeches?', *Phoenix* 36: 95-103

Wilson, J.B. (1979), *Pylos 425 BC: A Historical and Topographical Study of Thucydides' Account of the Campaign* (Warminster: Aris & Phillips).

Wilson, P.J. (1996), 'Tragic Rhetoric: The Use of Tragedy and the Tragic in the Fourth Century', in M.S. Silk (ed.): 310-31.

—— (1997), 'Leading the Tragic Khoros: Prestige in the Democratic City', in C.B.R. Pelling (ed.), 81-108.

—— (2000), *The Athenian Institution of the Khorêgia: the Chorus, the City and the Stage* (Cambridge: Cambridge University Press).

Winkler, J.J. (1990), 'The Ephebes' Song: Tragôidia and Polis', in J.J. Winkler and F.I. Zeitlin (eds): 20-62.

—— and F.I. Zeitlin (1990) (eds), *Nothing to do with Dionysos? Athenian Drama in its Social Context* (Princeton: Princeton University Press).

Winkler, M.M. (2001) (ed.), *Classical Myth and Culture in the Cinema* (Oxford: Oxford University Press).

Wise, J. (1998), *Dionysus Writes: The Invention of Theatre in Ancient Greece* (Ithaca, NY: Cornell University Press).

Woodman, A. J. (1988), *Rhetoric in Classical Historiography: Four Studies* (London and Sydney: Croom Helm).

Wohl, V. (2002), *Love Among the Ruins: The Erotics of Democracy in Classical Athens* (Princeton and Oxford: Princeton University Press).

Worman, N. (2002), *The Cast of Character: Style in Greek Literature* (Austin: University of Texas Press).

Worthington, I. and J.M. Foley (2002) (eds), *Epea and Grammata. Oral and Written Communication in Ancient Greece* (Leiden: E.J. Brill).

Young, D.C. (1968), *Three Odes of Pindar: a Literary Study of Pythian 11, Pythian 3, and Olympian 7* (Leiden: E.J. Brill).

Yunis, H. (1996), *Taming Democracy: Models of Political Rhetoric in Classical Athens* (Ithaca, NY: Cornell University Press).

—— (2003), 'Writing for Reading: Thucydides, Plato, and the Emergence of the Critical Reader', in his (ed.): 189-212.

—— (2003) (ed.), *Written Texts and the Rise of Literate Culture in Ancient Greece* (Cambridge: Cambridge University Press).

Zadorojnyi, A. V. (1998), 'Thucydides' Nicias and Homer's Agamemnon', *CQ* (n.s.) 48: 298-303.

Zagorin, P. (1990), 'Historiography and Postmodernism: Reconsiderations', *HT* 29: 263-74.

Index of Passages

References to the page and note numbers of this book are in bold type.

184

General Index

Names of modern scholars are cited in cases where they are mentioned in the main body of the text (citations in the notes are not included). Names of people and places that are mentioned only incidentally (e.g. Achilles, Aristogeiton, Hipparchus, Helenus, Panactum, Paralus, Scyros, Solon) are omitted.

acting 23, 83, 107, 156n110, 158n30
agôn, agônisma, agônismos (contest, rivalry) 21, 35, 38, 40, 139-40n75
Aineias Tacticus 28-9, 109, 138n48, 138n51, 156n1
Alcibiades 3, 39, 44, 49, 87, 90-4, 98, 99, 102, 106, 141n90, 152n26
alêtheia (truth, not forgetting) 37, 57-60, 64, 76-8, 146n25, 149n73
Allison, J. 5, 19, 77, 85
Amphipolis (second battle of) 26-30, 33, 43, 138n48
Antiphon 73, 90
apodeixis (exposition) 34, 63, 146n18
archaeology, the 46, 48, 58, 88, 142n15
Aristophanes 8, 22, 94, 128, 137n25, 153n46, 160n67
Aristotle 8, 106, 142n10, 143n23, 146n19, 153n57, 154n63
Austin, J.L. 4, 68

Boedeker, D. 63
Bowie, A. 99
Brasidas 24-33, 38, 138n41, 139 n57, 152n38
Budelmann, F. 101, 107

Cerdylium 26-28, 139n73
Chaireas 92, 96, 106
Chios 89, 90
cinema of war 19-20, 135n1
classic (work of literature) 6, 10, 109, 133n47
Cleon 3, 22, 26-9, 50-1, 55, 56, 95, 137n27, 138n41, 139n70, 143n28, 144n31, 145n55, 148n45
comedy 22, 94, 117, 120, 128
Connor, W.R. 3, 11, 85
contextualism 1-4, 9
Corcyra 50, 86, 132
Crane, G. 1, 2, 4, 5, 9, 27, 83

Debnar, P. 14, 19, 68
deception 39, 90, 92, 93, 103, 106-7, 138n52, 156n110

democratic ideology 73, 94, 95
Demosthenes (Athenian general, fifth-century) 3, 31, 34, 35-6, 138n55, 140n76
Demosthenes (Athenian orator and politician, fourth-century) 45, 68, 143n29
Dewald, C. vi, 5
didaskalia (lesson, rehearsal) 23-4, 137n31, 152n35
Diggins, J.P. 3
Diodotus 55, 142n10, 148n45, 155n99
Dionysius of Halicarnassus 4-5, 13, 21, 59, 71-2, 75-6, 109, 113, 131n15, 137n20, 145n12, 151n14, 156n1, 156-7n5
Dover, K.J. 15, 52

Edmunds, L. 6, 15, 25, 62, 67
Egesta / Egestaeans 39, 52, 118, 141n92, 148n49, 151n21
ekplêxis (stunned reaction) 35, 140n78
elpis (hope) 89, 152n31
epic 6, 7, 10, 38, 58, 87, 88, 99, 120, 125, 126-7, 132n35, 136n17, 138n54, 149n78, 151n23, 153n59, 154n64
epideixis (demonstration) 17, 34, 39
Epipolae 36
Euripides 22, 100, 137n35, 154n64
Eurymedon (Athenian general) 35

Feeney, D. 10
fiction, fictional 12, 21, 60, 66, 112, 115, 118-23, 125-7, 129, 147n30, 159n37
film, filmic 19-20, 66, 135n4, 136n9
Finley, J.H. 22
fleet, Athenian 35, 39, 52, 87, 90, 94, 96, 97, 98, 101-5, 141n91, 153n56
Flory, S. 84
foresight (see also *pronoia*) 27-8, 33, 43-4, 51-3, 55, 73, 139n65, 142n9, 144n45, 144n48
Fox, M. 115
funeral oration 23, 24, 30, 48, 74-5, 131n25, 138n52, 141n89

gaze 19, 26-7, 31, 34, 35, 40, 136n17, 137n38, 139n59

186

General Index

Goldhill, S. 22, 23, 112
Gorgias 57-61, 63, 145n1, 146n12
Gould, J. 107
Gylippus 35, 39

Hall, S. 1
Halliwell, S. 75
hamartia (flaw, error) 86
Hellanicus 62, 126, 142n13, 146n16
Hermocrates 4, 91
Herodotus 1, 2-3, 5, 6, 7, 10, 17, 21, 22, 27,
    47-8, 58, 61-3, 87, 97, 110, 111, 113-15,
    118, 122, 126-7, 129, 130n6, 131n10,
    132n27, 133n45, 136n17, 138n43, 142
    n4, 143n16, 145n56, 146n15, 149n78,
    150n80, 151n23, 152n25, 158n20, 159n46
Hesk, J. 99
hindsight 16, 20, 43, 44, 51, 52, 76
Hippocratic corpus 2, 6, 10, 144n49
Homer, Homeric epic 6-7, 22, 45, 58, 80, 88,
    99, 110-11, 117, 125-8, 132n29, 138n54,
    141n88, 143n23, 149n78, 150n79,
    151n23, 153n59, 154 n64, 158n34,
    160n63
Hornblower, S. vi, 12, 19, 52, 81, 88, 121
Hunter, V. 31, 84

incompleteness of the *History* 18, 87, 89,
    150n13
inscription, as metaphor for history 9-10, 16,
    116, 131n26, 132n27, 133n43
insight 9, 10, 13, 18, 20, 23-6, 28, 29, 33, 35,
    37, 41, 44, 50, 51, 53-5, 78-80, 120, 124
intertextuality 6-7, 9, 12, 22, 64, 80, 99, 112,
    114, 154n64

James, C.L.R. 1

Kagan, D. 52
Kallet, L. 12, 76, 79, 85, 98
kataplêxis (amazement) 35, 89, 140n78
kinêsis (political upheaval) 48, 86, 88,
    143n23, 151n20
kosmos (arrangement, order, refinement) 57-
    60, 140n76, 145n5
ktêma es aiei (possession for all time) 6, 15,
    18, 63, 109, 110, 116

Lang, M. 77
Lemnos 83, 98-102, 154n69
lesson 15, 20, 23-4, 30, 32, 52, 75, 136n14,
    137n32, 144n51, 148n44
letters 92, 152n39 (*see also* Nicias' letter)
logographos (prose-writer) 21, 57-8, 78,
    145n2
logos (speech, account, argument, word) 37,
    57-63, 70, 145n3, 146nn
Loraux, N. 3, 7, 15, 82
Ludwig, P. 22, 27

Macleod, C. 22, 51
Mantinea, battle of 48, 123-4
Marcellinus 84
mathêma (instruction) 23
Melian dialogue 21, 24, 86, 137n32, 144n36,
    148n44, 151n22
Melos 51-2, 86
Moles, J. 3, 5, 8-10, 41, 116, 120
Mononson, S. 94
monumentality 109, 116-17, 132n27,
    158n29
to muthodês (the realm of myth) 21
Mytilene debate 50, 55, 127, 148n45, 155n99

narratology 12, 25, 43, 147n30
Neoptolemus 100-7, 155n100, 156n101
Nicias 3, 34-9, 45, 49, 52, 71, 75, 87, 96, 127,
    140n78, 140n82, 140n86, 140-1n88,
    144n32, 144n35, 148n54, 149n74,
    149n76, 151n21
Nicias' letter 76-81, 140n86, 149nn, 150n80
nostos, Nostoi (return home) 88, 99, 102,
    152n30, 155n87
numbers, rhetoric of 121-4, 159n46

Ober, J. 7, 8, 84
oligarchic revolution 73, 83, 86, 90, 93-9, 102-
    3, 106-7, 151n19, 152n39
omniscience 127-8, 150n11
opsis (sight, vision) 30-1, 35, 39, 136n14,
    141n95; *epopsis* 13; *prosopsis* 34
oral performance 9, 14-17, 57, 77, 78, 80,
    133n44, 135n74, 145n3, 147n27
oratory 10, 38, 133n44, 137n27, 158n35

paradeigma (example, demonstration, para-
    digm) 23, 24, 137n32
Peisander 90, 93, 106, 152n41
Pelling, C. 22
Pentekontaëtia 48, 61, 63, 126, 146n13
perception 20, 23, 32, 34, 97, 139n60, 140n87,
    147n35
Perdiccas 30-1
Pericles 3, 23-4, 30, 34, 52-3, 55, 68-76, 78-80,
    86, 96, 98, 103, 131n25, 132n35, 138n52,
    139n57, 139n71, 140n81, 141n89,
    143n30, 144nn, 145n55, 147n42, 148nn,
    149nn, 155n99
persuasion 37, 44, 59-61, 67, 79, 87, 90-2,
    106, 118-19, 121, 147n35
Phaeax 42
phaneros (visible) 28-9, 31, 37, 140n82
Philoctetes 98-107, 154n70
photography 19, 135nn
Phrynichus 90, 92-3, 151n14
plague 50-1, 53, 73-5, 85, 113-14, 141n101
Plataea, Plataeans 33, 46, 54, 59, 76
Plato, platonic dialogues 8, 11, 16-17, 72-3,
    135n77, 157n13, 160n63

187

General Index

plot(s) 11, 18, 21, 24, 83-4, 89-93, 95, 103, 107, 120, 155n79
Plutarch 19, 52, 137n35, 140n76, 152n36, 155n93, 156n107
point of view (see also vantage point) 13, 25, 26, 38, 41, 127, 137n38
ponos (toil, exertion) 86, 117, 140n79, 147n28
posterity 5, 68, 111, 115, 117, 119, 120, 135n74
Price, J. 31, 88
pronoia (foresight, foreknowledge) 32-3, 53, 60, 139n65, 144nn
Ps.-Aristotle 97, 153n63
Ps.-Xenophon 8, 148n54
Pylos 20, 22, 31, 34, 138n54

Rawlings, H.R. 84
realism 59, 76, 132n34, 133n46, 145n8
reception 9, 10, 12, 17, 18, 109, 114, 134n61, 135n77, 157n14
rhetoric, rhetorical 3, 9, 10, 12, 14, 16, 31, 32, 38, 39, 54, 55, 57-60, 64, 67-73, 75, 76, 79, 82, 94, 96, 105, 106, 113-15, 117-18, 120, 137n27, 139n57, 140-1n88, 150n80, 158n30, 159n42
rhetoric of history 21, 24, 120, 121-5, 147n30
Rood, T. 7, 11, 12, 20, 23, 31, 32, 38, 51
Rotella, G. 116

Samos 86, 89-90, 92-7, 102-5, 153n58
saphes, to saphes (clear, a clear picture) 15, 25, 32, 36, 54, 78-9, 136n13
shaping 11-13, 18, 66, 109, 110
Sicilian expedition, Sicily 35, 36, 38, 42, 45, 49, 51-2, 77, 80, 84-8, 96, 137n35, 148n54, 151nn, 153n54
sight (see also *opsis*, firesight, insight, and hindsight) 20, 23-9, 31-7, 39-41, 54-5, 66, 124, 136nn, 137n26, 141n95
skopein (to observe, reflect on) 9, 10, 20, 25, 40, 54, 124
Small, J.P. 65
Socrates 16, 72-3, 128, 148n58
Sophocles 83, 89, 98-102, 105, 107, 153n51, 154nn, 155n84, 155-6n100
Sostratus of Cnidus 116, 158n26
speech culture (Athenian) 18, 64, 68, 69, 79
speeches in Thucydides 4, 14-15, 18, 24, 25, 37, 45, 57-61, 64, 66-70, 72, 74-87, 92, 95, 98, 120, 146n23, 147nn, 148nn, 149n68, 150n9, 151n14
Stahl, H.-P. 107
stasis (civil unrest, revolution) 48, 50, 86, 96
sumbouleutic oratory, *sumboulos* 45, 60-1, 145n10
superlative adjectives 39, 87-8, 140n84, 143n23, 152n36
suspicion 73, 90, 93, 95, 152n34
symposium 8, 132n38

Syracuse, battle in the harbour of 13, 38, 39, 42, 55, 141n98

Taplin, O. 99
Taylor, M. 93-4
theatre 19, 20-7, 35, 55-6, 96, 100-1, 104, 107, 137n27, 141n91, 156n106
theatre of war 18-20, 25-6, 32, 42, 86, 98, 107
Themistocles 53, 73, 97, 139n57, 148n60
theôria (contemplation, theorizing, speculation) 113, 118, 120, 158n32
Theramenes 90, 106, 152n36
Thomas, R. 2, 16-17
Thrace 31, 42
Thucydides: and Herodotus 1, 2-3, 6, 7, 10, 17, 21, 22, 27, 47-8, 61-3, 87, 126, 130n6, 132n27, 133n45, 143n16, 145n56, 146n17; as general 3, 33, 43, 110, 124, 130n10, 156n5; exile of 22, 56, 83, 98, 128, 145n56; as heroic researcher 150n82; rhetoric of history 3, 9, 10, 21, 24, 44, 67-73, 76, 121, 123-4, 134n54, 136n18; style 4-6, 16, 19, 22, 59, 76, 85, 131nn, 151n15
time, narrative 4, 18, 42-51
timelessness of the *History* 6, 9, 14, 16-17, 44, 45, 54, 74, 109, 110, 114, 128
Tissaphernes 44, 90-2, 106, 152n40
tragedy 3, 5, 10, 18, 22, 24, 38-9, 83, 87-9, 98, 101, 103, 106-7, 114, 120, 136n16, 140n83, 149n78, 151n24, 153n51, 154nn, 156n106
Trojan War, Troy 58, 61, 83, 88, 99-102, 105, 111, 117, 132n35, 136n17, 151nn, 155n79
trust, mistrust 83, 90-3, 95-6, 98, 100
truth (see also *alêtheia*) 9, 21, 33, 37, 38, 46, 48, 49, 57-61, 63-8, 76-82, 90, 93, 107, 114, 115, 117-22, 125-7, 129, 140n84, 144n34, 147n35, 157n8, 159n37

vantage point 17, 18, 25-7, 34-5, 41, 44, 47, 127-8, 139n73, 142n14
Vernant, J.-P. 20

Westlake, H.D. 77
White, H. 120
Williams, B. 33, 68, 115
writing, written word 6, 14-17, 37, 40-1, 57, 58, 61, 62, 65-8, 70, 76-8, 81, 109, 110, 132n37, 133-4n53, 140n86, 145n3, 149n68

Xenophon 106, 114, 153n53, 156n107
xungraphô (to write down, write up) 15, 62, 67, 76, 110, 147n34

Yunis, H. 11, 14

Zadorojnyi, A. 80

188

www.ingramcontent.com/pod-product-compliance
Lightning Source LLC
Chambersburg PA
CBHW071411100726
47908CB00004B/1133